MARGARET SANGER
and the
Birth Control Movement:

A Bibliography, 1911-1984

by
GLORIA MOORE
and
RONALD MOORE

The Scarecrow Press, Inc.
Metuchen, N.J., & London
1986

Library of Congress Cataloging-in-Publication Data

Moore, Gloria, 1932–1985.
    Margaret Sanger and the birth control movement.

    Includes index.
    1. Sanger, Margaret, 1879–1966--Bibliography.
2. Birth control--United States--History--Bibliography.
I. Moore, Ronald, 1932-   . II. Title. [DNLM:
1. Sanger, Margaret, 1879-1966. 2. Family Planning--
history--United States--abstracts. Z 7164.B5 M822m]
Z7164.B5M66   1986   [HQ763.6.U5] 016.3046'6'0973   86–10119
ISBN 0-8108-1903-1

Dedicated with gratitude and affection to

The Library Faculty and Staff
Skidmore College
Saratoga Springs, N.Y.

and

Marion V.C. Lippman
Teacher Extraordinary
George Washington High School, N.Y.C.

PREFACE

The purpose of this retrospective bibliography is to gather into one place the bibliographic citations connected with the birth control movement and Margaret Sanger; only those available through the American public and college libraries are included. Although this reference collection will probably be used primarily by college and research scholars, efforts were made to include materials for high school students as well.

Margaret Sanger is the major focus of this bibliography, and each entry was selected to reflect her actions and influence in the unfolding history of the birth control movement.

Many thousands of items are available to the public and are held in the Margaret Sanger collections. The locations of these collections are listed in the front of this book.

As an aid to the user, an OCLC (Online Computer Library Center) number has been added to the bibliographic description of each book and monograph. This number can be used for inter-library loans and occurs in college libraries located in the United States.

The annotations following the citations are meant to inform the reader about the content of the material. They are not intended to be critical of the content of any work. All materials were examined personally, except those few with citations marked "Not seen." M.S. is used to mean Margaret Sanger, since Margaret Sanger's name appears in almost every annotation.

The MLA Handbook for Writers of Research Papers, 2nd edition, was used as our guide for the bibliographic descriptions. The following article's guidelines were followed as closely as possible in the preparation of this bibliography:

"Guidelines for the Preparation of a Bibliography: Prepared by the Bibliographic Committee, Reference and Adult Service Division (RASD), American Library Association, Approved by the RASD Board of Directors, July 1982" RQ Fall 1982:pp. 31-2.

Except for OCLC and M.S., standard abbreviations were used and are listed in the front of this book.

A special feature of this bibliography is the arrangement of the citations covering the period 1911 to 1966, the latter date marking the conclusion of Margaret Sanger's life. These citations are arranged in chronological order, with each year comprising a separate unit. Each unit first lists items by Margaret Sanger, then lists all other items that reflect her work or influence. Within each unit, large items are followed by smaller items--for example, books are followed by articles.

This bibliography contains three other major groups of citations: Obituaries, major biographies, and citations covering the period 1967 to 1984. The citations within each of these groups are listed in alphabetical order.

Item numbers have been given to all bibliographic citations except those indicating either obituaries of Margaret Sanger or reviews. Obituaries of Margaret Sanger are treated as a separate group and are given one item number. Reviews generally follow major works reviewed and are included under the major work's item number. All item numbers correspond with those listed in the author and subject indexes and in the title index of Margaret Sanger's works.

Acknowledgements

Since I lost my beloved wife and co-author in May of this year due to lung cancer our daughters Ronda, Roxanne, and Cathrine have given me support and help, without which this book could not have been finished. Cathrine devoted three months of her time to complete the indexing, proofreading, and final preparation of the manuscript.

The entire staff at the Skidmore College Library, where Gloria worked as a librarian for the last fifteen years, gave us support and cheerful encouragement all the way.

Our special gratitude goes to Chris McGill who typed the entire work under very trying circumstances and who met us with a cheerful smile when we were mostly sad.

To all--we are most thankful.

Ronald Moore

November 26, 1985

Saratoga Springs

TABLE OF CONTENTS

A. Citations arranged in chronological order with each
    year comprising a separate unit. Each unit first
    lists items by Margaret Sanger, then lists all other
    items that reflect her work or influence. Within
    each unit, large items are followed by smaller items--
    for example, books are followed by articles. (Items
    1-1160)

SOURCES CONSULTED

America: History and Life, 1964-1981
Bibliography of the History of Medicine, 1964-1984
Biography Index, 1946-1984
Book Review Digest, 1915-1984
Book Review Index, 1970-1984
British Humanities Index, 1962-1984
Catholic Periodical and Literature Index, 1967-1984
Catholic Periodicals Index, 1930-1960
Cumulative Book Index, 1928-1984
Dissertation Abstracts (Data Base Search)
Document Catalogue, 1912-1940
Education Index, 1929-1984
Essay and General Literature Index, 1900-1984
General Science Index, 1978-1984
Historical Abstracts, 1955-1984
Humanities Index, 1974-1984
Index to Legal Periodicals, 1926-1984
International Index to Periodicals, 1907-1965
Monthly Catalog, 1941-1984
New York Times Index, 1912-1984
Public Affairs Information Service, 1915-1984
Readers' Guide to Periodical Literature, 1915-1984
Social Sciences and Humanities Index, 1965-1974
Social Sciences Index, 1974-1984
Subject Index to Periodicals, 1915-1961
United States Catalog, 1912-1927
Women Studies Abstracts, 1982-1984
Writings on American History, 1915-1974

PERIODICALS READ

Birth Control Review, 1917-1940
Family Planning Perspectives 1967-1975
Human Fertility, 1940-1948
Journal of Contraception, 1935-1939
Masses, 1911-1917
Milbank Memorial Fund Quarterly, 1923-1975
Mother Earth, 1906-1917
New Generation, 1925

New York Call, 1910-1916, Microfilm
Population Council Annual Reports, 1953-1975
Woman Rebel, 1914

COMPUTER SEARCHES CONDUCTED, 1982-1984

(Subjects: Margaret Sanger, Birth Control, and Contraception,
History of)

LOCATIONS OF SPECIAL COLLECTIONS

American Birth Control League Papers, Houghton Library, Harvard University, Cambridge, Massachusetts

Margaret Sanger Collection, Katharine Dexter McCormick Library, Planned Parenthood Federation of America, Inc., 810 Seventh Ave., New York City, N.Y. 10009

Margaret Sanger Papers, Library of Congress, Washington, D.C.

Margaret Sanger Papers, Sophia Smith Collection, Smith College, Northampton, Massachusetts

Planned Parenthood Federation of America Papers, Sophia Smith Collection, Smith College, Northampton, Massachusetts

ABBREVIATIONS

The following list includes the major abbreviations used in this book.
Various forms of publishers' names--and other signs and abbreviations--that need no explanation--have not been included.

AMA: American Medical Association
Approx.: Approximately
Assoc.: Association
bibl.: bibliography
bibliog.: bibliography
biog.: biography
c.: copyright
CA.: California
ca.: circa
CAT.: catalog
CBS: Corporate symbol for the Columbia Broadcasting System
ch.: chapter
co.: company
Col.: column
comp.: compiled, compiler
Cong.: Congress
cont.: content, continued
Ct.: Connecticut
DAI: Dissertation Abstracts International
D.A.R.: Daughters of the American Revolution
D.C.: District of Columbia
Del.: Delaware
diss.: dissertation
doc.: document
DOCT.: document
dr.: doctor
ed.: edition, editor
e.g.: for example
et al.: and others
fasc.: fascicle: part, number
H.: House
H.R.: House of Representatives
i.e.: that is
ill.: illustrated, illustrations
illus.: illustrated, illustrations
Inc.: Incorporated

Ind.: Indiana
introd.: introduction
I.P.P.F.: International Planned Parenthood Federation
IUD: Intrauterine Device
I.W.W.: Industrial Workers of the World
Jr.: Junior
Lieut.: Lieutenant
LL.D.: Doctor of Laws degree
Lt. Col.: Lieutenant Colonel
Ltd.: Limited
MA.: Massachusetts
Mag.: magazine
Mass.: Massachusetts
M.D.: Medical doctor
Minn.: Minnesota
Mrs.: Mistress
M.S.: Margaret Sanger
n.: number
N.B.C.: National Broadcasting Company
N.C.: North Carolina
N.D.: no date
N.J.: New Jersey
n.p.: no place, no publisher
N.S.: New Series
N.Y.: New York
N.Y.C.: New York City
OCLC: Online Computer Library Center (formerly the Ohio College
        Library Center, 1967-1977)
o.p.: out of print
p.: page
PA.: Pennsylvania
pa.: paper
Ph.D.: Doctor of Philosophy
Pr.: Press
pp.: pages
Pref.: Preface
priv. pr.: privately printed
pt.: part
Pub.: Publication, Published, Publisher
Rep.: Representative
repr.: reprint, reprinted
Rev.: review
rev.: revised
S.: Senate
Sect.: Section
sess.: session
S.J.: Society of Jesus
suppl.: supplement
tr.: translated, translator
Unesco: United Nations Educational, Scientific and Cultural Organ-
         ization

Univ.: University
U.S.: United States
U.S.A.: United States of America
U.S.G.P.O.: United States Government Printing Office
v.: versus
v.: volume
V.D.: venereal disease
vol.: volume
vols.: volumes
v.p.: various paging
vs.: versus
W.E.G.S.K.: What Every Girl Should Know
WFAB: Radio Station, Syracuse, New York
WNAC: Radio Station, Boston, Massachusetts
WWI: World War One
WWII: World War Two
Y.M.C.A.: Young Men's Christian Association
Y.W.C.A.: Young Women's Christian Association

THE BIBLIOGRAPHY

1. "Margaret H. Sanger." New York Call, 20 Nov. 1911: p. 4
   col. 6.
   One of the advertisements for "Margaret H. Sanger, 235 West
   135th Street, New York Women's Organizer."

2. Sanger, Margaret H. "The Fangs of the Monster at Lawrence."
   New York Call, 15 Feb. 1912: p. 6 col. 3.
   M.S. on the Lawrence, Mass. strike.
3. _____. "The Fighting Women of Lawrence." New York Call,
   18 Feb. 1912, Sun. ed.: p. 15 col. 6-7.
   M.S. describes the bravery of the Lawrence women and their
   understanding of "international solidarity."
4. _____. "An Evening with George De Forest Brush." New
   York Call, 4 Aug. 1912, Sun. ed.: p. 10 col. 2-6.
   M.S. reports a conversation with the American painter,
   George De Forest Brush. They discuss socialism.
5. _____. "What Every Girl Should Know; Introduction." New
   York Call, 17 Nov. 1912, Sun. ed.: p. 15 col. 6-7.
   M.S. provides an "Introduction" to her coming series of art-
   icles in which she will provide sex education for the young.
6. _____. "What Every Girl Should Know; Girlhood-Part I."
   New York Call, 24 Nov. 1912, Sun. ed.: p. 15 col. 1-2.
   Discusses the problems of the adolescent girl.
7. _____. "What Every Girl Should Know; Girlhood-Part II."
   New York Call, 1 Dec. 1912, Sun. ed.: p. 15 col. 1-3.
   M.S. continues discussion of adolescence.
8. _____. "What Every Girl Should Know; Puberty-Part I."
   New York Call, 8 Dec. 1912, Sun. ed.: p. 15 col. 1-2.
   M.S. discusses the female reproductive organs.
9. _____. "What Every Girl Should Know; Puberty-Part II."
   New York Call, 15 Dec. 1912, Sun. ed.: p. 15 col. 1-2.
   Continues the discussion of the female anatomy.
10. _____. "What Every Girl Should Know; Sexual Impulses-Part
    I." New York Call, 22 Dec. 1912, Sun. ed.: p. 15 col. 1-2.
    Points out the importance of the sexual impulse at puberty
    and the problems involved with masturbation.
11. _____. "What Every Girl Should Know; Sexual Impulses-Part
    II." New York Call, 29 Dec. 1912, Sun. ed.: p. 15 col.
    1-3.
    M.S. continues her discussion of sexual impulses.
12. United States. Cong. House. The Strike at Lawrence, Mass.:
    Hearings before the Committee on Rules of the House of Rep-
    resentatives on House Resolutions 409 and 433. H. Doc. 671.
    62nd Cong., 2nd sess. Serial Vol. 138; 6320. 2-7 Mar. 1912,
    Washington: GPO, 1912. p. 464.
    In these hearings to investigate the I.W.W. strike at Lawr-
    ence, Mass., M.S. testifies (pages 226-233) on the condition of
    the strikers' children and on her part in transporting them to
    New York City.

13. "Lawrence Strikers Send 250 Children." New York Call, 10
     Feb. 1912: p. 1 col. 6-7.
     M.S. is named as one of those who will speak at a Union
     Square meeting on behalf of the Lawrence strikers' children.
14. "Lawrence Children in New York Given Passionate Ovation."
     New York Call, 11 Feb. 1912, Sun. ed.: p. 1 col. 6-7--
     p. 2 col. 1-2.
     M.S. is on the committee that brings Lawrence children to
     New York.
15. "150 Strike Waifs Find Homes Here; Great Throng Waits in Cold
     to Give Warm Welcome to Children from Lawrence, Mass."
     New York Times, 11 Feb. 1912: Pt. 2, p. 1 col. 7--p. 2
     col. 1.
     M.S. is mentioned as one of those in charge of the distribu-
     tion in New York of the children of Lawrence, Mass. strikers.
16. "Strikers' Children Parade Fifth Ave; Second Batch of 103 from
     Lawrence Led by Band Playing the 'Marseillaise'." New York
     Times, 18 Feb. 1912: Pt. 2, p. 4 col. 1.
     M.S. is one of those who had already "assumed care" of
     three strikers' children and now has volunteered to take two
     more.
17. "Climax of Horror Reached in Probing Lawrence Strike." New
     York Call, 6 Mar. 1912: p. 1 col. 7--p. 2 col. 1.
     Reports on hearing held before the House Rules Committee on
     the Lawrence Strike. Portions of M.S.'s testimony are given.
18. "Mrs. Taft Listens to Strike Charges; Attends Inquiry Into
     Lawrence Police's Treatment of Women and Children in Riots."
     New York Times, 6 Mar. 1912: p. 6 col. 2-3.
     Reports on testimony given before the House Rules Committee
     on the Lawrence, Mass. strike. Some of M.S.'s testimony is
     included.
19. "New York Still Aiding Strikers." New York Call, 19 Mar. 1912:
     p. 2 col. 2.
     William Sanger is among those whose paintings are on exhibit
     to raise funds for the Lawrence strikers.
20. "Open Art Exhibit for Lawrence Children." New York Call, 2
     April 1912: p. 1 col. 2.
     William Sanger is one of the artists who have donated work
     to be sold for the benefit of the Lawrence children.
21. "Condition of the Lawrence Children." New York Call, 7 April
     1912, Sun. ed.: p. 14 col. 1-7.
     Reprints the testimony of M.S. before the Committee on Rules,
     House of Representatives on March 5, 1912. Portrait of M.S.
     included.
22. "Another Announcement." New York Call, 13 Oct. 1912, Sun.
     ed.: p. 15 col. 5.
     Announces that a series of articles by M.S. entitled "What
     Every Girl Should Know" will begin shortly.
23. Mrs. L. B. "A Mother Protests." New York Call, 22 Dec. 1912,
     Sun. ed.: p. 15 col. 3-4.
     Letter to the editor protests "What Every Girl Should Know"
     articles as unsuitable.

24. "Letters to the Editor." <u>New York Call</u>, 29 Dec. 1912, Sun.
    ed.: p. 15 col. 6-7.
    Letters opposing and supporting M.S.'s "What Every Girl
    Should Know" series.

                            1913

25. Sanger, Margaret H. "What Every Girl Should Know; Reproduc-
    tion-Part I." <u>New York Call</u>, 12 Jan. 1913, Sun. ed.: p.
    15 col. 6-7.
    M.S. explains how to teach the reproductive process to young
    people.
26. _____ . "What Every Girl Should Know; Reproduction-Part II."
    <u>New York Call</u>, 19 Jan. 1913, Sun. ed.: p. 15 col. 1-2.
    M.S. continues with her discussion of reproduction.
27. _____ . "What Every Girl Should Know; Some Consequences
    of Ignorance and Silence." <u>New York Call</u>, 26 Jan. 1913,
    Sun. ed.: p. 15 col. 1-2.
    Among other things, M.S. discusses the prevalence of ve-
    nereal disease.
28. _____ . "What Every Girl Should Know; Some Consequences
    of Ignorance and Silence-Part II." <u>New York Call</u>, 2 Feb.
    1913, Sun. ed.: p. 15 col. 1-3.
    M.S. continues her discussion of venereal disease.
29. _____ . "What Every Girl Should Know; Some Consequences
    of Ignorance and Silence-Part III (The Censored Article)."
    <u>New York Call</u>, 2 Mar. 1913, Sun. ed.: p. 15 col. 1-3.
    The <u>Call</u> prints the article on venereal disease that had been
    censored by the Post Office.
30. _____ . "With the Girls in Hazleton Jail." <u>New York Call</u>,
    20 April 1913, Sun. ed.: p. 15 col. 6-7.
    M.S. describes her jail experience in Hazelton, PA. where
    she was arrested on a picket line at the Duplin Silk Mill.
31. _____ . "The Eugenic Mother and Baby." <u>New York Call</u>,
    5 Oct. 1913, Sun. ed.: p. 15 col. 1-2.
    M.S. reviews the book <u>The Eugenic Mother and Baby</u> by Dr.
    W. Grant Hague. Although she considers the book "a gem,"
    she attacks the two chapters where "the writer idealizes the
    slave woman...."
32. "An Explanation to Our Readers." <u>New York Call</u>, 5 Jan. 1913,
    Sun. ed.: p. 15 col. 5.
    Editorial explains that M.S.'s "What Every Girl Should Know"
    installment "had to be postponed because of lack of space."
33. "Letters to the Editor." <u>New York Call</u>, 5 Jan. 1913, Sun. ed.:
    p. 15 col. 1-4.
    More letters pro and con concerning "What Every Girl Should
    Know" series.
34. "Letters to the Editor." <u>New York Call</u>, 12 Jan. 1913, Sun. ed.:
    p. 15 col. 1-3.
    Letters opposing and supporting WEGSK series.

35. "Letters to the Editor." New York Call, 19 Jan. 1913, Sun.
     ed.: p. 15 col. 3-4.
     Prints three letters in support of M.S.'s "What Every Girl
     Should Know" series.
36. "The Feelings of a Young Man." New York Call, 26 Jan. 1913,
     Sun. ed.: p. 15 col. 3.
     Letter praises "What Every Girl Should Know" series.
37. "A Valuable Letter." New York Call, 2 Feb. 1913, Sun. ed.:
     p. 15 col. 3-5.
     A letter from a young girl in praise of M.S.'s "What Every
     Girl Should Know" series.
38. "A Sufferer Makes a Plea." New York Call, 9 Feb. 1913, Sun.
     ed.: p. 15 col. 3.
     A woman suffering from venereal disease praises "What
     Every Girl Should Know" series.
39. "What Every Girl Should Know; NOTHING! By Order of the
     Post Office Department." New York Call, 9 Feb. 1913, Sun.
     ed.: p. 15 col. 1-2.
     Notice replaces M.S.'s What Every Girl Should Know" series.
40. "The Post Office Censorship." New York Call, 10 Feb. 1913:
     p. 6 col. 1-2.
     Editorial denouncing the post office censorship of M.S.'s
     "What Every Girl Should Know" articles in the Call.
41. "Decency and Indecency." New York Call, 11 Feb. 1913: p. 6
     col. 1-2.
     Editorial calls "What Every Girl Should Know" articles neces-
     sary knowledge and, therefore, "decent."
42. "Volkszeitung Severely Raps Ban Placed on the Sanger Articles
     in Sunday Call." New York Call, 11 Feb. 1913: p. 1 col.
     3-5.
     Reports that Volkszeitung, a German Socialist paper, has
     attacked the post office for banning M.S.'s "What Every Girl
     Should Know" articles from the Call. Article calls for a "fight"
     for "freedom of the press."
43. "The Post Office Censorship." New York Call, 12 Feb. 1913:
     p. 6 col. 1-2.
     The Call will "test" the ban on M.S.'s "What Every Girl
     Should Know" articles.
44. "Ignorance in Authority." New York Call, 14 Feb. 1913: p. 6
     col. 1-4.
     Long editorial attacks the post office for banning "What
     Every Girl Should Know" articles.
45. Block, Anita C. "Editorial Comment; Socialists and Bourgeois
     Morality." New York Call, 16 Feb. 1913, Sun. ed.: p. 15
     col. 3-5.
     Editorial defends the "What Every Girl Should Know" series
     and explains that a socialist newspaper can expect no help from
     "prominent citizens" or "women's clubs."
46. Kobbe, Herman. "What Every Girl Should Know." New York
     Call, 16 Feb. 1913, Sun. ed.: p. 15 col. 1-2.

Article praises M.S.'s "What Every Girl Should Know" series, attacks the postal censorship, and calls for more socialist-directed sex education.

47. "Letters to the Editor." New York Call, 16 Feb. 1913, Sun. ed.: p. 15 col. 1-4.
Letters are in support of "What Every Girl Should Know" series.

48. Bowers, Edwin F. "Against Stupidity, Even the Gods Fight in Vain." New York Call, 19 Feb. 1913: p. 6 col. 5.
Letter of praise for M.S. from a physician, and a call for more information to the public.

49. Block, Anita C. "Editorial Comment; A Few Final Remarks." New York Call, 2 Mar. 1913, Sun. ed.: p. 15 col. 3-5.
Editor explains that the post office has removed the ban against the final article of "What Every Girl Should Know" series. She claims the ban has made the socialists aware of the need for further sex education.

50. "Letters to the Editor." New York Call, 2 Mar. 1913, Sun. ed.: p. 15 col. 7-8.
More letters for and against "What Every Girl Should Know" series. Includes a short letter from M.S. offering help to a letter writer.

51. "Sex Knowledge and Socialist Propaganda; The 'Pure' Girl a Cause of Immorality." New York Call, 16 Mar. 1913, Sun. ed.: p. 15 col. 4-7.
Two more letters commenting on "What Every Girl Should Know" series.

1914

52. Sanger, Margaret H. Family Limitation. New York: 1914. Illus. 16 p. (OCLC: 2085990).
Written in simple English for "working men and women in America," M.S.'s article includes the birth control information she gathered from French and Dutch doctors.

53. _____. What Every Mother Should Know; Or How Six Little Children Were Taught the Truth. New York: The Rabelais Press, 1914. 59p. Not seen.

54. _____. "The Aim." Woman Rebel, 1.1 Mar. 1914: p. 1.
M.S. sets forth "the aims" of the Woman Rebel.

55. _____. "The New Feminists." Woman Rebel, 1.1 Mar. 1914: pp. 1-2.
Calls the new American feminism a middle class movement "lacking in vitality, force, and conviction."

56. _____. "On Picket Duty." Woman Rebel, 1.1 Mar. 1914: p. 3.
Little comments that attack the "feminists."

57. _____. "The Prevention of Conception." Woman Rebel, 1.1 Mar. 1914: p. 8.

States that the Woman Rebel will defy the law that forbids giving information on the prevention of conception.

58. _____ . "Why the Woman Rebel?" Woman Rebel, 1.1 Mar. 1914: p. 8.
M.S. lists her beliefs.

59. _____ . "Conventions." Woman Rebel, 1.1-2 April 1914: pp. 11-12.
A call to "defy conventions."

60. _____ . "Humble Pie." Woman Rebel, 1.2 April 1914: p. 9.
Some tongue-in-cheek comments on the banning of the Woman Rebel's first issue from the mails.

61. _____ . "Into the Valley of Death--For What?" Woman Rebel, 1.2 April 1914: p. 12.
Asks that women "revolt against introducing into the world another class of human beings to be starved, crippled and maimed for the masters."

62. _____ . "Marriage." Woman Rebel, 1.2 April 1914: p. 16.
In this call for free love, M.S. denies the importance of vows before church or state in relationships between men and women.

63. _____ . "On Picket Duty." Woman Rebel, 1.2 April 1914: p. 11.
Editorial comments on, among other things, the feminists, the suffrage movement, and the Triangle fire.

64. _____ . "Self Preservation." Woman Rebel, 1.2 April 1914: p. 16.
Editorializes on the courage of the workers in Union Square on April 4th, 1914.

65. _____ . "World Builders?" Woman Rebel, 1.2 April 1914: p. 15.
Floyd Dell is charged with underestimating the importance of Emma Goldman and Dora Marsden.

66. _____ . "Abortion in the United States." Woman Rebel, 1.3 May 1914: p. 24.
A cry against the horrors of illegal abortion.

67. _____ . "The Ban." Woman Rebel, 1.3 May 1914: p. 24.
M.S. promises that despite the postal ban subscribers will receive the Woman Rebel.

68. _____ . "Blood and Oil." Woman Rebel, 1.3 May 1914: pp. 17-18.
Attacks the capitalist encroachments into Mexico.

69. _____ . "Cannibals." Woman Rebel, 1.3 May 1914: p. 17.
Spurred by the strike in Colorado, M.S. attacks the Y.M.C.A., the Y.W.C.A., the Baptist Church, John D. Rockefeller, Jr., and Standard Oil.

70. _____ . "Civilization." Woman Rebel, 1.3 May 1914: p. 20.
Comments on a statement made by Charlotte Perkins Gilman at an antiwar meeting.

71. _____ . "Hunting Big Game." Woman Rebel, 1.3 May 1914: p. 23.

Questions why 12,000 children are arrested each year for playing on the New York streets.

72. _____. "Is This True?" Woman Rebel, 1.3 May 1914: p. 23.
Why is an American girl "... the last one out on strike and the first one back"?

73. _____. "'The Menace's' Advice." Woman Rebel, 1.3 May 1914: p. 23.
An attack on the Catholic Church and on the idea that a woman is only a childbearing machine.

74. _____. "Motherhood--Or Destruction." Woman Rebel, 1.3 May 1914: p. 22.
M.S. disputes the idea that motherhood is of vital importance to a woman.

75. _____. "On Picket Duty." Woman Rebel, 1.3 May 1914: p. 19.
Attacks John D. Rockefeller, Jr. (because of mining conditions in Colorado) and praises the hunger strike of Becky Edelsohn.

76. _____. "Sex Talks." Woman Rebel, 1.3 May 1914: p. 24.
A call for sex education for boys and girls.

77. _____. "Soldiers and Prostitution." Woman Rebel, 1.3 May 1914: p. 21.
Equates prostitution with the military.

78. _____. "Watchful Waiting." Woman Rebel, 1.3 May 1914: p. 24.
Proclaims that forty thousand Socialist Party women have protested to President Wilson about the strikebreaking in Colorado.

79. _____. "Choose!" Woman Rebel, 1.4 June 1914: p. 29.
The revolutionary woman can not be dominated by the materialism of "Things."

80. _____. "Class and Character, Article No. 1." Woman Rebel, 1.4 June 1914: p. 28.
Calls on the working woman to reject the standards and values of the upper classes.

81. _____. "Don't Miss It!" Woman Rebel, 1.4 June 1914: p. 32.
Encourages readers to subscribe to the new radical publication, Land and Liberty.

82. _____. "Mary, Mother Mary." Woman Rebel, 1.4 June 1914: p. 32.
Uses the plight of a fourteen-year-old mother to illustrate the need for "birth-control."

83. _____. "The Militants in England." Woman Rebel, 1.4 June 1914: pp. 25, 31.
Praises the militancy of the English feminists.

84. _____. "Not Suppressed." Woman Rebel, 1.4 June 1914: p. 32.
Cites a news story from the N.Y. Evening Mail that reports a death and suicide resulting from an illegal abortion.

85. _____. "Servile Virtues." Woman Rebel, 1.4 June 1914: p. 32.
Attacks the "servile virtues" being taught in the New York City schools.

86. _____. "Suppression." Woman Rebel, 1.4 June 1914: p. 25.
Suppression by the Post Office of the Woman Rebel is the suppression of "birth control."

87. _____. "Your Liberty." Woman Rebel, 1.4 June 1914: p. 32.
M.S. reprints the letter sent to her by Postmaster E. M. Morgan banning the May 1914 issue of Woman Rebel from the mails.

88. _____. "Are Preventive Means Injurious?" Woman Rebel, 1.5 July 1914: p. 40.
States that harmless means of birth control exist and should be available.

89. _____. "The Birth Control League." Woman Rebel, 1.5 July 1914: p. 39.
Announces the aims of the newly formed Birth Control League of America.

90. _____. "Cantankerous Katherine." Woman Rebel, 1.5 July 1914: p. 35.
An attack against Katherine B. Davis, commissioner of correction in New York.

91. _____. "Class and Character, Article No. 2." Woman Rebel, 1.5 July 1914: pp. 36-37.
A call for a strong, free woman.

92. _____. "Militants in England." Woman Rebel, 1.5 July 1914: p. 35.
M.S. admires the English "militants" and their demand for the right to vote but feels that a woman's control over her own body is more important.

93. _____. "No Gods." Woman Rebel, 1.5 July 1914: p. 40.
A denouncement of all the "gods" of society.

94. _____. "Save Rangel, Cline et al. from 'Texas Justice'." Woman Rebel, 1.5 July 1914: p. 40.
Asks that the sentencing of workers to the penitentiary in Texas be protested.

95. _____. "Tragedy." Woman Rebel, 1.5 July 1914: p. 33.
Calls for "Solidarity" and "Revolution."

96. _____. "Another Woman." Woman Rebel, 1.6 Aug. 1914: pp. 42-43.
Attacks women who exploit other women by acting as "detectives, policewomen and commissioners of correction."

97. _____. "The Birth Control League." Woman Rebel, 1.6 Aug. 1914: p. 47.
Lists the aims of the Birth Control League of America and asks for members and contributions.

98. _____. "Class and Character, Article No. 3." Woman Rebel,

1.6 Aug. 1914: p. 44.
Discusses a woman's need for a healthy body, and the effects of alcohol.

99. _____. "Confiscated." Woman Rebel, 1.6 Aug. 1914: p. 48.
Announces that the July issue of Woman Rebel has been banned and confiscated by the U.S. Post Office.

100. _____. "The History of the Hunger-Strike." Woman Rebel, 1.6 Aug. 1914: p. 46.
Tells the story of Becky Edelsohn and demands her release from prison.

101. _____. "More Justice!" Woman Rebel, 1.6 Aug. 1914: p. 48.
Asks help for the workers being tried in Texas.

102. _____. "No Masters." Woman Rebel, 1.6 Aug. 1914: p. 47.
Asks the working woman to live by the standard of the Woman Rebel, "No Gods, No Masters."

103. _____. "The Old and The New." Woman Rebel, 1.6 Aug. 1914: p. 48.
Compares "the woman of the past," Katherine B. Davis, with Rebecca Edelsohn, "the woman of the future."

104. _____. "One Woman's Fight." Woman Rebel, 1.6 Aug. 1914: p. 42.
The article sets forth Becky Edelsohn as an example to all rebel women. Two letters are included that were written by Becky during her hunger strike; the letters depict conditions on Blackwell's Island.

105. _____. "A Question." Woman Rebel, 1.6 Aug. 1914: p. 45.
An attack on Katherine B. Davis, commissioner of corrections.

106. _____. (Untitled Letter). Woman Rebel, 1.6 Aug. 1914: p. 45.
Letter asks for opinions on birth control propaganda. "Is it necessary? Is it important? Is it immoral? Is it futile?"

107. _____. "The War's Lesson." Woman Rebel, 1.6 Aug. 1914: p. 48.
"The war is good." It will show the need for worker "Solidarity."

108. _____. "Where Is Your Power Now?" Woman Rebel, 1.6 Aug. 1914: p. 48.
At the beginning of World War I. "Our feelings and sympathies must be with the French who have always labored as champions of human liberty."

109. _____. "Your Guardians." Woman Rebel, 1.6 Aug. 1914: p. 45.
Notifies subscribers that if copies of the Woman Rebel fail to arrive, the "United States Post Office has decided that [the magazine] is not fit for you to read."

110. _____. "Government." Woman Rebel, 1.7 Sept.-Oct. 1914:
     p. 51.
     Reprints a Land and Liberty article that protests M.S.'s
     indictment.

111. _____. "How to Manufacture Cannon-Fodder." Woman Rebel,
     1.7 Sept.-Oct. 1914: p. 54.
     Comments on incidents where breeding is being encouraged
     to offset war deaths.

112. _____. "Indictment." Woman Rebel, 1.7 Sept.-Oct. 1914:
     p. 49.
     Announces M.S.'s indictment for depositing copies of the
     Woman Rebel in the post office. Emphasizes the importance of
     the birth control issue and, even in the radical press, finds
     little support for the fight.

113. _____. "A Little Lesson for Those Who Ought to Know
     Better." Woman Rebel, 1.7 Sept.-Oct. 1914: p. 53.
     Questions and answers about birth control.

114. _____. "No Defense Fund." Woman Rebel, 1.7 Sept.-Oct.
     1914: p. 53.
     M.S. asks for help in forming birth control organizations
     but not for a defense fund to help her fight her own case.

115. _____. "Opinions." Woman Rebel, 1.7 Sept.-Oct. 1914:
     pp. 51-52.
     Presents opinions and letters concerning M.S.'s indictment.

116. _____. "Some Letters." Woman Rebel, 1.7 Sept.-Oct.
     1914: p. 55.
     Prints letters from women who have written in asking for
     birth control information.

117. _____. "What Makes Propaganda." Woman Rebel, 1.7 Sept.-
     Oct. 1914: p. 56.
     Revolutionaries must "act" for their cause and hope propa-
     ganda results bring that cause "to the attention of the people."

118. _____. "Women Awakening." Woman Rebel, 1.7 Sept.-Oct.
     1914: p. 56.
     Editorializes on the need to provide birth control information
     to working women.

119. DeCleyre, Voltairine. "Direct Action." Woman Rebel, 1.1
     March 1914: p. 3.
     Strikes and violence must go together.

120. Goldman, Emma. "Love and Marriage." Woman Rebel, 1.1
     Mar. 1914: p. 3.
     An emotional appeal for "fewer and better children."

121. Greig, Teresa Billington. "Feminism." Woman Rebel, 1.1 Mar.
     1914: p. 3.
     Feminism must be a "movement seeking to remodel social
     life...."

122. Holt, Catherine. "The Unemployed in New York." Woman
     Rebel, 1.1 Mar. 1914: p. 5.
     Deplores the arrest cf the unemployed in New York and
     calls for the end of the "profit-making system."

123. Howard, Marion. "Why Wait?" Woman Rebel, 1.1 Mar. 1914:
     p. 2.
     Calls on workers to hold a "Universal Eight Hour Strike."
124. "I.W.W. Preamble." Woman Rebel, 1.1 Mar. 1914: p. 7.
     Reprints the preamble of the Industrial Workers of the
     World.
125. Kelly, Dorothy. "Rulers, Judges, Soldiers and Hangmen."
     Woman Rebel, 1.1 Mar. 1914: p. 2.
     Attacks the "trend toward specialism and professionalism"
     as lacking humanity.
126. Kleen, Elizabeth. "To Be a Woman Rebel." Woman Rebel,
     1.1 Mar. 1914: p. 2.
     The woman rebel is seen as one who "gets out of the habits
     imposed on her by bourgeois convention."
127. Locke, Benita. "Mothers' Pensions: The Latest Capitalist
     Trap." Woman Rebel, 1.1 Mar. 1914: pp. 4-5.
     Attacks as a "Capitalist Trap" all plans to pay money to
     poor mothers.
128. Mann, Nora. "Mary Wollstonecraft--A Great Rebel." Woman
     Rebel, 1.1 Mar. 1914: pp. 5-6.
     A tribute to Mary Wollstonecraft.
129. Morgan, J. Edward. "My Song (A Prose Poem)." Woman
     Rebel, 1.1 Mar. 1914: p. 5.
     Morgan sings "the Song of the BOMB."
130. Chapelier, Emile. "To Working Girls." Woman Rebel, 1.2
     April 1914: p. 12.
     A call to working women to stop being "breeders of flesh
     and blood for the factories, ... for the cannons, for prostitu-
     tion, for mad houses and asylums."
131. Cole, Ethel. "Poverty and Children." Woman Rebel, 1.2
     April 1914: p. 10.
     "... poverty and large families go hand in hand."
132. Kelly, Dorothy. "Prevention and the Law." Woman Rebel,
     1.2 April 1914: p. 10.
     This is a call for legalized abortion.
133. Mann, Nora. "Louise Michel, the Red Virgin (1830-1905)."
     Woman Rebel, 1.2 April 1914: pp. 13-14.
     A tribute to the French revolutionary, Louise Michel.
134. Meric, Victor. "The First Right." Woman Rebel, 1.2 April
     1914: p. 10.
     A short paragraph proclaiming a woman's right to control
     her own body.
135. Mylius, Edward F. "Freedom in America." Woman Rebel, 1.2
     April 1914: p. 13.
     A description of "Union Square April 4, 1914" and the
     brutalization of the worker.
136. Ureles, Sonia. "Man's Law." Woman Rebel, 1.2 April 1914:
     p. 9.
     A story of a woman and her unwanted pregnancies.
137. "Bars Magazine from Mail; Mrs. Sanger is Notified to Take
     Away Copies of 'The Woman Rebel'." New York Times,
     4 April 1914: p. 19, col. 2.

Article also notes M.S.'s prominence in the Lawrence, Mass. strike, names her as a member of the I.W.W., and reports that she considers Charlotte Perkins Gilman "a conservative and a reactionary."

138. Aegyptus. "The Pauline Ideas vs. Woman." Woman Rebel, 1.3 May 1914: p. 20.
Charges St. Paul with imposing upon women a "... serfdom of sexual, intellectual, personal and spiritual bondage...."

139. Bobsien, O. "Book Review." Woman Rebel, 1.3 May 1914: p. 23.
A review of C. V. Drysdale's The Small Family System--Is It Injurious or Immoral?

140. Cole, Ethel. "Open Discussion." Woman Rebel, 1.3 May 1914: p. 18.
Asks for a discussion of control of conception.

141. Eastman, Max. "The Woman Rebel." The Masses, 5.8 May 1914: p. 5.
Eastman welcomes the first issue of M.S.'s Woman Rebel and thanks her "for speaking out clearly and quietly for popular education in the means of preventing conception." He criticizes the tone of the magazine, however, as having a "blare of rebellion for its own sake." "The Woman Rebel seems to give a little more strength to the business of shocking the Bourgeoisie than the Bourgeoisie really are worth."

142. Humane, Alixe. "Ellen Key's Ideal of Woman." Woman Rebel, 1.3 May 1914: p. 18.
Presents some of the ideas of Ellen Key.

143. Kleen, Elizabeth. "Can You Afford to Have a Large Family?" Woman Rebel, 1.3 May 1914: p. 23.
A call to regulate family size according to income.

144. Mann, Nora. "Louise Michel." Woman Rebel, 1.3 May 1914: pp. 21-22.
The conclusion of the tribute to Louise Michel.

145. Humane, Elixe. "Marriage." Woman Rebel, 1.4 June 1914: p. 31.
Equates marriage with slavery for women.

146. McKenna, Edmond. "To Mother Jones in Colorado and Elsewhere." Woman Rebel, 1.4 June 1914: p. 29.
A poetic salute to Mother Jones.

147. Nelson, Caroline. "Sacred Motherhood." Woman Rebel, 1.4 June 1914: p. 27.
Cites customs around the world that treat women as unclean and calls for control of childbirth.

148. Newcome, Clara. "Neo-Malthusianism--What It Is." Woman Rebel, 1.4 June 1914: p. 26.
The working classes must have control of their childbearing.

149. Wilkinson, Lily Gair. "Women in Freedom." Woman Rebel, 1.4 June 1914: pp. 29-30.
Advocates "free love" and an end to private property.

150. Groff, Alice. "The Marriage Bed." Woman Rebel, 1.5 July
        1914: p. 39.
        Marriage, as an institution, is "degenerating."
151. McKenna, Edmond. "To Emmeline Pankhurst." Woman Rebel,
        1.5 July 1914: p. 37.
        A poetic salute to Emmeline Pankhurst.
152. Mann, Nora. "Theroigne de Mericourt." Woman Rebel, 1.5
        July 1914: pp. 37-38.
        The story of Theroigne de Mericourt, French revolutionary.
153. Thorpe, Herbert A. "A Defense of Assassination." Woman
        Rebel, 1.5 July 1914: pp. 33-34.
        Defends violence as a means of reform.
154. Pratt, Robert E. "Becky and the Respectables." Woman
        Rebel, 1.6 Aug. 1914: pp. 41-42.
        A tribute to Becky Edelsohn who staged a hunger strike
        while imprisoned on Blackwell's Island.
155. Wilkinson, Lily Gair. "Sisterhood." Woman Rebel, 1.6 Aug.
        1914: pp. 45-46.
        The major division is one of class, not sex, but even rich
        women are slaves, owned by men.
156. Liber, B. "Birth and the War Machine." Woman Rebel, 1.7
        Sept.-Oct. 1914: pp. 49-50.
        Sets forth the principles of Malthus and calls for birth pre-
        vention, rather than war, as a check on population.
157. "Woman Rebel Editor on Trial." New York Call, 20 Oct.
        1914: p. 4 col. 4.
        Reports that M.S. will be put on trial for sending "inde-
        cent" material through the mails. Article quotes remarks of
        Inez Milholland Boissevain made in defense of M.S.
158. "Mrs. Sanger's Case on Trial Today." New York Call, 21
        Oct. 1914: p. 4 col. 1.
        Briefly reports that M.S.'s case was postponed.
159. "Margaret Sanger." The Masses, 6.2 Nov. 1914: p. 20.
        The Masses notes the indictment of M.S. and offers its sup-
        port. It urges its readers to help and offers to accept "com-
        munications" on Sanger's behalf.

                                1915

160. Sanger, Margaret H. Dutch Methods of Birth Control. New
        York: n.p., n.d. 16 p (1915?)
        Includes a reprint of a pamphlet printed by the Neo-
        Malthusian League of Holland, which describes methods of
        contraception and is entitled "Methods Used to Prevent Large
        Families."
        An introduction by M.S. gives a "Brief History of the
        League" and praises the league's accomplishments in Holland.
161. _____. What Every Girl Should Know. Preface by Joy
        Johannessen. New York: Belvedere, 1980. (Reprint of
        the 1920 ed. published by M. N. Maisel, N.Y.) 81 p.
        (OCLC: 6379519).

One of many printings of the pamphlet first published in 1915. An informative preface compares this work with What Every Boy and Girl Should Know (see item 645). M.S.'s early radical and socialist beliefs are apparent in this sexual guide. No index.

Browne, F. W. Stella. "The Message of the Margarets." New Generation, 1.7 July 1922: pp. 14-15.

Review of What Every Girl Should Know.

162. "Sanger Held for Trial as Comstock Testifies; Agent Admits He Obtained 'Family Limitation' Pamphlet at Own Request." New York Call, 3 Feb. 1915: p. 3 col. 5.

163. "Raise a Fund for Sanger; Free Speech Argument for Man Arrested by Comstock." New York Times, 6 Feb. 1915: p. 12 col. 5.

Leonard Abbott, president of the Free Speech League, proposes to raise funds for the defense of William Sanger.

164. Eastman, Max. "Margaret Sanger vs. Anthony Comstock." New York Call, 21 Feb. 1915, Sun. ed.: Sect. 2 p. 15 col. 1-4.

Discusses Post-Office censorship of the Woman Rebel and the What Every Girl Should Know series and reports the arrest of William Sanger, giving parts of his conversation with Anthony Comstock. Eastman calls for support for Sanger.

165. _____. "Is the Truth Obscene?" The Masses, 6.6 Mar. 1915: pp. 5-6.

This article deals with William Sanger's arrest for handing out a copy of Family Limitation and reports his conversation with Anthony Comstock. The article calls on the public to support the Sangers and asks physicians and leaders of the women's movement to appear in court on their behalf.

166. "Progress or Comstock?: By Our Readers." The Masses, 6.7 April 1915: pp. 23-24.

The Masses prints letters in reply to its article of March 1915 on the arrest of William Sanger (see item 165). All are in support of Sanger except one letter "From an Opponent." A letter from Upton Sinclair is included.

In a box on page 24, The Masses requests donations for "the Sanger Fund."

167. "Films on Births and Censorship." Survey, 34 3 April 1915: pp. 4-5.

The article reports on William Sanger's arrest for distributing a copy of Family Limitation. It names many of those "who have sprung" to the Sangers' defense as well as those who are calling for the formation of a birth control league.

168. "Birth Control." The Masses, 6.8 May 1915: p. 20.

This article announces the formation of the Birth Control League and includes the remarks made by Mary Ware Dennett at its organizational meeting. Dennett sees the league as having been created from several groups, "the impetus having been largely precipitated by the Sanger case."

169. "The Sanger Case." The Masses, 6.8 May 1915: p. 20.
   The Masses reports that $93.65 has been received for the
   Sanger Fund, it prints "a few characteristic letters" on the
   subject, and it asks for more contributions.

170. "The Question of Birth-Control." The Masses, 6.9 June 1915:
   pp. 21-22.
   Includes more letters of support for the Sangers.

171. O'Malley, Austin. "The Dog or the Baby." America, 13.9
   12 June 1915: pp. 223-24.
   This is a Catholic doctor's attack on the "Committee on
   Birth Control" which, it says, attempts to "further the work
   of one Margaret H. Sanger."

172. Eastman, Max. "Revolutionary Birth-Control: A Reply to
   Some Correspondents." The Masses, 6.10 July 1915: pp.
   21-22.
   The article is written in rebuttal to the letters received regarding the William Sanger case, which advise "self-control"
   rather than birth control. Eastman is pleased by the publicity
   that birth control has been receiving in the press.

173. "Clash Over Comstock; Purity Congress Refuses to Listen to
   Attack upon Anti-Vice Man." New York Times, 19 July
   1915: p. 16 col. 7.
   From the floor of the Ninth International Purity Congress
   in San Francisco, Leon Malmed and William C. Hall question
   Anthony Comstock concerning the arrest of William Sanger. It
   is also reported that Judge Swann denied Sanger the jury trial
   Sanger had asked for.

174. Abbott, Leonard D. "The Sanger Case." New York Times,
   25 July 1915: Sect. 2 p. 14 col. 7.
   In a letter to the editor, Leonard Abbott states that
   William Sanger was not denied a jury trial as reported by the
   Times on July 19, 1915. His appeal for a jury trial was dis-
   missed by the appellate division of the Supreme Court of New
   York.

175. _____. "Is William Sanger to Go to Jail?" The Masses,
   6.12 Sept. 1915: p. 19.
   Reports that the William Sanger trial is scheduled for Sept.
   3 and that "he has been denied a jury trial" by Judge Swann.

176. "To Fight in Court for Birth Control; Sanger, the Artist,
   Ready to Meet Comstock's Efforts to Suppress Discussion;
   Calls it a Human Right; Tells of Hardships to Parents and
   Children Through Ill-balanced Families." New York Times,
   5 Sept. 1915: Sect. 2 p. 8 col. 5.

177. Minor, Robert. "Anything But the Truth." New York Call,
   9 Sept. 1915: p. 6, col. 3-6.
   Cartoon shows William Sanger being led in chains to jail
   while the wealthy people, holding a leaflet entitled "Sterilize
   the Unfit," watch.

178. "'My Case Not Issue' Says Sanger on Eve of Trial." New York
   Call, 10 Sept. 1915: p. 1 col. 5.

Reports an interview with William Sanger on the day before his trial. (A picture of Sanger is included.)

179. "William Sanger On Trial." New York Call, 10 Sept. 1915: p. 6 col. 1-2.
    Editorial defends W. Sanger.

180. "The Case of Sanger." New York Call, 11 Sept. 1915: p. 6 col. 1-2.
    An editorial defense of William Sanger.

181. "Disorder in Court as Sanger is Fined; Justices Order Room Cleared When Socialists and Anarchists Hoot Verdict; Defends Birth Control, Prisoner Accuses Comstock of Violating the Law and Goes to Jail Rather than Pay." New York Times, 11 Sept. 1915: p. 7 col 2.
    The "turbulent" trial of William Sanger is reported. Sanger was tried for giving a copy of Family Limitation to Anthony Comstock's agent. (For reprint of Sanger's statement see item 265.)

182. "What They Say About Sanger Case." New York Call, 11 Sept. 1915: p. 1 col. 6.
    Reports statements defending Sanger that were made by Mary Ware Dennett, Henrietta Rodman, Anita C. Block, and William J. Robinson.

183. "William Sanger Sentenced to Thirty Days in Jail; Judge McInerney Denounces Birth Control Propaganda as Against the Laws of God and Man in Giving Verdict. Court Room Cheers Defendant's Bold Stand." New York Call, 11 Sept. 1915: p. 1 col. 7--p. 4 col. 2-3.
    Includes picture of Margaret Sanger.

184. "William Sanger's Full Statement, Banned by Court, Is Printed Here." New York Call, 11 Sept. 1915: p. 4 col. 4-7.
    Reprints William Sanger's court statement (see item 265).

185. "Sanger Poses as a Martyr; Hopes to Draw Public Searchlight upon Existing Conditions." New York Times, 12 Sept. 1915: Sect. 2, p. 15 col. 1.

186. "What They Said: The Sanger Trial." America, 13.23 18 Sept. 1915: pp. 567-68.
    A sarcastic look at the trial of William Sanger; linking birth control with the woman suffrage movement.

187. Block, Anita C. "The Sanger Case." New York Call, 19 Sept. 1915, Sun. ed.: Mag. Sect. p. 13 col. 2-3.
    Editorial expresses admiration for William Sanger but maintains that his tactics are wrong. Collective action, not individual action, is needed (see item 190 for response).

188. "The Age of Birth Control." New Republic, 4 25 Sept. 1915: pp. 195-97.
    Responding to the arrest and sentencing of William Sanger, the author of this editorial advocates birth control and eugenic control.

189. "Birth Control and the New York Courts." Survey, 34 25 Sept. 1915: p. 567.
    A brief report on the trial of William Sanger.

190. Ashley, Jessie. "Differs on the Sanger Case." New York
     Call, 26 Sept. 1915, Sun. ed.: Mag. Sect. p. 13 col. 1-2.
     This letter to the editor praises William Sanger and attacks
     the editorial of Sept. 19 (see item 187).
191. Dell, Floyd. "Criminals All." The Masses, 7.1 Oct.-Nov.
     1915: p. 21.
     William Sanger chooses to go to jail rather than pay $150
     fine. He gets thirty days. Dell criticizes the law and the
     court and warns that the trial of M.S. will be even more
     serious.
192. "The Battle Over Birth Control." Current Opinion, 59.5 Nov.
     1915: pp. 339-41.
     In this unsigned editorial, the words of Justice McInerney,
     when sentencing William Sanger, are quoted. These words
     are contrasted with those of Judge William N. Gatem, of Port-
     land, Oregon, who dismissed a case against two men who had
     been accused of the distributing of one of M.S.'s pamphlets.
193. Keller, Helen. "Helen Keller, Blind, Deaf and Dumb Genius,
     Writes for Daily Call on Defective Baby Case." New York
     Call, 26 Nov. 1915: p. 5 col. 1-3 (see item 1206).
     Citing the William Sanger case, Helen Keller puts forth a
     strong appeal for birth control.

                              1916

194. Sanger, Margaret. "Birth Control and the Working Woman."
     New York Call, 25 June 1916, Sun. ed.: Mag. Sect. p. 9
     col. 1-4.
     M.S. advocates birth control as a means of giving the
     working woman a better life and of creating a "happier hu-
     manity."
195. _____. "Mrs. Sanger's Magazine." The Masses, 9.2 Dec.
     1916: p. 36.
     This short letter from M.S. announces the coming publica-
     tion of the Birth Control Review, with M.S. as editor and
     Dr. Frederick A. Blossom as managing editor.
196. "Mrs. Sanger to Be Tried; Back from Abroad to Face Indict-
     ments for Misuse of Mails." New York Times, 7 Jan. 1916:
     p. 9 col. 4.
     Reports on M.S.'s "first public statement" after her return
     to the U.S.
197. "Mrs. Sanger Defends Birth Control Fight." New York Call,
     8 Jan. 1916: p. 5 col. 6.
     Reports on comments made by M.S. before "an invited
     audience at the Fireside Club."
198. Fawcett, James Waldo. "The Sanger Case." New York Call,
     13 Jan. 1916: p. 6 col. 3.
     This letter to the editor from the secretary of the Margaret
     Sanger Defense Committee asks the readers of the "liberal
     press" to support M.S. with letters to the President and to
     the "capitalist papers."

199. "Socialists Will Aid Mrs. Sanger." New York Call, 13 Jan.
    1916: p. 4 col. 1.
    Announces that "a series of open-air meetings" will be
held by Brooklyn Socialists to aid M.S. in her coming court
case. M.S. and Elizabeth Gurley Flynn will speak.

200. "Mrs. Sanger Speaks in Brooklyn Tonight." New York Call,
    14 Jan. 1916: p. 2 col. 2.
    M.S. and Elizabeth Gurley Flynn will speak in Brooklyn.

201. "On Trial for Urging Birth Control." Survey, 35.16 15 Jan.
    1916: pp. 446-47.
    Reports that M.S.'s trial for "circulating obscene matter
through the mails" in the Woman Rebel will be held January
18, 1916. The article also reports on the letter sent on
Sanger's behalf to President Woodrow Wilson from well-known
figures in England.

202. "Want Women to Try Her; Friends Petition Court for Mixed
    Jury in Mrs. Sanger's Case." New York Times, 15 Jan.
    1916: p. 5 col. 5-6.
    A petition asks that M.S.'s jury be "composed of six women
and six men."

203. Payne, Kenneth W. "Threat of Jail Won't Stop 'Woman Rebel'
    from Making 'Birth Control' a Big Issue!" New York Call,
    16 Jan. 1916, Sun. ed.: p. 2 col. 2-3.
    M.S. will go to court without a lawyer. Her remarks on
the case, and birth control, are reported.

204. "Friends Dine Mrs. Sanger; Advocate of Birth Control Goes on
    Trial Today." New York Times, 18 Jan. 1916: p. 7 col.
    5.
    A dinner to support M.S. was given at the Hotel Brevoort.
Parts of M.S.'s speech are quoted.

205. Lewis, Marx. "Pledge Support to Mrs. Sanger; Prominent Men
    and Women Will Aid Woman Editor in Birth Control Fight."
    New York Call, 18 Jan. 1916: p. 1 col. 3.
    Reports on a dinner held for M.S. at the Hotel Brevoort.

206. "What Chance Has Mrs. Sanger?" New York Call, 18 Jan.
    1916: p. 6 col. 1-2.
    Editorial warns that M.S. may be convicted.

207. "Margaret Sanger's Case Draws Record Crowd of Writers to
    Court Room; Birth Control Advocate is Promised Trial Soon
    and is Assured of Fair Treatment by Judge, Whose Bass
    Boom Dwindles to Soft Southern Drawl." New York Call,
    19 Jan. 1916: p. 1 col. 5-6.
    Trial of M.S. is postponed. Large numbers of reporters
and supporters crowd court (includes picture of M.S. with two
sons).

208. "Mrs. Sanger Draws Crowd; Court Sets Misuse of Mails Case
    for Trial Next Monday." New York Times, 19 Jan. 1916:
    p. 22 col. 4.

209. "Aid Mrs. Sanger for Brave Fight." New York Call, 21 Jan.
    1916: p. 2 col. 4-5.
    Prints a Birth Control League resolution that asks for M.S.'s
acquittal.

210. "Birth Control Advocate with Friends Who Approve Ideas."
     New York Call, 24 Jan. 1916: p. 2 col. 2-3.
     Picture shows M.S. on way to court with two friends. Re-
     ports that the trial is postponed until February 12.

211. "Noted Women of All Walks of Life Will Crowd Federal Court at
     Mrs. Sanger's Trial." New York Call, 2 Feb. 1916: p. 5
     col. 5-7.
     Reports on large demonstration to be held at trial of M.S.
     Also reports that rumors from the government are that the
     case will be dropped.

212. "The Sanger Case." America, 14 12 Feb. 1916: p. 431.
     This editorial attacks M.S. for breaking the laws and ac-
     cuses her and her followers of anarchy.

213. "Will Try Mrs. Sanger Soon." New York Call, 13 Feb. 1916,
     Sun. ed.: p. 3 col. 4-5.
     Reports on M.S.'s coming trial and on the arrest of Emma
     Goldman who was taken into custody for advocating birth
     control.

214. "Dr. Biggs for Birth Control." New York Call, 15 Feb. 1916:
     p. 3 col. 1.
     Reports that M.S.'s trial is postponed again and prints a
     letter from Dr. Herman Biggs, New York State Health Com-
     missioner, advocating a revision of the birth control laws.

215. "Drops Mrs. Sanger's Case; Federal Action Followed by Plans
     for a Celebration." New York Times, 19 Feb. 1916: p. 12
     col. 2.
     The case against M.S. for sending the Woman Rebel
     through the mails is dropped.

216. Field, James A. "Publicity by Prosecution: a Commentary on
     the Birth Control Propaganda." Survey, 35 19 Feb. 1916:
     pp. 599-601.
     Author states that the arrests and prosecutions of William
     and Margaret Sanger did not check the tide of birth control
     propaganda. A short history of the systematic agitation in
     favor of birth control is given to prove the author's state-
     ment.

217. "U.S. Drops Birth Control Suit Against Woman Rebel." New
     York Call, 19 Feb. 1916: p. 1 col. 4-5.
     Article prints remarks of M.S. made after the dismissal of
     her case.

218. "Mrs. Sanger and Friends Hold Jubilee." New York Call, 21
     Feb. 1916: p. 3 col. 3. (Same article appears 22 February
     1916: p. 3 col. 6.)
     A celebration was held at the Bandbox Theater. M.S.'s
     comments are included. It is also reported that M.S. will
     leave for the Middle Western and Pacific States where "she in-
     tends to establish birth control leagues."

219. "Mrs. Sanger in Theatre; Acquitted Woman's Friends Hold
     Meeting at Bandbox." New York Times, 21 Feb. 1916:
     p. 3 col. 1.
     Briefly reports on a meeting of celebration held at the
     Bandbox Theatre.

220. "Birth Control Meeting; Carnegie Hall Will Hear Propaganda
     Discussed on March 1." New York Times, 26 Feb. 1916:
     p. 11 col. 2.
     The Birth Control Committee, with Leonard D. Abbott as
     chairman, announces a mass meeting to be held at Carnegie
     Hall. Although M.S.'s case has been dropped, Emma Goldman
     still awaits trial.
221. "Indictments Quashed in Birth Control Case." Survey, 35.22
     26 Feb. 1916: p. 628.
     Notes that "twelve counts against Mrs. Sanger were dis-
     missed" on February 18, 1916.
222. "Emma Goldman to Women; Carnegie Hall Filled to Hear Birth
     Control Discussion." New York Times, 2 March 1916:
     p. 20, col. 4.
     Emma Goldman speaks on birth control at Carnegie Hall. A
     letter of support from M.S. was read.
223. "Birth Control." The Masses, 8.6 April 1916: p. 21.
     Notes that the National Birth Control League has prepared
     two bills to amend federal and New York obscenity laws and
     asks for their support. The dismissal of M.S.'s case shows
     that the voice of public opinion is important. However, the
     arrest of Emma Goldman indicates that the obscenity statute is
     still being used.
224. "Birth-Control." The Masses, 8.9 July 1916: p. 27.
     Comments on the steps made by William J. Robinson and
     M.S. to change the Comstock Law. Notes the imprisonment
     of Emma Goldman and the deliberate attempt by Emma Pastor
     Stokes and Ben Reitman, at the Carnegie Hall meeting, to be
     arrested for handing out birth control information.
225. "Mrs. Sanger Plans Clinic; Says She Will Advocate Birth Con-
     trol in Brownsville." New York Times, 22 July 1916: p. 4
     col. 3.
     M.S. announces her plan to open a Brownsville clinic.
226. "For Birth Control Clinic; Mrs. Sanger Will Renew Her Cam-
     paign on the East Side." New York Times, 12 Sept. 1916:
     p. 11 col. 4.
     Reports on M.S.'s decision to open a clinic on New York's
     lower East Side. Also notes her recent arrest in Portland,
     Oregon.
227. Van Epps, C., M.D. "The Birth Control Movement." Iowa
     Board of Control. Bulletin, 18 Oct. 1916: pp. 312-15.
     An article on the indictment of M.S., published in the
     Woman Rebel, sparked this plea for birth control.
228. "The Spreading Movement for Birth Control." Survey, 37
     21 Oct. 1916: pp. 60-61.
     Reports that birth control leagues have been organized in
     many American cities. In Cleveland, where one of the first
     "thoroughly" organized units was established after M.S. spoke
     there, is a league which includes doctors, nurses, social work-
     ers, clergymen, and others. This article also notes M.S.'s

arrest in Portland, Oregon, where she was taken into custody
for distributing leaflets.

229. "Police Arrest Mrs. Sanger in Her New Clinic; Raid on Browns-
ville Institute Results in Jailing of Birth-Control Advocate."
New York Call, 27 Oct. 1916: p. 2 col. 1.
M.S., Fannie Mindell, and Ethel Byrne are arrested.

230. "Mrs. Sanger Accepts Bail; Birth Control Advocate Reconsiders
Determination to Stay in Jail." New York Times, 28 Oct.
1916: p. 8 col. 4.
M.S., Fannie Mindell, and Ethel Byrne are arrested because
of Brownsville clinic activities; they are released on bail. Item
also reports on the arrest of Emma Goldman for spreading birth
control information.

231. "Fine Birth Control Agent; Justice McInerney Favored Sending
Miss Ashley to Prison." New York Times, 31 Oct. 1916:
p. 9 col. 5.
Jessie Ashley is said to have been fined for distributing
birth control information. The article also reports that M.S.'s
trial was postponed.

232. "Woman Fined $50 in Birth Control Case." New York Call,
31 Oct. 1916: p. 3 col. 1.
Among other things, this article reports that Jessie Ashley
was fined for distributing birth control information and that
M.S.'s case was postponed.

233. "Birth Control Advocates Face Trial." New York Times, 7 Nov.
1916: p. 8 col. 4.
Notes the arraignment of M.S., Fannie Mindell, and Ethel
Byrne.

234. "Mrs. Sanger to Reopen Clinic; Despite Arrest and Approach-
ing Trial, Birth Control Fight Will Go On in Brooklyn."
New York Call, 13 Nov. 1916: p. 5 col. 1-2.
Prints M.S.'s statement on her announcement to reopen
Brownsville Clinic.

235. "Mrs. Sanger Reopens Clinic." New York Times, 14 Nov.
1916: p. 4 col. 2.
Notes that M.S., despite her arrest, has reopened the
Brownsville Clinic.

236. "Birth Control Agitation is in Full Swing; Mrs. Sanger's
Second Clinic Open in Brownsville--Woman's Club Plans
Meeting." New York Call, 15 Nov. 1916: p. 3 col. 1.
M.S. reopens clinic. Article describes need for birth con-
trol.

237. "Mrs. Sanger Arrested for Second Time." New York Call,
16 Nov. 1916: p. 1 col. 6--p. 3 col. 4.
Gives M.S.'s statements after her second arrest for oper-
ating Brownsville Clinic.

238. "Mrs. Sanger Rearrested; Birth Control Advocate Charged
with Maintaining a Public Nuisance." New York Times, 16
Nov. 1916: p. 17 col. 1.

239. "Mrs. Sanger Reopens Clinic." New York Call, 17 Nov. 1916:
p. 2 col. 5.
Despite two arrests, M.S. reopens Brownsville Clinic.

240. "Vice Society Head Hissed by Women; J. S. Sumner's Views
on Birth Control Opposed at the Women's City Club; Mrs.
M. Sanger Assailed; Charge Made That Her Agents Have
Commercialized Her Propaganda." New York Times, 18 Nov.
1916: p. 5 col. 1-2.
John S. Sumner, secretary of the Society for the Prevention
of Vice, attacks M.S.'s "motives" and accuses her of having
"an eye to profit."

241. "Mrs. Sanger Rests Before Trials Begin; Undaunted by Persecution, She Will Reopen Clinic, No Matter What Results."
New York Call, 19 Nov. 1916, Sun. ed.: p. 7 col. 3.

242. "Mrs. Sanger and 2 Others Enter Pleas." New York Call,
21 Nov. 1916: p. 3 col. 1.
M.S., Ethel Byrne, and Fannie Mindell plead not guilty.
The National Birth Control League will "open an active organi-
zation campaign in New York City ... with Dr. Frederick A.
Blossom as director...."

243. "Judges May Try to Rush Sanger Trials; Hearing May Be Held
Monday, Giving Birth Control Advocate Little Time to Sum-
mon Witnesses." New York Call, 22 Nov. 1916: p. 3 col.
2.

244. "Mrs. Sanger Defies Court; Will Forfeit Bond Rather than Appear for Trial." New York Times, 27 Nov. 1916: p. 13
col. 6.
M.S. announces she will not appear in court. Says Justice
McInerney "has a personal animosity against birth control."

245. "Mrs. Sanger Not to Attend Trial; Thinks It Useless to Appear Before Judge McInerney, Who is Hostile to Birth
Control." New York Call, 27 Nov. 1916: p. 3 col. 1.
M.S. announces she will not appear before Judge J. J.
McInerney. Article also reports a meeting to be held by
prominent women in their attempt to take over the running of
the clinic if M.S. is not able to do so.

246. "McInerney May Not Try Her Case; Mrs. Sanger Calls Judge
Prejudiced--He Says He's Willing to Transfer Trial." New
York Call, 28 Nov. 1916: p. 4 col. 1.
Prints M.S.'s statement attacking Judge J. J. McInerney.

247. "Mrs. Sanger Wants a Jury; Application with That Object De-
fers Her Trial in Brooklyn." New York Times, 28 Nov.
1916: p. 24 col. 2.

248. "Women Unite to Aid Mrs. Sanger." New York Call, 29 Nov.
1916: p. 5 col. 1.
Two committees of women are organized. One will support
M.S.'s clinic. The other will arrange meetings on birth control.

249. "Pastor for Birth Control; The Rev. Mr. Hess Attacks Police
for Activity Against Its Advocates." New York Times, 4
Dec. 1916: p. 13 col. 3.
Rev. William Milton Hess of the Trinity Congregational
Church in the Bronx defends birth control in a sermon and
criticizes the police for arresting M.S. and others.

250. "Rules Against Mrs. Sanger." New York Times, 5 Dec. 1916:
p. 11 col. 2.
M.S. is denied an application to transfer her trial to the
county court.

251. "Mrs. Sanger Loses Appeal." New York Times, 12 Dec. 1916:
p. 15 col. 1.
M.S.'s appeal to transfer her trial is dismissed.

252. "Jury to Get Sanger Case; Nuisance Charge Against Woman is
Transferred by Court." New York Times, 13 Dec. 1916:
p. 11 col. 3.
M.S. trial for "maintaining a public nuisance" is transferred
to the grand jury.

253. "Mrs. Sanger to Get Probe of Her Charges; Judge Hylan Grants
Application Which May Change Venue of Case." New York
Call, 13 Dec. 1916: p. 5 col. 1.

254. "New League for Birth Control is Launched." New York Call,
20 Dec. 1916: p. 5 col. 3.
Birth Control League of New York is formed with Frederick
A. Blossom as president. One of its aims "will be to help
Margaret Sanger in her fight against the present laws on birth
control."

255. "Mrs. Sanger's Writ Fails; Birth Control Advocate Must Give
Bail or Go to Jail." New York Times, 23 Dec. 1916: p. 5
col. 3.

1917

256. Sanger, Margaret H. The Case for Birth Control: A Supple-
mentary Brief and Statement of Facts. New York: Modern
Art Printing Co., 1917, 251 p. (OCLC: 1132035).
This compilation of statistical, historical, and informative
data includes works and parts of works by numerous authors
as well as a speech, "The Case for Birth Control," given by
M.S. throughout the U.S.
As noted on the title page, the brief is meant "To aid the
court in its consideration of the statute designed to prevent
the dissemination of information for preventing conception."
The statute in question was Section 1142 of the New York State
Penal Law.

257. _____. "The People of the State of New York, Respondent,
against Margaret H. Sanger, Defendant-Appellant. Appellant's Statement and Points." New York: The Heela Press,
1917 71 p. Not seen.

258. _____. "An Open Letter to Judge J. J. McInerney."
Birth Control Review, 1.1 Feb. 1917: p. 16.
Presented as "an historic document," this letter from M.S.
accuses Judge McInerney of being "prejudiced against her."

259. _____. "Shall We Break This Law?" Birth Control Review,
1.1 Feb. 1917: p. 4.

M.S. proclaims that women will break the law to establish
their "right to voluntary motherhood."

260.   _____; Blossom, Frederick A.; Stuyvesant, Elizabeth. "To
the Men and Women of the United States." Birth Control
Review, 1.1 Feb. 1917: p. 3.
This open letter introduces the first issue of the Birth
Control Review "as the herald of a new freedom."

261. Sanger, Margaret. "Printed and Spurious Editions." Birth
Control Review, 1.4 June 1917: p. 6.
An announcement from M.S. stating that because she has
been unable to copyright some of her pamphlets, pirated editions are being circulated. Works that she never wrote are
also being circulated with her name.

262.   _____. "Woman and War." Birth Control Review, 1.4 June
1917: p. 5.
This article depicts women as victims of "unwilling motherhood" and as suppliers of sons for the "slaughter" of war.

263.   _____. "An Answer to Mr. Roosevelt." Birth Control Review, 1.5 Dec. 1917: pp. 13-14.
M.S. replies to an article by Theodore Roosevelt and refutes his argument that birth control will result in intelligent
people having fewer children.

264.   _____. "Birth Control and Woman's Health." Birth Control
Review, 1.5 Dec. 1917: pp. 7-8.
M.S. presents the argument that birth control will improve,
not impair, women's health.

265. Fawcett, James Waldo, ed. "Jailed for Birth Control; The Trial
of William Sanger September 10, 1915." New York: N.P.,
1917. 15 p. (OCLC: 8004311).
This pamphlet contains the full statement of William Sanger,
which he was unable to present in court. Originally, the
statement had been printed in the New York Call of September
11, 1915. (See item 184.) A reprint of the article featuring
coverage of the trial (New York Times of Sept. 11, 1915) is
also included. (See item 181.)

266. Roosevelt, Theodore. The Foes of Our Own Household. New
York: George H. Doran, 1917. 347 p. (no index, no
bibl.) (OCLC: 394557).
In a chapter entitled "Birth Reform," Roosevelt links birth
control with racial suicide.

267. "Birth Controllers Up Early for Trial; Women Give Mrs. Sanger
a Breakfast, Then Go to Brooklyn to Wait All Day in Court;
Mrs. Byrne's Case Begun." New York Times, 5 Jan. 1917:
p. 4 col. 2-3.

268. "Sanger Trial Begins Monday." New York Call, 5 Jan. 1917:
p. 3 col. 3.
Reports on M.S.'s pre-trial support.

269. "Mrs. Sanger's Aid Is Found Guilty; Mrs. Byrne Convicted on
Technicality in First of Birth Control Trials." New York
Times, 9 Jan. 1917: p. 11 col. 1.

270. "Mrs. Sanger's Case Set Back; Her Sister is Found Guilty."

New York Call, 9 Jan. 1917: p. 1 col. 2--p. 3 col. 5.
Reports on trial during which Ethel Byrne was found guilty. Also reports on the birth control trial of Emma Goldman, who was acquitted.

271. "Plan Ovation for Mrs. Sanger; Birth Control League Organizes Mass Protest Meeting Against Police Interference." New York Call, 14 Jan. 1917, Sun. ed.: p. 7 col. 3.
Announces a mass meeting at Carnegie Hall on January 29 on behalf of birth control movement.

272. "Mrs. Sanger's Clients Plan Demonstration; Women Who Have Been Helped Will Participate in Carnegie Hall Meeting." New York Call, 18 Jan. 1917: p. 5 col. 4.

273. "Paterson Fears Sanger Visit." New York Call, 19 Jan. 1917: p. 2 col. 4.
M.S. is scheduled to speak before Paterson Philosophical Society in Paterson, N.J., but "conservative elements" oppose her appearance.

274. O'Malley, Austin, M.D. "A Nauseous Philosophy and Poor Arguments." America, 16.15 20 Jan. 1917: pp. 348-49.
Dr. O'Malley rebuts arguments for birth control presented by Dr. S. Adolphus Knopf following an incident during which M.S. was not allowed to address a meeting in Philadelphia.

275. "Mrs. Sanger in Paterson; Police Do Not Interfere at Birth Control Lecture." New York Times, 22 Jan. 1917: p. 18 col. 2.
M.S. speaks in Paterson, N.J. at Institute Hall.

276. "Mrs. Sanger Lectures, Despite Opposition." New York Call, 22 Jan. 1917: p. 1 col. 2.
M.S. spoke in Paterson, N.J.

277. "Birth-Control Martyr, Sentenced to Prison, Plans Hunger Strike." New York Call, 23 Jan. 1917: p. 1 col. 2-3.
Ethel Byrne begins hunger strike after being sentenced to thirty days in prison.

278. "Mrs. Byrne Must Go to Workhouse; Sister of Mrs. Sanger Sentenced for Use of Birth Control Literature; Threatens Hunger Strike." New York Times, 23 Jan. 1917: p. 20 col. 3-4.

279. "Mrs. Byrne Loses on Constitutional Plea." New York Call, 24 Jan. 1917: p. 2 col. 2.
Ethel Byrne begins her sentence after plea is lost.

280. "Mrs. Byrne Starts Lots of Strikes; Won't Eat, Drink, Be Examined, or Bathed, and Says She Won't Work, Either!" New York Times, 24 Jan. 1917: p. 20 col. 2-3.

281. "Doctor's Care for Mrs. Byrne." New York Call, 25 Jan. 1917: p. 1 col. 6--p. 3 col. 5.
Ethel Byrne vows to continue her hunger strike on Blackwell's Island (picture of Ethel Byrne included).

282. "Mrs. Byrne Fasts in Workhouse Cell; But Commissioner Lewis Promises She'll Eat When It Becomes Necessary; She Spurns a Bath, Too; Committee of 100 Urges Prisoner to Take Up Feeding Again for the Cause's Sake." New York Times, 25 Jan. 1917: p. 20 col. 2-3.

Burdette G. Lewis, commissioner of correction, Women's Committee of One Hundred.

283. "Mrs. Byrne Weaker, Still Fasts in Cell; Birth-Control Prisoner May Be Fed by Force if Her Hunger Strike Continues; Her Sister is Indicted; Gov. Whitman Will Hear Plea for Woman-- Bail Ready for Mrs. Sanger." New York Times, 26 Jan. 1917: p. 1 col. 2.

284. "Mrs. Sanger Indicted As Sister Continues Heroic Hunger Strike." New York Call, 26 Jan. 1917: p. 1 col. 5-6.

285. "Mrs. Byrne in State of Coma, Attorney Says." New York Call, 27 Jan. 1917: p. 1 col. 5--p. 2 col. 2.

286. "Mrs. Byrne is Game as Strength Wanes; Workhouse Officials Testify to Her Fast, but Suspect She Has Had Water; Defer Forcible Feeding; But Physicians Watch Birth Control Prisoner Carefully--Visit by Her Sister Forbidden." New York Times, 27 Jan. 1917: p. 1 col. 4.

287. "Mrs. Byrne Fed Forcibly Twice; Doctors Fearful." New York Call, 28 Jan. 1917: p. 1 col. 5-6--p. 2 col. 6.

288. "Mrs. Byrne Now Fed by Force; Birth-Control Prisoner, Near Collapse, Revives After Food is Administered; Offered No Resistance; Mrs. Sanger Hears Her Sister Was in a State of Coma as a Result of Hunger Strike; Visitors Are Still Barred." New York Times, 28 Jan. 1917: pt. 1 p. 1 col. 3--p. 6 col. 2-4.

289. "Mrs. Sanger to Starve Also; Determined to Follow Her Sister's Course if She is Sentenced." New York Times, 28 Jan. 1917: pt. 1 p. 6 col. 4-5.
M.S. vows to go on hunger strike if imprisoned.

290. "Mrs. Byrne to Have a Feeding Schedule; Workhouse Physicians Decide Not to Wait Again till She is Near a Collapse; Diet is Milk, Eggs, Brandy; Mrs. Sanger's Trial Set for Today-- Birth Control Mass Meeting at Carnegie Hall Tonight." New York Times, 29 Jan. 1917: p. 1 col. 4--p. 3 col. 7.

291. "Mrs. Byrne Weak After Forceful Feeding." New York Call, 29 Jan. 1917: p. 1 col. 1--p. 2 col. 3.

292. "Judge Demands Crime Proof in Sanger Trial; Freschi Says State Must Show Intent." New York Call, 30 Jan. 1917: p. 1 col. 6--p. 3 col. 3-4.
(Justice John J. Freschi) reports on proceedings of M.S. trial (includes M.S. picture).

293. "Judge Demands Crime Proof in Sanger Trial; Mrs. Byrne Still Fed Through Tube; Refuses to Eat Voluntarily, Though She Shows Improvement after First Weakness." New York Call, 30 Jan. 1917: p. 1 col. 5--p. 3 col. 4.

294. "Judges Scored by Mrs. Sanger; 'Vortex of Persecution,' is Term She Uses in Carnegie Hall Meeting for Birth Control." New York Call, 30 Jan. 1917: p. 3 col. 3.
Reports on mass meeting at Carnegie Hall, and M.S. speech.

295. "Justices in Doubt in Sanger Case; Birth-Control Advocate Ex- pected Conviction, but Court Reserves Decision." New York Times, 30 Jan. 1917: p. 4 col. 3.

296. "Mrs. Byrne Fed Regularly; Continues to Offer No Resistance When Food is Administered." New York Times, 30 Jan. 1917: p. 4 col. 3-4.

297. "Mrs. Sanger Defies Courts Before 3,000; Carnegie Hall Mass Meeting Pledges Support in Her Birth-Control Fight; Women Cheer Her Speech; Dr. Mary Hunt Attacks 'Fifth Ave. Doctors' for Service to Rich Which She Says is Denied the Poor." New York Times, 30 Jan. 1917: p. 4 col. 2-3.

298. "Mrs. Byrne Declares 'General Strike'; Won't Eat, Talk or Move." New York Call, 31 Jan. 1917: p. 1 col. 2-3.

299. "Mrs. Byrne's Health Good; Officials Believe Workhouse Term Will Improve Physical Condition." New York Times, 31 Jan. 1917: p. 4 col. 3.

300. Goldstein, J. J. "The Birth Control Clinic Cases." Birth Control Review, 1.1 Feb. 1917: p. 8.
     The attorney for the defendants--Margaret Sanger, Ethel Byrne and Fannie Mindell--sets forth "in simple language the successive legal phases of the cases."

301. Margaret Sanger Defense Committee of the Birth Control League of New York. "To the People of the United States." Birth Control Review, 1.1 Feb. 1917: p. 16.
     This letter appeals for funds to defend M.S., Ethel Byrne, and Fannie Mindell.

302. "What the Birth Control Leagues are Doing." Birth Control Review, 1.1 Feb. 1917: pp. 10-11.
     Among other things, article reports on the organizational meeting of the Birth Control League of New York and the establishment of the Margaret Sanger Defense Committee to raise $5,000 to defend the clinic court cases.

303. "For State Inquiry into Birth Control; Whitman Tells Delegation of Women He is Willing to Appoint a Commission: Offers Mrs. Byrne Pardon; But Insists That She Must Refrain from Violating Law after Her Release." New York Times, 1 Feb. 1917: p. 22 col. 1-2.

304. "Whitman Will Name Commission to Study Birth Control Phases." New York Call, 1 Feb. 1917: p. 1 col. 3-4--p. 2 col. 3.
     M.S. and others protest treatment of Ethel Byrne. Gov. Whitman will name a commission to study birth control.

305. Day, Dorothy. "Mrs. Byrne, in Collapse, Is Pardoned by Whitman; Sister Finds Striker with Teeth Broken and at Death's Door." New York Call, 2 Feb. 1917: p. 1 col. 5-6--p. 2 col. 6.
     A dramatic account of Ethel Byrne's release from Blackwell's Island after Gov. Whitman's pardon (caricature of Ethel Byrne included).

306. "Mrs. Byrne Pardoned; Pledged to Obey Law; Birth Control Hunger-Striker Taken from Prison to Sister's Home in Ambulance." New York Times, 2 Feb. 1917: p. 11 col. 5.

307. Day, Dorothy. "Mrs. Byrne Too Weak to Eat After Ordeal at Workhouse." New York Call, 3 Feb. 1917: p. 1 col. 4--p. 2 col. 3.

Quotes M.S. on Ethel Byrne's condition and on Sanger and
Fannie Mindell's case.

308.   "Margaret Sanger and Miss Mindell Convicted in Birth Control
       Case." New York Call, 3 Feb. 1917: p. 1 col. 2-3.

309.   "Mrs. Sanger Guilty; Faces Prison Term; Court Will Sentence
       Woman in Birth Control Case Monday; May Go on Hunger
       Strike; Lewis Issues Statement Asserting Friends of Mrs.
       Byrne Have Misrepresented Case." New York Times, 3 Feb.
       1917: p. 8 col. 2-3.
       Commissioner of Correction Lewis says Ethel is in good
       physical condition.

310.   Day, Dorothy. "Mrs. Byrne Well When Sentenced Says Physi-
       cian." New York Call, 4 Feb. 1917, Sun. ed.: p. 4 col.
       3.
       Report by Ethel Byrne's physician, Dr. Morris H. Kahn.

311.   "Mrs. Sanger to Face Prison Sentence Today." New York Call,
       5 Feb. 1917: p. 1 col. 3.

312.   Day, Dorothy. "Mrs. Byrne Tells Her First Story of Life
       During Hunger Strike." New York Call, 6 Feb. 1917:
       p. 1 col. 2.
       Reports on conditions in women's section of Blackwell's
       Island (as seen by Ethel Byrne).

313.   "Mrs. Sanger Gets 30 Days; Refuses Alternative of a Fine, but
       She Will Not Go on Hunger Strike." New York Times, 6
       Feb. 1917: p. 20, col. 5.
       M.S. refuses to abandon birth control campaign and to ac-
       cept fine. Will go to workhouse.

314.   "Mrs. Sanger Starts Term; Her Sister, Mrs. Byrne, Condemns
       Conditions on Island." New York Times, 7 Feb. 1917: p.
       13 col. 5.
       Concerns M.S.'s stay at Blackwell's Island.

315.   Day, Dorothy. "Blackwell's Island Gray, Dead, Desolate,
       Declares Mrs. Byrne." New York Call, 8 Feb. 1917:
       p. 3 col. 3-4.
       Ethel Byrne describes conditions on Blackwell's Island.

316.   "Replies to Mrs. Byrne: Commissioner Lewis Says Workhouse
       Is Not Run to Please Inmates." New York Times, 8 Feb.
       1917: p. 12 col. 7.

317.   "Mrs. Sanger in Queens Jail; Transferred from Island Because
       Workhouse Was Crowded." New York Times, 9 Feb. 1917:
       p. 20 col. 2.
       M.S. is moved from Blackwell's Island to Queens County
       Jail in Long Island City.

318.   "Not Afraid, But Lewis Moves Mrs. Sanger." New York Call,
       9 Feb. 1917: p. 5 col. 2.
       M.S. is transferred from Blackwell's Island to Queens
       County Jail to serve out her thirty-day sentence. Commis-
       sioner Lewis cites overcrowding as reason (Burdette G. Lewis).

319.   "Editorial Notes." The New Republic, 10.119 10 Feb. 1917:
       p. 32.
       Because of the successful agitation of M.S. and the hunger

strike of Ethel Byrne, Gov. Whitman has offered to appoint a
committee that would investigate the matter of birth control
and report to the legislature. (Charles Whitman, Governor
of New York.)

320. "Trials of Birth Control Advocate." Survey, 37 10 Feb. 1917:
     p. 555.
     Notes the hunger strike of Ethel Byrne and includes de-
tails of raid on the Brownsville Clinic.

321. Day, Dorothy. "Mrs. Sanger Put Near Maniac." New York
     Call, 12 Feb. 1917: p. 5 col. 1-2.
     M.S. reports on poor conditions at Queens County Jail.

322. "Mrs. Sanger's Pen is Feared." New York Call, 14 Feb.
     1917: p. 3 col. 4.
     M.S.'s lawyer, Jonah Goldstein, describes poor jail condi-
tions.

323. Kosmak, George W., M.D. "Birth Control: What Shall Be the
     Attitude of the Medical Profession Toward the Present-Day
     Propaganda." Medical Record, 91 17 Feb. 1917: pp. 268-
     273.
     A call to physicians to ignore the "hysteria" of birth con-
trol propaganda. Individual decisions should be in the hands
of the doctor, and continence should be stressed.

324. "Asks Governor to Hurry; Mrs. Pinchot Urges Investigation
     of the Birth Control Question." New York Times, 19 Feb.
     1917: p. 18 col. 4.
     Mrs. Amos Pinchot urges Governor Whitman to appoint the
promised birth control committee.

325. "Birth Control League, Active; Margaret Sanger's Incarcera-
     tion Does Not Stop Work--Meetings Are Planned." New
     York Call, 26 Feb. 1917: p. 5 col. 1-2.
     The work of the New York Birth Control League continues
with meetings and propaganda.

326. Block, Anita C. "An Admirable Meeting." Birth Control Re-
     view, 1.2 Mar. 1917: p. 12.
     Describes the Carnegie Hall meeting as "a triumph of
women, for women, by women."

327. Blossom, Frederick A. "Growth of the Birth Control Movement
     in the U.S." Birth Control Review, 1.2 Mar. 1917: pp.
     4-5.
     A tribute to M.S. written while she was in jail. Simul-
taneously in the New York Call, 25 Feb. 1917, Sun. ed.:
Mag. Sect. p. 6 col. 1-4.

328. _____. "New York's Tribute." Birth Control Review, 1.2
     Mar. 1917: p. 11.
     Describes the mass meeting held at Carnegie Hall as a
tribute to M.S.

329. Hoyt, Kepler. "Carnegie Hall Mass Meeting." Birth Control
     Review, 1.2 Mar. 1917: p. 11.
     The Carnegie Hall meeting is seen as a protest against an
unjust law.

330. Margaret Sanger Defense Committee. "To the Friends of Birth

Control." Birth Control Review, 1.2 Mar. 1917: p. 16.
This article calls for more funds for defense counsel and
for appeals in the Sanger clinic cases.

331. Mylius, E. F. "Hunger-Striking Against an Unjust Law."
Birth Control Review, 1.2 Mar. 1917: p. 10.
The article praises Ethel Byrne for her hunger strike dur-
ing her imprisonment.

332. "New York Speaks Its Mind." Birth Control Review, 1.2 Mar.
1917: p. 12.
Concerns the "resolutions adopted at the Carnegie Hall
mass meeting Jan. 29, 1917."

333. "The Sanger Clinic Cases." Birth Control Review, 1.2 Mar.
1917: p. 13.
Chronological breakdown of happenings in the Sanger clinic
cases.

334. Stuyvesant, Elizabeth, with illustrations by William Sanger.
"The Brownsville Birth Control Clinic." Birth Control
Review, 1.2 Mar. 1917: pp. 6-8.
An account of the Brownsville Clinic; included are descrip-
tions of the women who were served.

335. "What Even a Judge Should Know." Birth Control Review, 1.2
Mar. 1917: p. 13.
Reports on the fifty-dollar fine Fannie Mindell received for
selling a copy of What Every Girl Should Know; the article
presents a few passages from this "obscene" work.

336. "Plan Welcome for Mrs. Sanger, Free Tomorrow." New York
Call, 5 Mar. 1917: p. 2 col. 4.
M.S. to be released from Queens County Jail. Testimonial
dinner is planned.

337. "Mrs. Sanger Free Today; Birth Control Advocate Did Not Try
to Spread Her Doctrines in Jail." New York Times, 6 Mar.
1917: p. 11 col. 4.

338. "Mrs. Sanger Flays Miss Davis's Plans; Birth Control Crusader, Her Imprisonment Ended, Brings Jail Women's
Plaint; Inmates 'Learn to Hate'; Will Deliver Her Message
to Miss Davis's Club--Resists All Attempts to Take Her
Fingerprints." New York Times, 7 Mar. 1917: p. 20 col.
5-6.
M.S. charges cruelty to women prisoners. Will speak at
Women's City Club where Katherine B. Davis, former commissioner of corrections, is an officer.

339. "Mrs. Sanger Out after Balking at Fingerprints; Birth Control Propagandist Struggles with Guards to Prevent Meas-
urements." New York Call, 7 Mar. 1917: p. 1 col. 2--
p. 2 col. 2.

340. "Lewis Replies to Mrs. Sanger; He is Glad When Mates Hate
Prison--Birth Control Leader Attacks Miss Davis." New
York Call, 8 Mar. 1917: p. 2 col. 7.
M.S. charges Katherine B. Davis, "former commissioner of
correction," with cruelty to prisoners. Commissioner Burdette
G. Lewis defends Davis.

341. "Miss Davis Denies She Was Heartless; Parole Board Chairman
     Says Mrs. Sanger's Charges Are Unfounded." New York
     Times, 8 Mar. 1917: p. 20 col. 2.
342. "Welcome For Mrs. Sanger; Birth Control Luncheon Marks Her
     Release from Jail." New York Times, 16 Mar. 1917: p. 12
     col. 5.
     Luncheon given by National Birth Control League at the
     Plaza Hotel.
343. "Mrs. Sanger Tells of Prison; Describes Her Life in Workhouse
     at Testimonial Which is Attended by 350." New York Call,
     17 Mar. 1917: p. 3 col. 1.
     Reports on a testimonial held for M.S. and Ethel Byrne at
     the Plaza Hotel.
344. Stuyvesant, Elizabeth. "The Brownsville Birth Control
     Clinic." New York Call, 18 Mar. 1917, Sun. ed.: Mag.
     Sect. p. 12 col. 1-4.
     Describes the methods used to open the Brownsville Clinic.
345. "Birth Control League Incorporated." New York Times, 20
     Mar. 1917: p. 13 col. 1.
     Birth Control League of New York City is chartered.
346. "Mrs. Sanger to Tour with Her Film." New York Times, 28
     Mar. 1917: p. 11 col. 2.
     M.S. "has been engaged by B. S. Moss for a tour of the
     country in conjunction with the exhibition of a motion picture
     of which she herself will be the star."
347. Debs, Eugene V. "My Dear Comrade Sanger:--? Birth Con-
     trol Review, 1.3 April-May 1917: p. 9.
     This letter from Debs praises M.S. for "a brave fight
     against the wolves of the system."
348. "An Honest Birth Control Film at Last!" Birth Control Review,
     1.3 April-May 1917: p. 11.
     This full page advertisement for the film "Birth Control"
     shows two stills of M.S. in scenes from the movie.
349. "Morsels from a Hunger Strike." Birth Control Review, 1.3
     April-May 1917: p. 9.
     Included are brief excerpts taken from publications
     throughout the U.S.; Ethel Byrne's hunger strike is discussed
     in the excerpts.
350. Sanger, William. "Birth Control." Birth Control Review, 1.3
     April-May 1917: p. 7.
     A short plea from William Sanger calling for birth control
     as "the message of a new philosophy dedicated primarily to the
     proposition of voluntary motherhood and racial betterment."
351. "To a Jailbird." Birth Control Review, 1.3 April-May 1917:
     p. 16.
     This article describes a "series of tributes" paid to M.S. on
     her release from Queens County Penitentiary.
352. "What the Birth Control Leagues Are Doing." Birth Control
     Review, 1.3 April-May 1917: pp. 14-15.
     Reports on activities of leagues throughout the country.
     A lecture by M.S. in Washington D.C. sparked the organization

of the league there. Her speech in Pittsburgh "brought many recruits."

353. Ellis, Havelock. "Birth Control and Eugenics." Eugenics Review, 9 April 1917: pp. 32-41.

In his concise review of birth control and eugenics, Ellis concludes that birth control is an invaluable instrument for "social betterment" and "eugenic aims." He deplores M.S.'s need to break the law.

354. "Publicity." The Masses, 9.6 April 1917: p. 16.

An editorial salute to Ethel Byrne and her hunger strike.

355. "Editorial Notes." The New Republic, 10.127 7 April 1917: p. 279.

This article comments on an "ordinary case" before the Supreme Court of New York in which a father (of eleven children) who earned less than ten dollars per week was granted a separation from his wife. The article also points out that M.S.'s sister, Ethel Byrne, was imprisoned on Blackwell's Island and was charged with disseminating birth control information.

356. "Dismisses Mrs. Sanger's Charges." New York Times, 6 May 1917: Pt. 1 p. 15 col. 3.

Mayor J. W. Stevens of Albany, New York dismissed charges against J. Sheldon Frost, commissioner of public safety. Charges were brought by M.S. because Frost refused to let Sanger lecture on April 10.

357. "Bars Birth Control Film; Mrs. Sanger's Agents to Appeal to Court from Bell's Order." New York Times, 7 May 1917: p. 18 col. 4.

Commissioner of Licenses Bell stopped the Park Theatre showing of M.S.'s film "Birth Control."

358. "Would Restrain Commissioner Bell." New York Times, 10 May 1917: p. 11 col. 5.

Message Photoplay Co., Inc., owner of "Birth Control," applied to the Supreme Court for an injunction to restrain Commissioner Bell from interfering with the film's showing.

359. "A Decision for Liberty." Birth Control Review, 1.4 June 1917: pp. 2, 8.

This article reproduces the opinion of Justice Nathan Bijur of the Supreme Court of New York in the case of Message Photoplay Co. v. Bell. The case centered on the showing of film "Birth Control" which presents M.S., her clinic, and her persecution. The supreme court opinion allowed the film to be shown.

360. "Upholds Mrs. Sanger Film; Justice Bijur Differs from Greenbaum on Birth Control Movies." New York Times, 7 June 1917: p. 10 col. 7.

Justice Nathan Bijur approves the film "Birth Control" for showing.

361. "Bars 'Birth Control' Film; Court Also Rules Against 'The Hand That Rocks the Cradle." New York Times, 14 July 1917: p. 7 col. 3.

Appellate division of the supreme court reversed Justice
Bijur's decision.

362. "Editorial Comment." Birth Control Review, 1.5 Dec. 1917:
p. 16.
Comments that although Fannie Mindell's appeal was won and
What Every Girl Should Know was no longer "indecent," the
appeal process had been expensive.

363. "Status of Birth Control Cases." Birth Control Review, 1.5
Dec. 1917: p. 5.
Reports on the status of the cases against M.S., Ethel
Byrne, and Fannie Mindell.

1918

364. Sanger, Margaret, H. "Morality and Birth Control." Birth
Control Review, 2.2 Feb.-Mar. 1918: pp. 11, 14.
M.S. links "morality" with birth control, sees birth control
as a way "to uplift" the human race.

365. _____. "Clinics, Courts and Jails." Birth Control Review,
2.3 April 1918: pp. 3-4.
M.S. reviews the opening of the Brownsville Clinic and
the arrests of Fannie Mindell, Ethel Byrne, and herself.

366. _____. "Let's Have the Truth." Birth Control Review,
2.7 Aug. 1918: p. 8.
In this editorial, M.S. calls for monies to be sent for a defense fund for I.W.W. workers on trial in Chicago.

367. _____. "A Statement of Facts--An Obligation Fulfilled."
Birth Control Review, 2.7 Aug. 1918: pp. 3-4.
M.S. relates the beginnings of the Birth Control Review as
well as her experiences with Frederick A. Blossom as manager.
She condemns Blossom for resigning and for taking with him
all office furnishings and records. Blossom also refused to
turn over records to the New York Birth Control League
(see items 380 and 381).

368. _____. "How Nature Gets Even." Birth Control Review,
2.8 Sept. 1918: p. 13.
M.S. presents statistics from the Queens County Penitentiary and attempts to show that most women in prison come
from large families.

369. _____. "All Together--Now!" Birth Control Review, 2.9
Oct. 1918: p. 7.
This open letter to the readers of the Birth Control Review asks women to join the battle for women and to work
for birth control.

370. _____. "Trapped!" Birth Control Review, 2.9 Oct. 1918:
p. 3.
The article gives an account of the arrest of Kitty Marion.

371. _____. "An Open Letter to Alfred E. Smith." Birth Control Review, 2.10 Nov. 1918: pp. 3-4.
This open letter to Alfred E. Smith, candidate for governor

of New York, asks Smith to "go on record in favor of Birth
Control."

372. _____. "When Should a Woman Avoid Having Children?"
Birth Control Review, 2.10 Nov. 1918: pp. 6-7.
M.S. spells out when and why a woman should not have a
child. Age, health, poverty, and other factors are examined.
Above all, she calls out for "mothers of workers" to stop pro-
ducing "cheap labor for the labor market."

373. _____. "Birth Control or Abortion?" Birth Control Review,
2.11 Dec. 1918: pp. 3-4.
M.S. cites the large number of abortions being performed
and suggests birth control as an alternative to abortion.

374. Brennesen, Ernest I. "Impressions of a Debate." Birth Con-
trol Review, 2.1 Jan. 1918: p. 12.
The article reports on a debate between Sanger and
Dr. Elmer Lee, editor of Health Culture: "Resolve that Birth
Control is Conducive to the Virility and Welfare of the Human
Race." The debate was sponsored by the Brooklyn Philosophi-
cal Society; it was held on November 18, 1917.

375. "A Twentieth-Century Opinion! The People of the State of
New York, Respondent, v. Margaret H. Sanger, Appellant.
(Decided January 8, 1918)." Birth Control Review, 2.2
Feb.-Mar. 1918: p. 15.
This article reprints the decision granting M.S.'s appeal.
Opinion grants an exception to physicians and those "acting
upon the physician's prescription or order" to supply birth
control "for the cure or prevention of disease."

376. Weitzenkorn, Louis. "The Dynamite of an Idea." Birth Control Review, 2.2 Feb.-Mar. 1918: p. 8.
Author links M.S. and the birth control movement with
radical and revolutionary movements.

377. "The Fight from Coast to Coast." Birth Control Review, 2.3
April 1918: pp. 5-11.
Reports from birth control leagues throughout the United
States. The leagues were formed as a result of the clinic
M.S. "founded and her subsequent arrest, trial and prison
sentence."

378. Debs, Eugene V. "Freedom is the Goal." Birth Control Review, 2.4 May 1918: p. 7.
Debs calls for "a million woman rebels to catch the clarion
cry of Margaret Sanger and proclaim the glad tidings of
woman's coming freedom throughout the world!"

379. "Editorial Comment." Birth Control Review, 2.4 May 1918:
p. 16.
This interesting editorial attacks an article written by Dr.
Arthur C. Jacobson for the Medical Times. Jacobson views
the New York Court of Appeals decision as a call for doctors
to take over the operation of birth control clinics. This editorial sees Jacobson as advising the medical profession "to
take charge and monopolize the credit."

380. "Mrs. Sanger Out of League; Birth Control Members Stand

By Dr. Blossom in Quarrel." New York Times, 8 July 1918: p. 11 col. 1.

After a disagreement between M.S. and Dr. Frederick A. Blossom over the management of the Birth Control League of New York, it was announced that the league had severed its relationship with M.S. (see items 367 and 381).

381. Myers, Hiram. "My Dear Mrs. Sanger:" Birth Control Review, 2.7 Aug. 1918: p. 4.

This letter from Hiram Myers, newly elected president of the Birth Control League of New York, explains why he has requested the district attorney to investigate the finances of the New York Birth Control League (see 367 and 380).

382. "The Birth Control Review on Broadway." Birth Control Review, 2.8 Sept. 1918: pp. 7, 10.

An interesting account of Kitty Marion's experiences selling the Birth Control Review on Broadway.

383. "Judges with Small Families Jail Kitty Marion." Birth Control Review, 2.10 Nov. 1918: p. 5.

Reports that Kitty Marion has been jailed, but that other women will sell the Birth Control Review on the streets.

1919

384. Sanger, Margaret. "Are Birth Control Methods Injurious? Birth Control Review, 3.1 Jan. 1919: pp. 3-4.

M.S. denies that "scientific" birth control methods are injurious to a woman's health, or that they cause cancer and other diseases.

385. _____. "Birth Control and Racial Betterment." Birth Control Review, 3.2 Feb. 1919: pp. 11-12.

Without birth control, eugenics cannot lead to "racial betterment." A woman's first duty is not to the state, as eugenists maintain, but to herself.

386. _____. "A Victory, A New Year and a New Day." Birth Control Review, 3.2 Feb. 1919: pp. 3-4.

M.S. discusses the events of the past year as well as the obscenity charges leveled against birth control.

387. _____. "A Parents' Problem or Woman's?" Birth Control Review, 3.3 Mar. 1919: pp. 6-7.

M.S. explains why the birth control movement's propaganda has been aimed at women and not at men. "The basic freedom of the world is woman's freedom. A free race cannot be born of slave mothers." Sanger sees birth control as a "woman's problem."

388. _____. "Why Not Birth Control Clinics in America?" American Medicine, N.S., 14 Mar. 1919: pp. 164-67. Also in: Birth Control Review, 3.5 May 1919: pp. 10-11.

A plea, aimed at physicians, to end unnecessary abortions and to initiate a system of birth control clinics such as the clinic in Holland four ;d in 1881 by Dr. Aletta Jacobs.

389.   . "The Tragedy of the Accidental Child." <u>Birth Control Review</u>, 3.4 April 1919: pp. 5-6.
M.S.'s impassioned, emotional plea for birth control.

390.   . "Western Women Demand Information." <u>Birth Control Review</u>, 3.6 June 1919: p. 5.
M.S. recounts her experience at a lecture she gave in San Francisco and concludes that California women are anxious for birth control information.

391.   . "How Shall We Change the Law." <u>Birth Control Review</u>, 3.7 July 1919: pp. 8-9.
M.S. examines the way in which Section 1142 of the New York state law should be changed. She rejects the "unlimited bill" and advocates "the Doctor's and Nurse's bill"; Sanger also suggests that midwifes be included.

392.   . "Vanderlip's Speech--A Warning Note." <u>Birth Control Review</u>, 3.7 July 1919: pp. 3-4.
In this editorial, M.S. comments on the problems of over-population and praises a statement made by Frank A. Vanderlip, former head of the City National Bank of New York.

393.   . "Meeting the Need Today." <u>Birth Control Review</u>, 3.10 Oct. 1919: pp. 14-15.
M.S. calls for the adoption in New York of the "doctor's and nurse's bill."

394.   . "A Lawbreaking Policeman." <u>Birth Control Review</u>, 3.11 Nov. 1919: p. 17.
M.S. discusses the police tactics used to suppress the <u>Birth Control Review</u>; she cites the arrest of Kitty Marion.

395.   . "Breaking into the South--A Contrast." <u>Birth Control Review</u>, 3.12 Dec. 1919: pp. 7-8.
M.S. contrasts the warm reception given her in Elizabeth City, North Carolina with the hostile reactions of an audience of women physicians in New York City.

396. Ellis, Havelock. <u>Philosophy of Conflict: and Other Essays in War-Time</u>. (Second Series). Freeport, N.Y.: Books for Libraries Press, 1970, 299 p. Index. (First published, 1919). (OCLC: 74582)
Volume contains an essay entitled "Birth Control and Eugenics" that outlines methods and points of view of the birth control movement. M.S.'s efforts are commended.

397. Robinson, Victor, PH.C. M.D. <u>Pioneers of Birth Control in England and America</u>. New York: Voluntary Parenthood League, 1919, 107 p. No index. (OCLC: 3760147)
Brief discourses on birth control leaders. Early career of M.S. is included (pp. 93-102).

398. "Arrests Women Agents; Solicitors for <u>Birth Control Review</u> Charged with Blocking Traffic." <u>New York Times</u>, 14 Oct. 1919: p. 23 col. 2.
Mrs. Genevieve Grandcourt, a writer, and Miss Kitty Marion, formerly an English actress, were arrested in Times Square.

399. "Margaret Sanger's Tour." <u>Birth Control Review</u>, 3.11 Nov. 1919: p. 4.

Announces that M.S. will tour New York state to discuss the birth control movement and birth control legislation. Asks for club groups to sponsor her.

400. "Dismisses Birth Control Case." New York Times, 18 Nov. 1919: p. 17 col. 3.

Supreme court dismissed M.S.'s appeal "on the constitutionality of the New York State Birth Control Act."

401. "Making People Think." Birth Control Review, 3.12 Dec. 1919: pp. 3-4.

The success of M.S.'s trip to Elizabeth City, N.C. is credited to W. O. Saunders, newspaper editor of the Independent.

1920

402. Sanger, Margaret H. Woman and the New Race. With a preface by Havelock Ellis. New York: Brentano's, 1920, 234 p. No index. (OCLC: 3313462)

In this eugenic plea, M.S. sees birth control as the means of creating a better society, of advancing the laboring classes, of ending war, and of setting women free both physically and sexually. This American edition also views birth control as a major component of the "melting pot." (For English edition see item 474.) Reviewed in Booklist, 17 May 1921; p. 284; The Dial, 70.1 May 1921: p. 594; Eliot, T. D. and S. W. American Journal of Sociology, 26 Mar. 1921: pp. 635-37; Freeman, 2 8 Dec. 1920: p. 310; Nation, 111.2890 24 Nov. 1920: p. 597; Survey, 45.20 12 Feb. 1921: p. 706.

403. _____. "A Birth Strike to Avert World Famine." Birth Control Review, 4.1 Jan. 1920: p. 3.

M.S. calls on the women of the world to avoid world famine by refusing to have children for five years.

404. _____. "From Woman's Standpoint." Birth Control Review, 4.1 Jan. 1920: p. 12.

Viewing women's problems during the steel strike, M.S. advises women and labor to limit the labor supply through birth control.

405. _____. "The Call to Women." Birth Control Review, 4.2 Feb. 1920: pp. 3-4.

M.S. calls again for a five-year halt to births. She stresses the threat of world famine predicted by R. C. Martens," an authority upon the world food situation."

406. _____. "Put Your Hosue in Order." Birth Control Review, 4.3 Mar. 1920: pp. 3-4.

A further discussion of the five-year halt to births and R. C. Martens' theories on world famine.

407. _____. "Wasting Our Human Resources." Birth Control Review, 4.3 Mar. 1920: pp. 9-11.

M.S. links crime, tuberculosis, and hereditary diseases to the lack of birth control.

408. _____. "Preparing for the World Crisis." Birth Control
      Review, 4.4 April 1920: pp. 7-8.
      Urges a five-year halt to births to help limit the effects of
      the coming financial and food crisis.
409. _____. "Women and the Rail Strike." Birth Control Review,
      4.5 May 1920: p. 3.
      M.S. links the railroad strike with the coming financial
      "panic"; she urges birth control.
410. _____. "The Legal Right of Physicians to Prescribe Birth
      Control Measures." American Medicine, N.S., 15 June
      1920: pp. 321-23.
      M.S. describes "the rights of physicians" (under Section
      1145 of the Penal Law of New York) to prescribe contraceptives
      to "cure or prevent disease."
411. _____. "Clinics the Solution." Birth Control Review, 4.7
      July 1920: pp. 6-8.
      M.S. discusses the birth control movement in England and
      the need for clinics both there and in the U.S.
412. _____. "Taking the Message to Working Women." Birth
      Control Review, 4.8 Aug. 1920: pp. 5-6.
      M.S. relates her experiences in London at meetings with the
      Women's Co-operative Guild, the International Socialist Club,
      and the Emily Davidson Club.
413. _____. "London Birth Control Meetings." Birth Control
      Review, 4.9 Sept. 1920: pp. 7-8.
      M.S. reports on audience reactions to her lectures in
      England.
414. _____. "Women in Germany." Birth Control Review, 4.12
      Dec. 1920: pp. 8-9.
      M.S. reports on her visit to Germany and tells of the
      hunger and suffering there.
415. Fielding, William J. Sanity in Sex. New York: Dodd, Mead
      and Co., 1920, 333 p., Index, Bibl. (OCLC: 1456777)
      This book discusses the sex-education movement that sprang
      from and followed World War I. A chapter on birth control
      traces M.S.'s role in the movement and makes a plea for birth
      control on the basis of "morality."
416. "Mrs. Sanger to England." Birth Control Review, 4.5 May
      1920: p. 4.
      Announces that M.S. sailed to England on April 24 "to
      deliver a series of lectures" "arranged by the leaders of the
      neo-Malthusian movement."
417. "Mrs. Sanger in England." Birth Control Review, 4.6 June
      1920: p. 6.
      Reports that M.S. was warmly welcomed by Dr. Stopes and
      Mrs. Bessie Drysdale. The article also reports on a meeting
      she attended in Cleveland before leaving for England.
418. "The People of the State of New York, Respondent, vs.
      Margaret H. Sanger, Appellant." Birth Control Review,
      4.6 June 1920 p. 3.

Reprints the decision of January 8, 1918, which allowed physicians to dispense birth control information.

419. "Mrs. Margaret Sanger in Germany." The Malthusian, 15 Oct. 1920: p. 70.
    "Notes" section gives a message from M.S. in Germany concerning: a request from Austria for a lecture, the growth of the birth control movement during the war, the adoption by Radicals of birth control, and the use of neo-Malthusianism in propaganda.

1921

420. Sanger, Margaret, ed. Appeals from American Mothers. New York: Womans Publishing Co., Inc., 1921, 16 p.
    Calls for help from women throughout the United States. Many of the letters were written in response to M.S.'s book, Woman and the New Race (see item 402).

421. _____ and Russell, Winter. Debate Between Margaret Sanger, Negative and Winter Russell, Affirmative. Subject: Resolved that the Spreading of Birth Control Knowledge Is Injurious to the Welfare of Humanity. Dr. S. Adolphus Knopf, Chairman. Parkview Palace, New York City, Sunday afternoon, 12 Dec. 1920 under the auspices of the Fine Arts Guild.... New York: The Fine Arts Guild, 1921, 36 p. Not seen.

422. Sanger, Margaret, ed. Sayings of Others on Birth Control. New York: Womans Publishing Co., Inc., 1921, 20p.
    Brief quotes from notable advocates of birth control.

423. _____. (Speeches) in: First American Birth Control Conference. Birth Control: What It Is, How It Works, What It Will Do. Proceedings. New York: Birth Control Review, 1921: pp. 14-18, 170-174.
    M.S.'s speeches before the conference include the welcoming address, (pp. 14-18) as well as one of the principal speeches on morality (pp. 170-174) in which she equates morality with responsibility (see item 434 for complete entry).

424. _____. "Women in Germany." Birth Control Review, 5.1 Jan. 1921: pp. 8-10.
    M.S. continues her report on her visit to Germany.

425. _____. "No Healthy Race Without Birth Control." Physical Culture, 45 Mar. 1921: pp. 41+.
    An appeal for a "new," physically strong woman and for an end to artificial beauty standards. Birth control will help make this possible.

426. _____. "Politicians vs. Birth Control." Birth Control Review, 5.5 May 1921: pp. 3-4.
    M.S. attacks politicians for refusing to help birth control.

427. _____. "Birth Control--Past, Present and Future." Birth Control Review, 5.6 June 1921: pp. 5-6, 11-13.
    M.S. looks at the history of birth control, stresses

Malthusian thought, and summarizes the situation existing throughout Europe and the U.S. (see items 428 and 429).

428. _____ . "Birth Control--Past, Present and Future." Birth Control Review, 5.7 July 1921: pp. 5-6, 15.
M.S. continues her review of the birth control situation (see items 427 and 429).

429. _____ . "Birth Control--Past, Present and Future." Birth Control Review, 5.8 Aug. 1921: pp. 19-20.
This is the concluding part of a three-part article (see items 427 and 428).
In this part Sanger stresses the need to end abortion via birth control; Sanger sees birth control as a means to a better world.

430. _____ . "Woman's Error and Her Debt." Birth Control Review, 5.8 Aug. 1921: pp. 7-8.
Sees birth control as part of woman's struggle "against sex servitude."

431. _____ . "The Eugenic Value of Birth Control Propaganda." Birth Control Review, 5.10 Oct. 1921: p. 5.
Emphasizes the necessity for eugenics and birth control to unite in order "to limit and discourage the overfertility of the mentally and physically defective."

432. _____ . "Impressions of the Amsterdam Conference." Birth Control Review, 5.11 Nov. 1921: p. 11.
Reports briefly on a conference held in Holland (Aug. 29-30, 1921).

433. _____ . "Mrs. Sanger's Opinion; To the Editor of the New York Times." New York Times, 19 Nov. 1921: p. 12, col. 5.
Letter from M.S. criticizes editorial of November 15, 1921 (see item 448).

434. First American Birth Control Conference. Birth Control: What It Is, How It Works, What It Will Do. Proceedings. New York: Birth Control Review, 1921, 212 p. Index.
Considered a landmark in the history of the American birth control movement, the First American Birth Control Conference was held in New York at the Hotel Plaza, November 11, 12, and 13, 1921. Margaret Sanger was chair of the conference committee. The twenty-four papers presented covered the scientific, economic, political, and social aspects of birth control. The medical aspects were discussed at a meeting open only to doctors; its papers were not published.

435. "Birth Control: a Discussion." Eugenics Review, 12 Jan. 1921: pp. 291-98.
Report of a meeting of the Eugenics Education Society in England (October 19, 1920). M.S. discussed the positive efforts of the birth control movement among poor women in Rotherhithe. Dr. Alice Drysdale Vickery related what she had experienced while promoting birth control during the preceding forty years and emphasized that poor women deliberately had been deprived of birth control information.

436. "Editorial Comment." Birth Control Review, 5.1 Jan. 1921:
      pp. 3-4.
      The editorial reports that M.S. addressed the New York
      Women's Publishing Company about her trip to Europe. It
      also reports that M.S. debated Winter Russell. The debate
      was sponsored by the Fine Arts Guild (see item 421). The
      Fine Arts Guild had sponsored M.S. in a series of four lec-
      tures.
437. "Mrs. Sanger's Lectures." Birth Control Review, 5.2 Feb.
      1921: p. 16.
      Reports on M.S.'s numerous lectures.
438. "Birth Control in Japan: Issue Forced into Prominence by
      Rapid Increase in Population." New York Times, 5 June
      1921: Sect. 6 p. 10 col. 1-3.
      A women's group invited M.S. to make a tour of Japan and
      to lecture on the birth control question.
439. Fisher, Irving. "Impending Problems of Eugenics."
      Scientific Monthly, 13 Sept. 1921: pp. 214-31.
      Birth control practiced mainly by the intelligent may lead
      to "race suicide." This situation can be prevented if the
      "propaganda of Sanger" and others is successful enough to
      limit lower class births.
440. "Birth Control Clinics: Mrs. Rublee Says Several Will Be
      Opened in the South." New York Times, 13 Oct. 1921:
      p. 15 col. 2.
      Plans for the First American Birth Control Conference were
      announced. M.S. named as chairman of the conference com-
      mittee.
441. Gleason, Arthur. "Birth Control." Survey, 47 22 Oct. 1921:
      pp. 113-14.
      Notes the announcement of the Voluntary Parenthood
      League, that Marie C. Stopes will speak in Town Hall in
      October, and that the First American Birth Control Confer-
      ence will be held in November, as announced by the committee
      chaired by M.S. Author compares and contrasts the actions
      and aims of the Voluntary Parenthood League and the American
      Birth Control League. A list of sponsors for the conference
      is given. Page 114 contains reprint of Section 211 of the
      Federal Penal Code, which had been passed in 1873.
442. "Is it Moral?" Birth Control Review, 5.11 Nov. 1921: p. 10.
      Announces the discussion "Birth Control: Is It Moral?" to
      be held at a mass meeting at Town Hall on November 13, 1921
      and led by M.S. and Harold Cox; asks for opinions.
443. "Birth Control League: Body Formally Organized to Assist
      Conference with Campaign." New York Times, 10 Nov.
      1921: p. 12 col. 2.
      M.S. chosen president of American Birth Control League.
444. "Urge Birth Control to Aid World Peace; Advocates, in First
      American Meeting, Ask Congress and Arms Conference to
      Act." New York Times, 12 Nov. 1921: p. 18 col. 1.
445. "First Birth Control Clinic to Open Here; Staff of 40 Physicians,

Says Mrs. Margaret Sanger, Selected for Institution." <u>New York Times</u>, 13 Nov. 1921: Pt. 1 p. 18 col. 2.

At First American Birth Control Conference, M.S. announced that clinic would open at 317 East Tenth Street.

446. "Police Veto Halts Birth Control Talk; Town Hall in Tumult; Mrs. Sanger and Mary Winsor, Leaders in Movement, Arrested at Meeting; Audience Swarms Stage; Sergeant Seizes Mrs. Sanger as She Starts to Speak--Police Buffeted by Crowd." <u>New York Times</u>, 14 Nov. 1921: p. 1 col. 1--p. 7 col. 2-3.

447. "Birth Control Raid Made by Police on Archbishop's Order; Capt. Donohue's Only Instructions from Headquarters were to 'Look for Mgr. Dineen'; Suppressed Before Start; Policeman Testifies That Donohue Ordered Him to Get Mrs. Sanger off the Stage; The Two Prisoners Freed; Evidence Lacking, Says Magistrate--Mgr. Dineen Explains Catholic Church's Attitude." <u>New York Times</u>, 15 Nov. 1921: p. 1 col. 3--p. 9 col. 1-2.

448. "Topics of the Times; Resistance Was Not the Remedy." <u>New York Times</u>, 15 Nov. 1921: p. 18 col. 5.

The editorial claims that birth control advocates at Town Hall behaved somewhat like "anarchists." It asserts that the birth controllers should have obeyed the police (see item 433 for M.S. reply).

449. "Asks Police Aid for Birth Control Talk; Robert McC. Marsh Requests Enright to Safeguard Bryant Hall Meeting Friday." <u>New York Times</u>, 16 Nov. 1921: p. 17 col. 1-2.

(Police Commissioner Richard E. Enright. Robert McC. Marsh, lawyer "representing the First American Birth Control Conference.")

450. "Topics of the Times; No Basis Found for Action." <u>New York Times</u>, 16 Nov. 1921: p. 18 col. 4-5.

Editorial protests "action of the police in forbidding the meeting" at Town Hall.

451. "Police Denounced for Stopping Meeting; Birth Control Committee Endorses Mrs. Sanger and Calls for Redress." <u>New York Times</u>, 17 Nov. 1921: p. 5 col. 3.

Committee of the First American Birth Control Conference.

452. "Birth Control Raid To Be Investigated; Enright Also Promises 'Appropriate Action' on Police Suppression of Town Hall Meeting; Protection Asked Tonight; Mrs. Sanger and Harold Cox, London Editor, to Lead Discussion at Park Theatre." <u>New York Times</u>, 18 Nov. 1921: p. 18 col. 2-3.

453. "Birth Control and War." <u>Survey</u>, 47.8 19 Nov. 1921: p. 267.

Reports on the final session of the First American Birth Control Conference held at New York City Town Hall. The session was broken up by the police, who prevented M.S. from speaking and arrested her. Also reported is M.S.'s announcement that the American Birth Control League will open a birth control clinic in New York during the week.

454. "Birth Control Talk Guarded by Police; Program Cut Off at
     Town Hall Carried Out at Park Theatre Without Interrup-
     tion; 3,000 Jam Street Outside." New York Times, 19 Nov.
     1921: p. 1 col. 4--p. 5 col. 4-5.
     First American Birth Control Conference.

455. "Hayes Denounces Birth Control Aim; Archbishop Declares that
     Law, Science, Policy and Experience Condemn Theory, Mrs.
     Rublee Cites Holland; Fifty Clinics There, Says Birth Con-
     trol Advocate, and Infant Mortality Lowest in Europe."
     New York Times, 21 Nov. 1921: p. 1 col. 4--p. 6 col. 2-3.
     Reprints lengthy statement of Archbishop Patrick J. Hayes
     protesting "propaganda of birth control." Juliet Barrett
     Rublee replies on behalf of First American Birth Control Con-
     ference.

456. "Birth Control Aid Denied by Academy; Public Health Committee
     Declares It Is Opposed to League's Principles and Methods;
     Police Hearing Today Many Witnesses Ready to Testify at
     Inquiry into Suppression of Town Hall Meeting." New York
     Times, 22 Nov. 1921: p. 16 col. 2.
     Public Health Committee of the Academy of Medicine declared
     itself opposed to American Birth Control League.

457. "Digs into Leader's Birth-Control Past; Chief Inspector Lahey
     Questions Mrs. Sanger on Clinic Conviction in 1916; Sup-
     pression Charge Heard; Preliminary Inquiry into Police
     Action at Town Hall Continued to Dec. 2." New York
     Times, 23 Nov. 1921: p. 9 col. 1-2.

458. "Ask Police to Call Dineen; Liberties Union Wants Alleged Com-
     plainant at Birth Control Hearing." New York Times, 25
     Nov. 1921: p. 7 col. 1.
     American Civil Liberties Union asks police to call Mgr.
     Joseph P. Dineen (secretary to Archbishop Hayes) to testify
     at Town Hall hearing.

459. "Birth Control and Free Speech." Outlook, 129 30 Nov. 1921:
     p. 507.
     This editorial, although not in agreement with M.S. on the
     birth control issue, denounces the roles played by the
     Catholic Church, Archbishop Hayes, and the New York City
     Police Force in denying "free speech" in Town Hall (New York,
     Nov. 13, 1921).

460. "Birth Control and Taboo." New Republic, 29.365 30 Nov.
     1921: p. 9.
     This editorial attacks Archbishop Hayes for using the police
     to break up the first birth control conference in New York
     City and for denying M.S. and others an "open forum."

461. "The American Birth Control League." Birth Control Review,
     5.12 Dec. 1921: p. 18.
     Prints the principles of the newly formed American Birth
     Control League, M.S., president.

462. "Church Control?" Birth Control Review, 5.12 Dec. 1921:
     pp. 3-5.
     An editorial attack against the Catholic Church. In the

article, Archbishop Patrick J. Hayes is blamed for suppressing the New York Town Hall meeting of Nov. 13, 1921.

463. "First American Birth Control Conference." Birth Control Review, 5.12 Dec. 1921: p. 9.
Gives the agenda of the First American Birth Control Conference (Nov. 11-18, 1921).

464. "The Press Protests." Birth Control Review, 5.12 Dec. 1921: pp. 16-17.
New York newspaper excerpts that protest the raid on New York Town Hall meeting.

465. "Arrest Mrs. Rublee for Views on Birth; Woman Who Took Issue with Archbishop Hayes is Soon Dismissed: She Will Fight the Case; District Attorney's Office Ordered Arrest, Then Told Court There Was No Evidence; Police Malice Is Charged." New York Times, 3 Dec. 1921: p. 9 col. 1-2.
Juliet Barrett Rublee arrested following her testimony at police hearing.

466. "Plan to Test Police Power over Speech; Birth Control Advocates to Bring Legal Action to Prevent Breaking Up Meetings." New York Times, 4 Dec. 1921: Pt. 1, p. 20 col. 1-2.

467. "Mrs. Rublee Plans False Arrest Suit; May Bring Action Against Policeman and Assistant Corporation Counsel." New York Times, 6 Dec. 1921: p. 19 col. 3.

468. "Marsh Denounces Inquiry by Police; Counsel for Birth Control Conference Protests Against Secret Hearing." New York Times, 8 Dec. 1921: p. 16 col. 2.

469. "See Plot by Police to Bar Free Speech; Ten Citizens Demand Inquiry by Mayor on 'Outrages' Against Birth Control Advocates." New York Times, 10 Dec. 1921: p. 15 col. 6.

470. "Archbishop Hayes on Birth Control; Pastoral to 'The Faithful' Calls Murder Horrible, but Terms Prevention Satanic." New York Times, 18 Dec. 1921: Pt. 1 p. 16 col. 1.

471. "Mayor Orders an Inquiry; Hirshfield to Investigate Closing of Birth Control Meeting." New York Times, 18 Dec. 1921: Pt. 1 p. 16 col. 1.
David Hirshfield, commissioner of accounts, is directed by Mayor Hylan to investigate police action.

472. "Mrs. Sanger Replies to Archbishop Hayes; Pastoral Letter Shows Church Clearly Understands Birth Control, She Says." New York Times, 20 Dec. 1921: p. 20 col. 2.

1922

473. Sanger, Margaret H. "Individual and Family Aspects of Birth Control: President, Mrs. Margaret Sanger." In Pierpoint, Raymond, ed. Report of the Fifth International Neo-Malthusian and Birth Control Conference; Kingsway Hall, London. July 11th to 14th, 1922: pp. 30-32. (OCLC: 989909)

M.S.'s opening address to the conference as president of the section on Individual and Family Aspects of Birth Control. (For complete conference entry, see item 488.)

474. _____. The New Motherhood; with introductions by Harold Cox and Havelock Ellis. London: Jonathan Cape, 1922, 243 p. No index. (OCLC: 3924048)

The English edition of Woman and the New Race (see item 402). Emphasis, however, in the form of two new chapters and the elimination of one American-oriented chapter has been placed on the United Kingdom. Reviewed by Browne, F. W. Stella. "The Message of the Margarets." New Generation 1.7 July 1922: pp. 14-15.

475. _____. The Pivot of Civilization. New York: Brentano's, 1922, 284 p. No Index. (OCLC: 3713879)

In this work (introduction by H. G. Wells), M.S. ties birth control to eugenics and neo-Malthusianism. "Principles and Aims of the American Birth Control League" on pp. 277-284. Reviewed in Booklist, 19 Jan. 1923: p. 112; Rev. of Pivot of Civilization by Margaret Sanger, Brentano's, 1922. The Bookman, 56.1 Sept. 1922: p. 103; East, E. M. and Harold Cox. "Margaret Sanger's Pivot of Civilization." Birth Control Review, 6.12 Dec. 1922: pp. 253-54; Hollingworth, Leta S. "For and Against Birth Control." New Republic, 32.410 11 Oct. 1922: p. 178; Nation, 115.2976 19 July 1922: p. 77.

476. _____. "Public Meeting: Mrs. Margaret Sanger." in Pierpoint, Raymond, ed., Report of the Fifth International Neo-Malthusian and Birth Control Conference, Kingsway Hall, London, July 11th to 14th, 1922: pp. 198-206. (OCLC: 989909)

In this address before the conference, M.S. relates incidents of her trips to Japan, China, and Korea. (For complete conference entry, see item 488.)

477. _____. "Woman, Morality, and Birth Control." New York: Women's Publishing Co., 1922, 55p. (OCLC: 5725610)

Reprinted from the Birth Control Review. Not seen.

478. _____. "Reply by Margaret Sanger to Archbishop Hayes' Statement." Birth Control Review, 6.1 Jan. 1922: p. 16.

M.S. protests attempts by the Catholic Church to make its "ideas legislative acts and force their opinions and code of morals upon the Protestant members of this country...."

479. _____. "The Morality of Birth Control." Birth Control Review, 6.2 Feb. 1922: pp. 11-12.

This is "an address delivered at the Park Theatre, New York City, on November 18, 1921." It is the address that was to have been delivered at Town Hall the night the hall was raided.

480. _____. "Margaret Sanger in Japan." Birth Control Review, 6.6 June 1922: pp. 101-104.

M.S. recounts her experiences in Japan. Excerpts "From the Japanese Press" are also included.

481. _____. "War and Population." Birth Control Review, 6.6
      June 1922: pp. 106-7.
      The address given at the Tokyo Y.M.C.A. on March 14,
      1922. Not allowed to speak on birth control, Sanger blames
      war on overpopulation.

482. _____. "Margaret Sanger in China." Birth Control Review,
      6.7 July 1922: pp. 123-25.
      In a letter, M.S. tells of her visit to China. Article reports
      that the visit resulted in extensive Chinese newspaper coverage
      of the birth control movement.

483. _____. "Margaret Sanger to the Readers of The Review."
      Birth Control Review, 6.11 Nov. 1922: pp. 217-218.
      M.S. thanks those who took over the movement during her
      absence and comments on the growing interest in birth control.

484. Abe, Isoo. "The Birth Control Movement in Japan." in
      Pierpoint, Raymond, ed. Report of the Fifth International
      Neo-Malthusian and Birth Control Conference: Kingsway
      Hall, London, July 11th to 14th, 1922: pp. 192-95.
      Professor Isoo Abe gives a brief report on Japan's birth
      control movement, noting the part played by M.S. (For com-
      plete conference entry, see item 488.)

485. Drysdale, B. I. "Reports: Great Britain" in Pierpoint,
      Raymond, ed. Report of the Fifth International Neo-
      Malthusian and Birth Control Conference: Kingsway Hall,
      London, July 11th to 14th, 1922: pp. 7-9. (OCLC:
      989909)
      Summarizes the work being done by the Malthusian League.
      Mrs. Drysdale mentions that the conference was funded by a
      "handsome personal gift" from M.S. (For complete conference
      entry, see item 488.)

486. Drysdale, C. V. "Opening of the Conference." in Pierpoint,
      Raymond, ed. Report of the Fifth International Neo-
      Malthusian and Birth Control Conference: Kingsway Hall,
      London, July 11th to 14th, 1922: pp. 1-7. (OCLC:
      989909)
      These are the conference president's opening remarks. He
      sums up the progress made by the birth control movement and
      praises M.S. for the part she has played in that progress.
      (For complete conference entry, see item 488.)

487. Kennedy, Anne. "Reports: United States of America." in
      Pierpoint, Raymond, ed. Report of the Fifth International
      Neo-Malthusian and Birth Control Conference: Kingsway
      Hall, London, July 11th to 14th, 1922: pp. 19-23.
      (OCLC: 989909)
      Kennedy summarizes M.S.'s historical connection with the
      birth control movement and outlines the work being done by
      the newly formed American Birth Control League. (For com-
      plete conference entry, see item 488.)

488. Pierpoint, Raymond, ed. Report of the Fifth International
      Neo-Malthusian and Birth Control Conference: Kingsway
      Hall, London, July 11th to 14th, 1922. London: William
      Heinemann Ltd., 1922, 308 p. (OCLC: 989909)

Includes papers presented at the Fifth International neo-Malthusian and Birth Control Conference organized by the New Generation League. Some of the papers have been abstracted separately; see items 473, 476, 484, 485, 487, 489.

489. Porritt, Annie G. "Publicity in the Birth Control Movement." in Pierpoint, Raymond, ed. Report of the Fifth International Neo-Malthusian and Birth Control Conference: Kingsway Hall, London, July 11th to 14th, 1922: pp. 301-07. (OCLC: 989909)

The managing editor of the Birth Control Review discusses the uses of publicity and propaganda in the birth control movement. (For complete conference entry see item 488.)

490. Sutherland, Halliday, G. M.D. Birth Control: A Statement of Christian Doctrine Against the Neo-Malthusians. New York: P. J. Kennedy & Sons, 1922. 160 p. Bibl. (no index) (OCLC: 4820980)

This anti-birth control work provoked Maria Stopes' libel suit against Sutherland.

491. "Mrs. Rublee's Arrest: A Record and A Protest." Birth Control Review, 6.1 Jan. 1922: pp. 5-7.

This article reports and protests the arrest of Juliet Barrett Rublee on December 2, 1921. The arrest occurred after Rublee testified during an inquiry into the action of the police at the New York Town Hall raid.

492. "Notes for the New Year." Birth Control Review, 6.1 Jan. 1922: p. 3.

Announces, among other things, that M.S. has been invited to visit Japan.

493. "Notes from the Field." Birth Control Review, 6.1 Jan. 1922: p. 15.

Reports on meetings attended by M.S. in New York and Massachusetts on behalf of the American Birth Control League.

494. "City Will Inquire into Birth Control; Hirshfield Announces He Will Conduct Public Hearing Next Monday." New York Times, 18 Jan. 1922: p. 36 col. 3.

495. "Cravath for Full Inquiry; Urges Hirshfield to Go Thoroughly into Birth Control Case." New York Times, 21 Jan. 1922: p. 24 col. 3.

496. "Hirshfield to Cravath; Accuses Lawyer of Trying to 'Sidestep Responsibility' for Police Inquiry." New York Times, 22 Jan. 1922: pt. 1 p. 5 col. 2.

497. "Hirshfield Cuts Off Free Speech Inquiry; Accuses Counsel for Birth Control Leaders of 'Sidestepping' and Insulting Him; Bars Him from Hearing; Resentment of Attorney Justified and No Insult Given, Cravath Tells Commissioner." New York Times, 24 Jan. 1922: p. 1 col. 5--p. 5 col. 2.

Marsh put out of court. Cravath defends Marsh.

498. "A Difference Hard to Explain." New York Times, 25 Jan. 1922: p. 14 col. 5.

Editorial questions Hirshfield's reason for barring Marsh from hearing.

499. "Protection Planned at Birth Control Talk; Mrs. Sanger to Deliver Farewell Address Before Lecture Tour in Japan and China." New York Times, 25 Jan. 1922: p. 36 col. 3.

500. "Mrs. Sanger Says Superman Is the Aim of Birth Control." New York Times, 31 Jan. 1922: p. 19 col. 2.
Speech on January 20 at Pennsylvania Conference of Birth Control.

501. "Birth Control As a Conquering Movement." Current Opinion, 72.2 Feb. 1922: pp. 212-3.
Includes portrait of M.S. (p. 213) with caption ("She may yet be canonized where once she was incarcerated."). Unsigned article gives a brief summary of the birth control movement in England and in the United States.

502. "Quizzes Witnesses over Birth Control; Hirshfield Asks if All the Persons Advocating the Movement Are Not Old." New York Times, 3 Feb. 1922: p. 9 col. 1.
Police hearing resumes. J. N. H. Slee is the first witness called.

503. "Police Admit Error in Town Hall Raid; Only Authority for Breaking Up Meeting Was Unknown Voice from Headquarters." New York Times, 18 Feb. 1922: p. 4 col. 2-3.

504. "Tokio Bars Mrs. Sanger from Making Tour of Japan to Lecture on Birth Control." New York Times, 18 Feb. 1922: p. 1 col. 4-5.

505. "Birth Control League; Justice Bijur Withholds Approval of Application for Incorporation." New York Times, 19 Feb. 1922: pt. 1 p. 20 col. 2.

506. "San Francisco." New York Times, 19 Feb. 1922: pt. 1 p. 20 col. 2.
Reports that M.S. was granted visas to China and India.

507. "Our Undesired Emigrant." New York Times, 20 Feb. 1922: p. 10 col. 4.
An editorial comment on the Japanese refusal to grant M.S. a visa.

508. "Birth Control Raid Is Laid to Donohue; Police Captain Acted on His Own Responsibility at Town Hall, Witnesses Say." New York Times, 21 Feb. 1922: p. 13 col. 1-2.

509. "Japan Has No Desire to Bar Mrs. Sanger; But Warns That She Cannot Be Admitted to Spread Birth Control Propaganda." New York Times, 21 Feb. 1922: p. 2 col. 5.

510. Dennett, Mary Ware. "Birth Control's Hunt for Sponsor; Suffragette Days Outdone by Side-Stepping of Congressmen Asked to Introduce Bill of Voluntary Parenthood League." New York Times, 26 Feb. 1922: pt. 7 p. 3 col. 1-4--p. 10 col. 1-2.
Dennett discusses the difficulties involved in trying to obtain a congressman to sponsor a bill to nullify the Comstock Law.

511. "News Notes." Birth Control Review, 6.3 Mar. 1922: pp. 28-30.
Announces M.S.'s coming trip to Japan, reports on meetings

she has attended throughout the country, and reports on
hearings held concerning the Town Hall meeting.

512. Rout, Ettie A. "Birth Control in Relation to V.D." Birth
Control Review, 6.3 Mar. 1922: pp. 36, 38.
This relates some of M.S.'s ideas concerning birth control
and venereal disease.

513. "Important News Condensed; Foreign." New York Times, 1
Mar. 1922: p. 4 col. 7.
While lecturing in Honolulu, M.S. announced she will go to
Japan despite ban on birth control propaganda.

514. "Mrs. Sanger Arrives in Japan." New York Times, 11 Mar.
1922: p. 8 col. 1.
M.S. arrived in Japan on March 10. Has pledged not to
lecture. Forty copies of her book were confiscated.

515. "Mrs. Sanger's Tokio Visit Uneventful." New York Times, 22
Mar. 1922: p. 26 col. 3.
Will address physicians' meetings in Osaka and Kyoto.

516. "Mrs. Sanger Ill in Yokohama." New York Times, 25 Mar.
1922: p. 11 col. 2.

517. "Mrs. Sanger on Way to China." New York Times, 29 Mar.
1922: p. 4 col. 3.

518. "Brief Submitted in Behalf of Paul D. Cravath and Others."
Birth Control Review, 6.4 April 1922: pp. 54-56.
This is "the brief prepared by Messrs. Emory R. Buckner
and Robert P. Patterson in connection with the complaint
against the police for stopping the Birth Control Meeting on
Nov. 13th."

519. "Editorial." Birth Control Review, 6.4 April 1922: p. 53.
Comments on the publicity being received by M.S. following the Japanese Government's denying her a visa and then
granting her one on the condition that she not discuss birth
control; the government then withdrew the ban.

520. "News Notes." Birth Control Review, 6.4 April 1922: p. 56.
Reports on M.S.'s addresses in San Francisco and Honolulu
and on her arrival in Japan.

521. "Birth Control Body Wins Charter Fight; Justice Bijur Decides
Favorably on Application to Incorporate the League." New
York Times, 14 April 1922: p. 36 col. 2.
The American Birth Control League is incorporated. See
"Lovett Reference Wrong." New York Times, 16 April 1922:
pt. 1 p. 18 col. 2 for correction in article.

522. "Birth Control League Incorporated." New York Times, 23
April 1922: pt. 1 p. 2 col. 3.
Birth Control League incorporation is finalized.

523. "Margaret Sanger in Japan." Birth Control Review, 6.5 May
1922: pp. 77-78.
The article reports on M.S.'s activities in Japan and announces that she will be a principal speaker at the International neo-Malthusian Congress in London in July.

524. Canto, Arturo C. "Birth Control in Mexico." Nation, 114.2965
3 May 1922: pp. 546-48.

By order of the governor, the district attorney of Merida Yucatan refused to prosecute those who had published a pamphlet on birth control written by M.S. and had translated the booklet into Spanish.

525. "Mrs. Sanger Shocks Her; Chinese Girl Interpreter Breaks Off Birth Control Lecture." New York Times, 10 June 1922: p. 3 col. 2.

526. Porritt, Annie G. "The Fifth International Birth Control Conference." Birth Control Review, 6.9 Sept. 1922: pp. 171-176.
Reports on the conference held in London, July 11-14, 1922. A section includes "M.S.'s Impressions."

527. "Mrs. Sanger Tells of Trip; Says Japanese and Chinese Hailed Birth Control." New York Times, 11 Oct. 1922: p. 19 col. 4.

528. "Mrs. Sanger Found Chinese Police Kind; Birth Control Advocate Contrasts Their Courtesy with 'Unthinkable Stupidity' Here; Her Speech Taken Down; Police Department Assigns Stenographers to Meeting but Speakers Are Not Molested." New York Times, 21 Oct. 1922: p. 36 col. 3.
Speaks of trip to Japan and China at meeting in Carnegie Hall.

529. Kennedy, Anne. "The Birth Control Movement in the United States." Birth Control Review, 6.11 Nov. 1922: pp. 222-23.
A paper presented at the International Birth Control Conference. Emphasizes M.S.'s role in the movement.

530. "World Aspects of Birth Control." Birth Control Review, 6.12 Dec. 1922: pp. 244-245, 256.
An account of the speech given by M.S. on October 30, 1922 at Carnegie Hall; it relates her experiences in Japan.

1923

531. Sanger, Margaret H. "Facing the New Year." Birth Control Review, 7.1 Jan. 1923: pp. 3-4.
M.S. editorializes on the events of 1922 and on the difficulties lying ahead.

532. _____. "Birthday of the Review and of Havelock Ellis." Birth Control Review, 7.2 Feb. 1923: pp. 27-28.
M.S. marks the sixth anniversary of the Birth Control Review with a tribute to Havelock Ellis.

533. _____. "The English Birth Control Case." Birth Control Review, 7.4 April 1923: pp. 84-85.
M.S. comments on the case directed against Family Limitation in England.

534. _____. "Hail! Not Farewell!" Birth Control Review, 7.4 April 1923: p. 84.
A tribute to Charles V. Drysdale and Bessie Drysdale on their resignation from the New Generation League in London.

535. _____. "A Review by Margaret Sanger." Birth Control Review, 7.4 April 1923: p. 95.
M.S. reviews Havelock Ellis' Little Essays of Love and Virtue New York: George H. Doran & Co., 1922.

536. _____. "Intelligence Tests for Legislators." Birth Control Review, 7.5 May 1923: pp. 107-108.
M.S. attacks the New York State legislators who refused to approve an amendment that would have allowed birth control information to be disseminated.

537. _____. "The Responsibility of an Idea." Birth Control Review, 7.7 July 1923: p. 171.
An emotional appeal for birth control.

538. _____. "The Vision of George Drysdale." Birth Control Review, 7.7 July 1923: pp. 177-179.
M.S.'s tribute to George Drysdale.

539. _____. "The Vision of George Drysdale." Birth Control Review, 7.8 Aug. 1923: pp. 198-201, 210.
Part 2 of George Drysdale article.

540. _____. "The Vision of George Drysdale." Birth Control Review, 7.9 Sept. 1923: pp. 225-227.
Part 3 of George Drysdale article.

541. _____. "The Vision of George Drysdale." Birth Control Review, 7.10 Oct. 1923: pp. 258-261.
Part 4 of George Drysdale article.

542. East, Edward M. Mankind at the Crossroads. New York: Charles Scribner's Sons, 1923. 360 p. Index. (OCLC: 3617329)
East presents Malthusian ideas and fears of overpopulation in terms of "racial dangers" and calls for eugenic control of population. He quotes M.S.'s Pivot of Civilization (see item 475).

543. Stopes, Marie Carmichael. Contraception: Its Theory, History and Practice. London: John Bale, Sons and Danielsson, Ltd., 1923. 418 p. Index. (OCLC: 3048413)
Marie Stopes, pioneer of the English birth control movement, makes brief mention of her contacts with Margaret Sanger. Stopes criticizes M.S. for her break with the Voluntary Parenthood League (see item 754 for third edition).

544. "Mrs. Sanger's Book Barred: London Court Orders Copies of 'Family Limitation' Destroyed." New York Times, 12 Jan. 1923: p. 3 col. 4.

545. "Says Mrs. Sanger Was Ill: Formal Statement Denies Caution Kept Her from Albany." New York Times, 26 Jan. 1923: p. 8 col. 6.
Item concerned M.S.'s failure to attend the opening meeting of the American Birth Control League at Albany.

546. Russell, Bertrand. "The Case of Margaret Sanger." Nation and the Athenaeum, 32.17 27 Jan. 1923: p. 645.
In a letter to the editor, Russell asks for funds to defend the publication and distribution of M.S.'s Family Limitation. Copies had been ordered destroyed by a London court. (See items 548, 549, and 550.)

547. Rout, Ettie A. "Calling Margaret Sanger to London." Birth
     Control Review, 7.2 Feb. 1923: pp. 30-31.
         Rout asks M.S. to come to London to give evidence regard-
     ing the prosecution of Family Limitation.
548. Stopes, Marie C. "The Aldred Prosecution." The Nation and
     the Athenaeum, 32.18 3 Feb. 1923: p. 685.
         Reply by M. Stopes to B. Russell's letter. Stopes claims
     that the "method of publication" was on trial--not the pamphlet,
     Family Limitation--and that there was no threat to the birth
     control movement (see items 546, 549, and 550).
549. R.S.P. "Birth-Control Prosecutions." The Nation and the
     Athenaeum, 32.19 10 Feb. 1923: pp. 718-9.
         Author disagrees with the opinions given by M. Stopes in
     her earlier letter and gives several pertinent examples from
     the history of birth control in England (see items 546, 548,
     and 550).
550. Russell, Bertrand. (Letter). The Nation and the Athenaeum,
     32.19 10 Feb. 1923: p. 719.
         Reply to letter of Marie Stopes (see items 546, 548, and
     549).
551. "Birth Control Bill Hearing in Hartford: Intense Interest
     Shown in the Measure Personally Championed by Mrs.
     Sanger." New York Times, 14 Feb. 1923: p. 8 col. 2.
552. "Backward Connecticut." New York Times, 15 Feb. 1923:
     p. 18 col. 5.
         At a public hearing, M.S. speaks before the judiciary com-
     mittee of the lower house.
553. Rout, Ettie A. "Family Limitation." Outlook (London), 51
     17 Feb. 1923: pp. 142-143.
         Letter by author abhors the order made in a West London
     court to destroy two thousand copies of M.S.'s Family
     Limitation.
554. "Sanger Meeting in Albany: Birth Control Advocates Gather
     in a Private Home." New York Times, 21 Feb. 1923: p. 15
     col. 3.
         M.S. speaks at home of Mrs. Ernest Pittman. Mayor had
     declared he would prevent her from speaking in Albany.
555. "A Calling of the Clan." Birth Control Review, 7.3 Mar.
     1923: pp. 59-60.
         This editorial presents the tactics used by the Knights of
     Columbus throughout the U.S. to stop M.S. from speaking.
556. "The Hearing at Hartford." Birth Control Review, 7.3 Mar.
     1923: pp. 63-64.
         The article describes M.S.'s appearance before a joint com-
     mittee of the Connecticut legislature during hearings on a bill
     to legalize birth control.
557. "News Notes." Birth Control Review, 7.3 Mar. 1923: pp.
     61-62.
         Reports that it was unnecessary for M.S. to go to London
     to defend Family Limitation. Notes also report on meetings
     where M.S. was speaker.

558. Rout, Ettie A. "Family Limitation." Outlook (London), 51 10
     Mar. 1923: p. 203.
     Another letter continuing the writer's support for birth
     control.
559. Porritt, Annie G. "Publicity in the Birth Control Movement."
     Birth Control Review, 7.4 April 1923: pp. 88-89, 99.
     Paper presented at the International Birth Control Con-
     ference. Discusses the publicity value to the movement of the
     words "birth control."
560. "State, Child, and Parent." Spectator, 130 7 April 1923:
     p. 590.
     This reaction to M.S.'s Pivot of Civilization calls for birth
     control as a means to ending child neglect and also as a
     means of eugenic control (see item 475).
561. "Apostle of Birth Control Sees Cause Gaining Here: Hearing
     in Albany on Bill to Legalize Practice a Milestone in Long
     Fight of Margaret Sanger--Even China Awakening to Need
     of Selective Methods, She Says." New York Times, 8 April
     1923: Sect. 8 p. 11 col. 1.
562. "Mrs. Sanger Urges Birth Control Law: Assembly and Senate
     Committeemen at End of Hearing Oppose the Measure."
     New York Times, 11 April 1923: p. 3 col. 2.
     M.S. and scores of others appear at public hearing on the
     Rosenman bill, which would permit physicians to give birth
     control information.
563. Bronson, Sonia Joseph. "Birth Control Campaigns." New
     York Times, 22 April 1923: Sect. 8 p. 8 col. 6.
     Letter to editor by Sonia Joseph Bronson opposes M.S.'s
     ideas as reported in New York Times of April 8, 1923 (see
     item 561).
564. "Synagogue Forbids Birth Control Talk: Rabbi Mischkind,
     Who Invited Mrs. Sanger to Address Forum, Resigns."
     New York Times, 22 April 1923: p. 5 col. 7.
565. "Back Their Pastor on Free Speech: Members Protest
     Trustees' Action in Accepting Resignation--Mrs. Sanger at
     Forum." New York Times, 23 April 1923: p. 15 col. 2.
566. "Resent Birth Control Ban. Tremont Temple Men's Club
     Condemns Action of Trustees." New York Times, 28 April
     1923: p. 4 col. 2.
567. "The Case of Birth Control: The National Woman's Party."
     Birth Control Review, 7.6 June 1923: pp. 141-42.
     Describes speeches given by Dr. Dorothy Bocker, Annie
     Porritt, and M.S. before the National Woman's Party in
     Washington on May 21.
568. "The Case for Birth Control: The Social Workers." Birth
     Control Review, 7.6 June 1923: pp. 140-41.
     Describes the speech given by M.S. in Washington, D.C.
     on May 20 at a social workers' conference.
569. "Progress of the Birth Control Movement." Birth Control Re-
     view, 7.8 Aug. 1923: pp. 195-96.
     Reviews the progress made by birth control movement, with
     emphasis on work of M.S.

570. "The Chicago Birth Control Conference." Birth Control Re-
     view, 7.12 Dec. 1923: pp. 316-22.
     Gives an account of the proceedings of the Middle Western
     States Birth Control Conference (Oct. 29-31, 1923, Chicago).
     M.S.'s speech "sounded the keynote."
571. "Birth Control Aid Told Before Police: Learn All about Clinic
     in Fifth Avenue at Luncheon Given by League. 900
     Patients in 11 Months. Director Tells of Institution's
     Need--$5,000 is Raised for Fund to Continue Work." New
     York Times, 6 Dec. 1923: p. 10 col. 1.

1924

572. Sanger, Margaret H. "A Personal Glimpse of Havelock Ellis."
     Birth Control Review, 8.2 Feb. 1924: pp. 40-41.
     M.S. heaps praise on Havelock Ellis.
573. _____. "The Case for Birth Control." Woman Citizen, N.S.
     8.17 23 Feb. 1924: pp. 17+.
     M.S. writes this as president of the American Birth Control
     League. Her "case" has a eugenic slant and an interesting
     postscript endorsing the control of birth control by the medi-
     cal profession. (For reprint, see item 605.)
574. _____. "A Review by Margaret Sanger." Birth Control
     Review, 8.3 Mar. 1924: pp. 87-88.
     M.S. reviews Hugh de Sélincourt's One Little Boy, New
     York: Albert and Charles Boni, 1923.
575. _____. "The Meaning of Radio Birth Control." Birth
     Control Review, 8.4 April 1924: pp. 110-11.
     A radio address given by M.S. on WFAB Syracuse (Feb.
     29, 1924).
576. _____. "The War Against Birth Control." American Mer-
     cury, 2.6 June 1924: pp. 231-6.
     Reprinted in Birth Control Review, 8.9 Sept. 1924: pp.
     245-248, 269.
     M.S. recalls ten years of mostly illegal suppression. She
     lists the psychological and humanistic characteristics of her
     movement. Finding the American public in a "mental coma"
     and at the mercy of the "professional meddlers," she calls on
     courage for victory.
577. _____. "The Passing of a Hero." Birth Control Review,
     8.10 Oct. 1924: pp. 288-289.
     M.S.'s tribute to Holland's Dr. J. Rutgers (at his death).
578. _____. "Editorial." Birth Control Review, 8.12 Dec. 1924:
     pp. 339-340.
     M.S. recounts her trip to London and praises the work
     being done there by the Walworth Clinic.
579. "Birth Control: University of North Carolina Versus North
     Carolina State College." in University Debaters' Annual,
     E. M. Phelps, ed. 1924-25: pp. 221-76.
     "Resolved: That the dissemination of knowledge of birth

control by contraceptive methods should be legalized throughout the United States. An interesting debate presenting both sides of the argument. An extensive bibliography is included.

580. U.S. Congress. Joint Committees on the Judiciary <u>Cummins-Vaile Bill</u>. Joint Hearings Before the Subcommittees of the Committees of the Judiciary. 68th Congress, 1st Session on H.R. 6542 and S.2290. April 8 and May 9, 1924. Serial 38. Washington, D.C.: U.S.G.P.O., 1924: 79 p.
Hearings held on bills to amend the Comstock Law so that the law would permit the circulation of birth control information sponsored by the Voluntary Parenthood League. Mary Ware Dennett testifies. In a short but interesting bit of testimony given by an opponent of the bills, M.S. is quoted in an attempt to show the unreliability of contraceptive methods (p. 52).

581. "Mrs. Sanger Reported Wed; Birth Control Advocate is Said to be Wife of J. N. H. Slee." <u>New York Times</u>, 18 Feb. 1924: p. 4 col. 4.
Reports that M.S. and J. Noah H. Slee "have been married for the past year and a half."

582. "Birth Control and Federal Legislation." <u>Birth Control Review</u>, 8 Mar. 1924: pp. 68-69.
Expresses the position of the American Birth Control League on federal birth control legislation. The league "has set itself against the indiscriminate dissemination of so-called Birth Control information." The bill that the league proposes would give only physicians access to the mails.

583. "Birth Control in Syracuse." <u>Birth Control Review</u>, 8.4 April 1924: pp. 100-01, 119.
Gives an account of the birth control conference held in Syracuse, New York, February 1924, despite attempts to prevent the conference from taking place.

584. Siddal, R. S., M.D. "The Intrauterine Contraceptive Pessary--Inefficient and Dangerous." <u>American Journal of Obstetrics and Gynecology</u>, 8 July 1924: pp. 76-79.
The paper views the use of the pessary as medically dangerous and finds it regrettable "that this is the method which one of the leading proponents of birth control in this country is said to recommend as being both certain and harmless."

585. "What We Stand For: Principles and Aims of the American Birth Control League, Inc." <u>Birth Control Review</u>, 8 Sept. 1924: pp. 256-57.

586. Fishbein, Morris. "Birth Control; An Unsolved Problem." <u>American Mercury</u>, 3.10 Oct. 1924: pp. 210-12.
Author notes Dr. William Allen Pusey's support for birth control, as evidenced in his presidential address before the American Medical Association. Essay discusses many problems blocking the success of birth control; among them, the lack of a practical method and the fact that the government has made unlawful the dissemination of information about any

method. The major problem involved the working classes. Dr. Pusey selected M.S.'s documents of the working classes printed in her Birth Control Review as evidence that "continence does not work among the poor."

587. Dickinson, Robert L., M.D. "Contraception: A Medical Review of the Situation: First Report of the Committee on Maternal Health of New York." American Journal of Obstetrics and Gynecology, 8 Nov. 1924: pp. 583-604.
     This paper was read at the Forty-ninth Annual Meeting of the American Gynecological Society (May 15, 1924). It details the use and effectiveness of various contraceptive methods, reports on the work of the birth control clinics, and points out the "need of investigation by the medical profession" (for response by M.S., see item 593).

588. "Editorial." Birth Control Review, 8.11 Nov. 1924: p. 307.
     Comments on M.S.'s short trip to England taken in October 1924 during which time Sanger arranged for the program of the Sixth International neo-Malthusian and Birth Control Conference to be held in New York, March 26-31, 1925.

589. "Mrs. Sanger Talks at Yale; Invited to Return after Lecture to Divinity Students on Birth Control." New York Times, 5 Dec. 1924: p. 21 col. 7.

590. "Birth Control Meeting; Two Doctors, a Lawyer and a Clergyman Speak--Police in Hall." New York Times, 7 Dec. 1924: Sect. 1 p. 2 col. 6.
     M.S. presided over a meeting at Carnegie Hall where Dr. James F. Cooper, Dr. Dorothy Bocker, I. N. Thurman, and Rev. Charles Potter spoke.

1925

591. Sanger, Margaret H., ed. The Sixth International Neo-Malthusian and Birth Control Conference. 4 vols. New York: American Birth Control League, Inc., 1925-26.
     These four volumes are the proceedings of the New York Conference of 1925.
     Vol. 1, International Aspects of Birth Control, 1925: 244 p. (OCLC: 5427123). Presents papers by birth control notables which deal with the movement throughout the world. There is also a report by Anne Kennedy, executive secretary of the American Birth Control League. An introduction by M.S., her "Address of Welcome" to the conference, and her letter to President Calvin Coolidge are included (see item 597).
     Vol. 2, Problems of Overpopulation, 1926: 208 p.
     Vol. 3, Medical and Eugenic Aspects of Birth Control, 1926: 247 p.
     Vol. 4, Religious and Ethical Aspects of Birth Control, 1926: 240 p.
     These three volumes contain more papers. Volumes 2 and

3 also contain resolutions passed by the conference. Volume
4 includes "The Children's Era," a presentation by M.S. (see
item 635).

592.   _____. "The Need of Birth Control in America." In:
Meyer, Adolf, M.D., ed. Birth Control; Facts and Responsibilities; A Symposium Dealing With This Important Subject
From a Number of Angles. Baltimore: Williams & Wilkins
Co., 1925: pp. 11-49.
A paper given at the Baltimore Conference on Birth Control,
1923. M.S. stresses many subjects, including: infant mortality, maternal mortality, the "feeble-minded," eugenics, and
the failure of "self-control" (see Meyer, item 606).

593.   _____. "Contraception: A Medical Review of the Situation."
Birth Control Review, 9.1 Jan. 1925: pp. 20-21.
M.S. reviews Robert L. Dickinson's "First Report of the
Committee on Maternal Health of New York." She agrees with
his appeal for "investigation by the medical profession" into
the status of birth control. However, she accuses his report
of being "tainted with bias" (see item 587).

594.   _____. "Margaret Sanger on Impressions and Comments."
Birth Control Review, 9.2 Feb. 1925: pp. 48-49.
M.S. reviews Havelock Ellis' Impressions and Comments,
New York: Houghton Mifflin Co., 1924.

595.   _____. "Radiant." Birth Control Review, 9.2 Feb. 1925:
pp. 35-36.
A birthday tribute to Havelock Ellis.

596.   _____. "Editorials." Birth Control Review, 9.3 Mar. 1925:
pp. 67-68.
M.S. comments on the growing discussion of birth control
in medical journals and on the relations between birth control,
overpopulation, and war.

597.   _____. "Address of Welcome to the Sixth International Neo-
Malthusian and Birth Control Conference." Birth Control
Review, 9.4 April 1925: pp. 99-100.
This is Sanger's welcoming speech to the conference (see
item 591).

598.   _____. "From Mrs. Sanger." Survey, 54.2 15 April 1925:
p. 116.
A letter written in reply to an article by Gertrude M.
Pinchot of the Committee on Maternal Health (see item 609).
M.S. admits that clinical birth control records are lacking.
She says her aim has been to help the individual woman, not
to amass records. That, she continues, is the job of the
medical profession (see item 623 for comment by Robert L.
Dickinson).

599.   _____. "Message to the President of the United States."
Birth Control Review, 9.5 May 1925: p. 131.
An open letter to President Calvin Coolidge asking that
Coolidge establish a Federal Birth Rate Commission.

600.   _____. "Editorial." Birth Control Review, 9.6 June 1925:
pp. 163-64.

M.S. disclaims the "eugenic" resolution adopted by the conference. Resolution was adopted at a "sparsely attended meeting" and "was out of order."

601. _____. "One Week's Activity in England." Birth Control Review, 9.8 Aug. 1925: pp. 219–20.
M.S. describes one week's activity of the birth control movement in England.

602. _____. "Is Race Suicide Probable?" Collier's, 76 15 Aug. 1925: p. 25.
M.S. attacks the concept of birth control as "race suicide"; she stresses birth control as a eugenic weapon.

603. _____. "The Incident at Williamstown." Birth Control Review, 9.9 Sept. 1925: pp. 246–47.
M.S. replies to Count Antonio Cippico, an Italian senator who demanded the U.S. liberalize its immigration laws to admit Italy's surplus population. Sanger praises Edward M. East for responding to this demand by advocating birth control.

604. Fishbein, Morris, M.D. The Medical Follies: An Analysis of the Foibles of Some Healing Cults, Including Osteopathy, Homeopathy, Chiropractic, and the Electronic Reactions of Abrams; with Essays on the Antivivisectionists, Health Legislation, Physical Culture, Birth Control, and Rejuvenation. New York: Boni & Liveright, 1925: 223 p. No Index.
Written by the editor of the Journal of the American Medical Association, the volume contains the essay "Birth Control," (pp. 141–49), which discusses the failure of M.S. and other "chief advocates of birth control" to find an ideal method of birth control.

605. Johnsen, Julia E., Compiler. Selected Articles on Birth Control. New York: H. W. Wilson, Co., 1925: 369 p. No Index. Bibliography. (OCLC: 1362106)
The introduction to this "handbook" contains a reference to "the Sanger case" as well as a discussion of the efforts to change federal and state legislation concerning birth control. The volume includes M.S.'s "Case for Birth Control" (pp. 134–37) (see item 573).

606. Meyer, Adolf, M.D., ed. Birth Control; Facts and Responsibilities; A Symposium Dealing with This Important Subject from a Number of Angles. Baltimore: Williams & Wilkins Co., 1925: 157 p. Index. No Bibliography. (OCLC: 2133419)
A collection of some of the papers presented at the Baltimore Conference on Birth Control (1923) and at the Chicago Birth Control Conference (1923). M.S.'s paper, "The Need of Birth Control in America," is included (see item 592).

607. Shaw, G. Bernard. "Two Notable Occurrences." Birth Control Review, 9.1 Jan. 1925: p. 5.
In a letter to M.S., George Bernard Shaw advocates birth control and comments on the decision against Marie Stopes in the Sutherland Case.

608. "The Annual Meeting." Birth Control Review, 9.2 Feb. 1925:
pp. 44-45, 58, 60.
Reports on the Third Annual Meeting of the American Birth
Control League.

609. Pinchot, Gertrude Minturn. "Surprises in an Investigation of
Birth Control." Survey, 53.12 15 Mar. 1925: pp. 751-53.
Reports methods used by the Committee on Maternal Health
in New York to conduct research on birth control. The rec-
ords of Dr. Dorothy Bocker and the American Birth Control
League are criticized as being "scant" and without follow-up
(see items 598 and 623 for replies from M.S. and Robert L.
Dickinson).

610. "Neo-Malthusians to Confer Here on Race Betterment."
New York Times, 22 Mar. 1925: Sect. 8 p. 18 col. 1-2.
Reports that the Sixth International neo-Malthusian and
Birth Control Conference will be held in New York beginning
March 25.

611. "Birth Control Conference; Noted Advocates from Abroad to
Attend Sessions Opening Today." New York Times, 25
Mar. 1925: p. 12 col. 2.

612. "Conference Opens on Birth Control; First International Meeting Here Brings Delegates from Many Lands; Message from
G. B. Shaw." New York Times, 26 Mar. 1925: p. 18
col. 1-6.

613. "Population Rise No Menace, He Says; Dr. Louis I. Dublin
Attacks Movement at Birth Control Conference." New York
Times, 27 Mar. 1925: p. 8 col. 1-2.
M.S. invited Dr. Louis I. Dublin to the conference to
"present the 'other side'."

614. "Asks League to Aid in Population Ills; Birth Control Con-
ference Also Seeks Help of Labor and Child Welfare
Bodies; Speakers Predict War; Dr. Goldstein and Harold
Cox Say Over-Population Will Bring Next Great Conflict."
New York Times, 28 Mar. 1925: p. 9 col. 1.

615. "Finds Excitement Injures the Race; Dr. Schlapp Says Unfit
Are Being Born to Women Who Plunge into Business;
Havelock Ellis's Views; Paper by British Author Read at
Birth Control Conference--Physicians Meet Today." New
York Times, 29 Mar. 1925: Sect. 1 p. 16 col. 1-3.

616. "Scientists Plead for Birth Control Idea; Leaders of Thought
in Many Lands State Why They Think the Restricting of
Population Has Become a World Necessity." New York
Times, 29 Mar. 1925: Sect. 9 p. 6 col. 1-5.
Gives statements by George Bernard Shaw, Havelock Ellis,
Dr. Corrado Gini, Raymond Pearl, Edward M. East, and
William F. Ogburn.

617. "Doctors in Shut Meetings; Exclude Even Mrs. Sanger from
Two Birth Control Discussions." New York Times, 30 Mar.
1925: p. 10 col. 2.
Also reports that M.S. "sent a telegram to President
Coolidge ... urging him to establish a Federal Birth Rate Com-
mission...."

618. "Ask Churches' Aid for a Better Race; Ministers Speak in Support of Movement for a Higher Order of Human Society; Favor Wider Knowledge; Physicians Express Their Views on the Subject at Birth Control Conference." New York Times, 31 Mar. 1925: p. 7 col. 1.

619. "Favors Increase of 'Super-Persons'; Birth Conference Resolution Calls for Larger Families among that Class: Roosevelt Draws Reply; Mrs. Sanger Says Colonel's Criticisms Are Unworthy--Week's Work Summarized." New York Times, 1 April 1925: p. 15 col. 1.

620. "Mrs. Sanger Heads New League." New York Times, 2 April 1925: p. 17 col. 2.
    Reports that M.S. was chosen president of the new International Neo-Malthusian Birth Control League.

621. "Are There Too Many of Us." Literary Digest, 85.2 11 April 1925: pp. 10-11.
    Notes the public's quiet and informed reaction to the Sixth International Neo-Malthusian and Birth Control Conference.

622. "The Child Who Was Mother to a Woman." New Yorker, 1 11 April 1925: pp. 11-12.
    This well-written "profile" links an incident occurring when M.S. was barred from speaking in Albany, New York with an incident occurring during her childhood when her father, Michael Higgins, was barred from presenting Robert Ingersoll in Corning, New York.

623. Dickinson, Robert L. "Dr. Dickinson Replies." Survey, 54.2 15 April 1925: p. 116.
    This short letter comments on an article by Gertrude M. Pinchot (see item 609). Dr. Dickinson was head of the Committee on Maternal Health, New York. He feels "there is need of one or more special clinics" until the medical profession can provide the necessary services (for M.S.'s reply to article see item 598).

624. Langdon-Davies, John. "Race-Suicide No Murder." New Republic, 42.541 15 April 1925: pp. 209-11.
    This article presents a discussion of the International Neo-Malthusian and Birth Control Conference held in New York from March 25 to 31, 1925.

625. "Neo-Malthusians." Nation, 120 15 April 1925: p. 401.
    An editorial tribute appearing after the neo-Malthusian and Birth Control Conference in New York. The editorial pays tribute to "Margaret Sanger and to the few men and women--chiefly women--who have faced notoriety and attack to make birth control a breathing issue."

626. Ross, Mary. "Up to the Doctors." Survey, 54.2 15 April 1925: p. 73.
    Reports on the International Conference on Birth Control held in New York in 1925. The article states that M.S. has offered to place "the medical activities of the American Birth Control League in the hands of a representative medical group."

627. "The Birth Control Conference." Woman Citizen, 9 18 April
     1925: p. 24.
       A report of the program presented at the Sixth Internation-
     al Neo-Malthusian and Birth Control Conference.
628. "A Great Sociological Congress: The Sixth International Con-
     ference March 25-31." Birth Control Review, 9.5 May 1925:
     pp. 137-139, 156.
629. "Legislators Wake to a Vital Problem: Hearing on the New York
     Birth Control Bill." Birth Control Review, 9.5 May 1925:
     pp. 143-155.
       Reports on testimony given by M.S. and others in the New
     York state legislature.
630. East, Edward M. "Menace of Overpopulation." World's Work,
     50 June 1925: pp. 174-78.
       Author discusses the history of the problems of overpopula-
     tion and also talks about the importance of the Sixth Inter-
     national Neo-Malthusian Conference held in New York City.
     Raymond Pearl made some interesting remarks at the confer-
     ence; they are included.
631. Dickinson, Robert L., M.D. "Correspondence: American Birth
     Control League." Journal of the American Medical Associa-
     tion, 85.15 10 Oct. 1925: pp. 1153-54.
       In this letter to the editor, Dr. Dickinson discusses M.S.'s
     work to obtain the affiliation of doctors associated with the
     American Birth Control League and also discusses her support
     of "doctor's only" legislation.
632. "Fights for Birth Control; Dr. Little of Michigan University
     Criticizes Church Attitude." New York Times, 29 Nov.
     1925: Sect. 1 p. 26 col. 2.
       Clarence C. Little, president of University of Michigan,
     spoke at the annual convention of the New York branch of the
     American Birth Control League.
633. Tagore, Rabindranath. "Dear Margaret Sanger." Birth Con-
     trol Review, 9.12 Dec. 1925: p. 341.
       In this letter, Tagore praises the birth control movement,
     saying that it is a means of lessening suffering.
634. "Mrs. Sanger at Columbia; Discusses Birth Control for an
     Audience Largely of Girl Students." New York Times, 4
     Dec. 1925: p. 8 col. 2.

1926

635. Sanger, Margaret H. "The Children's Era." in Sixth Inter-
     national Neo-Malthusian and Birth Control Conference.
     Vol. 4, Religious and Ethical Aspects of Birth Control.
     New York: American Birth Control League, Inc., 1926:
     pp. 53-58.
       This paper was presented at the 1925 New York Conference.
     It is a plea for eugenic control. (See item 591 for complete
     conference proceedings.)

636. _____. Happiness in Marriage. New York: Brentano's,
      1926: 231 p. (OCLC: 1469137)
      Much like a marriage manual. Deals with the normal prob-
lems of sex, love, and marriage. Reviewed by Booklist, 23
Jan. 1927: p. 151; Dell, Floyd. "Happiness in Marriage."
Birth Control Review, 11.1 Jan. 1927: pp. 18-22; Parsons,
Alice Beal. "Signposts in a Wilderness." Books (New York
Herald Tribune), 8 Aug. 1926: p. 4; Saturday Review of
Literature, 3.13 23 Oct. 1926: pp. 241-242; "Some Notes on
How to Be Happy If Married." New York Times Book Review,
4 July 1926: p. 8 col. 2; Survey, 56.10 15 Aug. 1926:
p. 550; Woolsey, D. H. "Sex in Home and State." New
Republic, 48.615 15 Sept. 1926: p. 102.

637. _____. "The Function of Sterilization." Birth Control
      Review, 10.10 Oct. 1926: p. 299.
      Part of an address given by M.S. to the Institute of
Euthenics at Vassar College (Aug. 5, 1926). Sanger advocates
sterilization for the insane and the feebleminded.

638. Adelman, Joseph. Famous Women: An Outline of Feminine
      Achievement Through the Ages with Life Stories of Five
      Hundred Noted Women. New York: Ellis M. Lonow Co.,
      1926: 328 p. Index. Illus. (OCLC: 1074345)
      Pages 323-24 contain brief mention of M.S.'s efforts for
women's rights in regard to childbearing.

639. Dennett, Mary Ware. Birth Control Laws: Shall We Keep
      Them Change Them or Abolish Them. New York:
      Frederick H. Hitchcock, 1926: 309 p. (OCLC: 802505)
      Another leader of the birth control movement traces the
development of the birth control laws, describes attempts to
change them, and makes a plea to abolish them. Stresses
Dennett's break with Sanger over "doctor's only" bill.
M.S.: pp. 40 (William Sanger's arrest), 49-50, 54-55, 66-73,
80, 89-91, 95, 101, 168-175, 187-89, 200-09, 230, 238, 253-54,
265, 279.

640. Popenoe, Paul. The Conservation of the Family. Baltimore:
      Williams & Wilkins Co., 1926: 266 p. Index. References.
      (OCLC: 323029)
      A call for the eugenic improvement of society. The book
accuses M.S. and the birth controllers of limiting the births
of "superior children."

641. "The Town Hall Revisited: November 1921-November 1925."
      Birth Control Review, 10.1 Jan. 1926: pp. 14-15.
      "Just four years after the famous raid, the American Birth
Control League holds a public meeting at Town Hall, reviews
the years between and looks forward into the future."

642. "Hits Humanitarian Work; Mrs. Sanger Says Birth Control Is
      Only Way to End Problem." New York Times, 11 Jan. 1926:
      p. 3, col. 5.
      M.S. speaks at the Washington Square Methodist Episcopal
Church. Meeting was sponsored by the Judson Sunday Club.

643. "For Birth Control Pension; Margaret Sanger Urges Payments

to Unfit Who Forego Parenthood." New York Times, 6 Aug.
1926: p. 30 col. 6.
Speech given at Vassar College Institute of Euthenics.

1927

644. Sanger, Margaret H., ed. Proceedings of the World Population Conference. Geneva, 1927. London: Edward Arnold
& Co., 1927: 383 p. Index and Who's Who of the congress.
Papers given by biologists and sociologists from around the
world. Contains a short preface by M.S.

645. _____. What Every Boy and Girl Should Know. Fairview
Park Elmsford, New York: Maxwell Reprint Co., 1969.
(Reprint of the 1927 ed. published by Brentano's, New
York) 140 p. (OCLC: 104470)
M.S. provides the same basic information as in the earlier
What Every Girl Should Know (see item 161), but her involve-
ment with the eugenic movement can be seen.

646. Broun, Heywood and Leech, Margaret. Anthony Comstock:
Roundsman of the Lord. New York: Albert and Charles
Boni, 1927: 285 p. Index. Bibliography. (OCLC:
2588816)
Brief mention of the arrest and conviction of William Sanger.

647. "New Notes." Birth Control Review, 11.7 July 1927: p. 210.
Reports that M.S. is in Europe and that she attended the
sessions of the economic conference held in Switzerland.

1928

648. Sanger, Margaret H. Motherhood in Bondage. New York:
Brentano's, 1928: 446 p. No index. (OCLC: 1269266)
A book of representative letters chosen from the thousands
sent to M.S. that included pleas for birth control information.
Mary Sumner Boyd's statistical analysis of 5000 letters is
also included. Reviewed by Booklist, 25 Mar. 1929: pp. 231-
32; "Brief Reviews." New York Times Book Review, 2 Dec.
1928: Sect. 4 p. 22 col. 2; Kirchwey, Freda. "Out of
Bondage." Nation, 127.3310 12 Dec. 1928: p. 661; Lind,
John E. "Motherhood in America." Saturday Review of Lit-
erature, 5.47 15 June 1929: p. 1114; "Motherhood in Bondage."
Birth Control Review, 13.3 Mar. 1929: p. 86; "Motherhood in
Bondage: Some Appreciations of Margaret Sanger's New Book."
Birth Control Review, 13.2 Feb. 1929: pp. 51-52; Parsons,
Alice Beal. "Mother America." Books (New York Herald
Tribune), 6 Jan. 1929: p. 12; Survey 61.8 15 Jan. 1929:
p. 515; Temple, Jean B. "Motherhood in Bondage." New
Republic, 57.737 16 Jan. 1929: p. 252.

649. _____. "Havelock Ellis." Birth Control Review, 12.7 July
1928: pp. 210-11.

A review of <u>Havelock Ellis: Philosopher of Love</u> by Houston Peterson. New York: Houghton Mifflin Co., 1928.

650. _____. "The Need for Birth Control." <u>Birth Control Review</u>, 12.8 Aug. 1928: pp. 227-28.

A call to educate the poor to the advantages of using birth control.

651. Cooper, James F., M.D. <u>Technique of Contraception: The Principles and Practice of Anti-Conceptional Methods</u>. New York: Day-Nichols, Inc., Publishers, 1928: 271 p. Bibl. (OCLC: 831605)

Cooper was medical director of the Birth Control Clinical Research Bureau. His conclusions are based on the study of 1600 cases taken there. This book details contraceptive methods and is intended for physicians. Its distribution was limited to physicians and those "whose professional standing is approved by the publishers." It is dedicated to M.S.

652. Peterson, Houston. <u>Havelock Ellis, Philosopher of Love</u>. New York: Houghton Mifflin Co., 1928: 432 p. Index. (OCLC: 363138)

Very brief mention of M.S. and of Ellis's influence on her work.

653. "Report Progress on Birth Control; Speakers at Annual Meeting of American League Tell of Educational Work." <u>New York Times</u>, 13 Jan. 1928: p. 7 col. 3.

Dr. Henry Pratt Fairchild reported on the World Population Conference.

654. Smedley, Agnes. "Margaret Sanger Comes to Berlin." <u>Birth Control Review</u>, 12.2 Feb. 1928: pp. 50-51, 54, 66.

Describes the experiences M.S. underwent during a trip to Berlin in December 1927.

655. Stone, Abraham. "Speaking of the Conference." <u>Birth Control Review</u>, 12.2 Feb. 1928: pp. 48-49, 59.

Dr. Stone comments on events at the World Population Conference. He describes an ovation given to M.S., despite her not seeking "active participation in any of the meetings."

656. "Says Europe's Future Lies in Birth Control; Mrs. Sanger, Back, Says Over-Population Threatens to Lead to Food Riots and War." <u>New York Times</u>, 15 Mar. 1928: p. 17 col. 1.

M.S. returns after two years in Europe.

657. "Support for Birth Control: A Welcome to Margaret Sanger." <u>Birth Control Review</u>, 12.4 April 1928: pp. 107-109.

Describes a mass meeting held at the engineering auditorium, New York on March 15, 1927. Gives excerpts from M.S.'s speech.

658. "School Show Bars Birth Control Body; League Invited Last Fall to Take Part Is Now Asked to Stay Away; Education Board Objects; Threatens to Withdraw from the Exhibition Opening Tomorrow--Mrs. Sanger, Indignant, May Sue." <u>New York Times</u>, 20 April 1928: p. 11 col. 1.

American Birth Control League barred from Parents'

Exposition at Grand Central Palace. N.Y.C. Board of Education objected to birth control league's presence.

659. "Birth Control Ban Arouses Protests; Kenneth Macgowan Declines Invitation to Speak at the Parents' Exposition; Objects to Censorship." New York Times, 24 April 1928: p. 12 col. 2-3.

660. "Mrs. Sanger Calls Catholics Bigots; Birth Control Leader Assails Church 'Tyranny' for Ban at Parents' Exposition; Attacks Smith Candidacy." New York Times, 25 April 1928: p. 14 col. 2-3.

661. "Editorial." Birth Control Review, 12.5 May 1928: p. 138. Notes that M.S. is on the "Honor List" of those excluded by the D.A.R.'s blacklist.

662. "A Question of Policy: Shall the Birth Control Review be Combined With a Eugenics Magazine?" Birth Control Review, 12.6 June 1928: p. 188. Prints letters in response to a question posed by M.S. regarding merging Birth Control Review with a eugenics magazine.

663. Smedley, Agnes. "A Berlin Birth Control Clinic." Birth Control Review, 12.6 June 1928: p. 179. Reports on the opening of a birth control clinic in Berlin; the opening of the clinic had been sparked by M.S.'s visit.

664. "Editorial." Birth Control Review, 12.7 July 1928: p. 199. Prints an open letter from M.S. to Cardinal Hayes in which Sanger asks that the Catholic Church "be kept out of politics."

665. "The Future of the Birth Control Review," Birth Control Review, 12.7 July 1928: p. 214. More letters addressed to the question of merging the Birth Control Review with a eugenics magazine.

666. "The Future of the Birth Control Review." Birth Control Review, 12.8 Aug. 1928: p. 238. More eugenics magazine letters.

667. Smith, Helena Huntington. "Birth Control and the Law." Outlook, 149 29 Aug. 1928: pp. 686-87+. Article focuses on the overriding influences of the Comstock Law (as regards birth control), on the lack of judicial precedent, and on the problems involved in dealing with the heterogeneous laws of forty-eight states.

668. "Mrs. Sanger Quits Birth Control Post; Resigns Presidency of League She Founded--To Study Ways to Lower Maternal Deaths." New York Times, 12 Sept. 1928: p. 11 col. 1-3.

669. "Succeeds Mrs. Sanger; Mrs. F. Robertson Jones Becomes Head of Birth Control League." New York Times, 13 Sept. 1928: p. 29 col. 8.

670. "Editorial." Birth Control Review, 12.10 Oct. 1928: p. 273. Gives M.S.'s reasons for resigning as president of the American Birth Control League. Sanger plans, through birth control, to concentrate on reducing "maternal mortality."

671. "Eugenics and Birth Control: More Replies to Margaret Sanger's Letter." Birth Control Review, 12.10 Oct. 1928: pp. 290-91.

672. "News Notes: United States." Birth Control Review, 12.10
Oct. 1928: p. 292.
Reports on the resignation of M.S. as president of the
American Birth Control League and on the election of Mrs. F.
Robertson Jones to the position.

673. "Editorial." Birth Control Review, 12.11 Nov. 1928: p. 306.
Reports that the first issue of a periodical published by
the American Eugenics Society ends the question of the fusing
of the Birth Control Review with a eugenics magazine. Also
announces that M.S. is planning a tour of the western states
on behalf of birth control clinics.

674. "Eugenics and Birth Control: More Opinions from Correspond-
ents Re the Two Movements." Birth Control Review, 12.11
Nov. 1928: pp. 323, 329.
"Final installment" of letters.

1929

675. Sanger, Margaret H. "Laws Concerning Birth Control in the
United States." New York: Committee on Federal Legislation for Birth Control, 1929. 38 p. (OCLC: 1541025)
Gives the federal statute on contraception and surveys and
interprets the state laws dealing with birth control. The
preface is written by M.S.--she is president of the Committee
on Federal Legislation for Birth Control. (For reprint, see
item 846.)

676. _____. "Editorial: Havelock Ellis." Birth Control Review,
13.2 Feb. 1929: pp. 37-38.
M.S. pays tribute to Havelock Ellis as "the foremost" of
the "contemporary saints."

677. _____. "Women and Birth Control." North American Review, 227.5 May 1929: pp. 529-34.
An answer to an article written by Marjorie Wells (see item
686). M.S. insists that the letters in Motherhood in Bondage
(see item 648) are typical of American women. She calls for
the spacing of births--the births of those women who desire
large families--and describes birth control as a social responsibility.

678. _____. "The Birth-Control Raid." New Republic, 58 1 May
1929: pp. 305-6.
M.S. calls on the people of New York to find out how and
where the police raid originated that was led by Policewoman
Mary Sullivan against the Birth Control Clinical Research
Bureau.

_____. "Editorial." Birth Control Review, 13.5 May 1929:
p. 123.
M.S. attacks the raid on the Birth Control Clinical Research
Bureau (April 15, 1929). (Reprinted from the New Republic,
58 1 May 1929.)

679. _____. "The Next Step." Birth Control Review, 13.10
     Oct. 1929: pp. 278-79.
     An appeal to readers to work toward amending the federal
     laws that hinder birth control.

680. Haywood, William D. Bill Haywood's Book: Autobiography
     New York: International Publishers, 1929: 368 p. No
     Index. (OCLC: 1012506)
     Haywood, of the I.W.W., mentions M.S.'s union activities
     (p. 268).

681. Vreeland, Francis McLennon. "The Process of Reform with
     Especial Reference to Reform Groups in the Field of Popu-
     lation." Diss. University of Michigan, 1929. Not seen.

682. "News Notes: California." Birth Control Review, 13.1 Jan.
     1929: p. 26.
     Reports on M.S.'s lecture tour in California.

683. Wolfe, A. B. "The Population Problem since the World War:
     A Survey of Literature and Research--Concluded."
     Journal of Political Economy, 37.1 Feb. 1929: pp. 87-120.
     Wolfe traces the literature of population. He also comments
     on M.S.'s place in the birth control movement and examines
     the birth control literature, finding very little of "scientific
     value."

684. "Mrs. Sanger Resigns Editorship." Birth Control Review, 13.3
     Mar. 1929: p. 95.
     M.S. resigns as editor of the Birth Control Review "to de-
     vote herself to the work of the Clinical Research Bureau."

685. "News Notes: California." Birth Control Review, 13.3 Mar.
     1929: pp. 90-91.
     Reports on M.S.'s experiences in California.

686. Wells, Marjorie. "Are Ten Too Many?" North American Review,
     227.3 Mar. 1929: pp. 262-268.
     This article was written by a mother of ten children in
     response to M.S.'s book, Motherhood in Bondage (see item
     648). Wells presents arguments for the large family and ac-
     cuses M.S. of collecting untypical letters of "abnormalities and
     horrors." (For M.S.'s reply to Mrs. Wells, see item 677.)

687. "The 'Black Plague'." Nation, 128.3323 13 Mar 1929: pp.
     301-2.
     Documents Catholic misrepresentation of the Remer bill.

688. "Birth Control." Time, 13.11 18 Mar. 1929: pp. 36, 38.
     Comments on tax deductions taken by James Noah Henry
     Slee for contributions made to the American Birth Control
     League. Also, reports on a fund-raising meeting for the
     "well-to-do" held by M.S. at New York's Hotel Plaza.

689. Lovejoy, Owen R. "Motherhood in Bondage." Birth Control
     Review, 13.4 April 1929: pp. 107, 119.
     An address given at a dinner of the Clinical Research
     Bureau, Hotel Plaza, New York, February 26, 1929. It
     praises M.S.'s Motherhood in Bondage.

690. "Raid Sanger Clinic on Birth Control; Police Seize Two
     Women Doctors and Three Nurses in West 15th Street

Bureau; Founder Is Not Arrested; But She Goes to Court and Aids in Planning Defense for Trial Friday--Dismissal Predicted." New York Times, 16 April 1929: p. 31 col. 3.
Birth Control Clinical Research Bureau is raided. Drs. Hannah M. Stone and Elizabeth Pissont are among those arrested.

691. "Doctors Aroused over Raid on Clinic; Dr. Harris May Be One of Those to Come to Support of Birth Control Bureau; Hearing for Five Today; Clergy and Women Leaders Send Pledges of Support to Mrs. Sanger." New York Times, 19 April 1929: p. 27 col. 2.

692. "500 in Court to Aid 5 Seized at Clinic; Indignation Expressed When Hearing Is Put Over Until Monday." New York Times, 20 April 1929: p. 21 col. 6.

693. "Clinic File Seizure Held to Be Illegal; McAdoo Officially Finds Police Exceeded Their Authority and Orders Return of Records." New York Times, 21 April 1929: pt. 1 p. 9 col. 2-3.

694. "Legal Comment on Current Events; The Law of Birth Control." New York Times, 21 April 1929: Sect. 3 p. 7 col. 5-6.
Comments on legal questions arising from the police raid on the Clinical Research Bureau.

695. "Medical Society to Sift Clinic Raid; County Body to Study Police Methods Tonight in Seizures at Birth Control Bureau." New York Times, 22 April 1929: p. 18 col. 2-3.
At its monthly meeting, the New York County Medical Society will discuss police raid.

696. "Rabbi Wise Assails Stock Speculation." New York Times, 22 April 1929: p. 28 col. 5.
Dr. Stephen S. Wise calls the raid on the Clinical Research Bureau an "outrage."
In Carnegie Hall, he spoke to the congregation of the Free Synagogue.

697. "Doctors Condemn Birth Control Raid; Medical Association of County Attacks Seizure of Records of Patients by Police; Academy Also Will Act." New York Times, 23 April 1929: p. 3 col. 5.
Dr. Robert L. Dickinson "offered a resolution protesting against the seizure of the records." The resolution was unanimously approved by the New York County Medical Society, New York Academy of Medicine.

698. "Editorial Paragraphs." Nation, 128.3329 24 April 1929: p. 495.
Notes the police raid on the Birth Control Clinical Research Bureau in New York City, the arrest of two doctors and three nurses, and the seizure of medical records.

699. "Uproar Interrupts Clinic Raid Hearing; 200 are Ejected for Laughing at Magistrate and Cheering Birth Control Defense." New York Times, 25 April 1929: p. 31 col. 6.
Also reports on Morris L. Ernst's examination of physician witnesses.

700. "Medical Council Decries Clinic Raid; See Freedom of Profession Menaced by Action Against Birth Control Centre; Asks Academy to Act; Finds Confidential Relations Between Physicians and Patients Endangered." New York Times, 26 April 1929: p. 13 col. 2-3.

701. Tompkins, Jean Burnet. "The Birth Control Clinic." New York Times, 30 April 1929: p. 28 col. 7.
Letter from the chair of the legislative committee of the New York State League of Women Voters, written to protest the raid on the clinic.

702. Jones, Eleanor Dwight. "Editorial." Birth Control Review, 13.5 May 1929: pp. 123-24.
The president of the American Birth Control League condemns the raid on the Clinical Research Bureau.

703. "Press Comments." Birth Control Review, 13.5 May 1929: p. 138.
Reprints an editorial from the New York Herald Tribune and a Heywood Broun column from the New York Telegram. Both condemn the raid on the Clinical Research Bureau.

704. "The Raid." Birth Control Review, 13.5 May 1929: p. 139.
Describes the raid on the Clinical Research Bureau.

705. "Birth Control Raid Assailed by Women; City Club Directors 'Shocked' at Interference with Clinic Operated Within Law." New York Times, 3 May 1929: p. 14 col. 5-8.
The Women's City Club protests both the clinic raid and the recent trial of Mary Ware Dennett.

706. Broun, Heywood. "It Seems to Heywood Broun." Nation, 128.3331 8 May 1929: p. 551.
Mr. Broun recalls the words of Justice Crane at the sentencing of Margaret Sanger, "that she was liable to punishment because she was a registered nurse and not a doctor."

707. Nichols, Dudley. "Sex and the Law." Nation, 128.3331 8 May 1929: pp. 552-54.
This article compares and contrasts the arrests and trials of Mary Ware Dennett and Margaret Sanger.

708. "Woman Police Head Demoted by Whalen in Birth Clinic Raid; Mrs. Mary Sullivan, Who Led Seizures at Sanger Office, Removed as Bureau Chief." New York Times, 12 May 1929: Sect. 1 p. 1 col. 3--p. 15 col. 3-4.

709. "Criticize Whalen in Clinic Raid Move; Backers of Birth Control Bureau Hold Demotion of Woman Is Not Enough." New York Times, 13 May 1929: p. 25 col. 2.

710. "Doctors Are Freed in Birth Clinic Raid; Court Holds Prosecution Failed to Show that Giving of Information Violated Law; Mrs. Sanger Sees Victory; Defense Counsel Criticizes Decision in Limiting Instruction to Married Women." New York Times, 15 May 1929: p. 20 col. 4-5.

711. "Editorial Paragraphs." Nation, 128.3332 15 May 1929: pp. 574-75.
Notes that Mary Ware Dennett was fined for sending "The Sex Side of Life" through the mails, that the International

Federation of Catholic Alumni attempted to have M.S. and her birth control clinic removed from a Fox Movietone "current-events reel," and that Carl Rave was arrested for selling a copy of M.S.'s Family Limitation.

712. "Editorial Paragraphs." Nation, 128.3334 29 May 1929: p. 635.

Notes the dismissal of the case (which arose from the police raid) against the Birth Control Clinical Research Bureau--and reports that Policewoman Sullivan was demoted.

713. Ward, Patrick J. "The Catholics and Birth Control." New Republic, 59.756 29 May 1929: pp. 35-38.

The New Republic invited Mr. Ward to write a definite statement of the Catholic attitude; this article represents that attitude.

"In Reply to Mr. Ward." New Republic, 59.756 29 May 1929: pp. 32-33.

Editorial reply to Mr. Ward's "The Catholics and Birth Control." "Strongest of all the indictments of the Catholic position in regard to birth control is its policy, which in the United States has been largely successful, of having its views embodied in legislation which applies to all citizens."

Ward, Patrick J. "Catholics and Birth Control." New Republic, 59.758 12 June 1929: pp. 100-01.

Mr. Ward's answer to the New Republic reply to his article on the Catholic position on birth control.

714. Drysdale, C. V. "The Birth Control Movement after a Century's Agitation." Current History, 30.3 June 1929: pp. 381-86.

Records M.S.'s "onslaught on the Comstock Law," as well as her success in widening the sphere of birth control.

715. "Editorial." Birth Control Review, 13.6 June 1929: p. 147.

Scores the results of the raid on the Clinical Research Bureau as vindicating the clinic. "The medical profession was forced to rally to the aid of the Clinic."

716. "News Notes: Illinois." Birth Control Review, 13.6 June 1929: pp. 171-72.

Reports M.S.'s address to the Illinois Birth Control League on April 30 and announces the tentative program for the International Conference on Population (June 17-28, Chicago).

717. "News Notes: United States." Birth Control Review, 13.6 June 1929: pp. 170-71.

Among other things, reports the formation of a committee (under M.S.'s chairmanship) to amend the federal laws.

718. "The Raid." Birth Control Review, 13.6 June 1929: pp. 154-55.

More discussion of the raid, of the publicity, and of the resultant support by the medical community.

719. "Judge Rosenbluth's Opinion." Birth Control Review, 13.7 July 1929: p. 194.

Reprints the opinion handed down by Judge Abraham

Rosenbluth on May 14, 1929, concerning the Clinical Research
Bureau case.

720. "The Raid and the Press." Birth Control Review, 13.7 July
1929: p. 206.
Excerpts from the American press concerning the birth control raid.

721. "Story of Margaret Sanger: Every Child a Wanted Child."
World Tomorrow, 12 July 1929: pp. 296-99.
An anonymous but highly favorable snapshot of M.S.

722. "News Notes: United States." Birth Control Review, 13.10
Oct. 1929: p. 295.
Reports that M.S. is chair and Mrs. Benjamin Carpenter is
vice-chair of the Committee for Federal Legislation on Birth
Control.

723. Bromley, Dorothy Dunbar. "This Question of Birth Control."
Harper's Magazine, 160 Dec. 1929: pp. 34-45.
This article covering aspects of birth control concludes that
the welfare of society rests on women's "well-being." Among
the many sources mentioned is M.S.'s Motherhood in Bondage.

724. "Birth Control." Nation, 129.3361 4 Dec. 1929: p. 649.
When Dr. Shirley Wynne, commissioner of health of New
York, refused to address a conference of the American Birth
Control League, and when the National Broadcasting Company
refused to air the league's major speeches, "the glare of publicity that these incidents turned upon the conference must
have delighted the hearts of M.S., Hannah M. Stone, and the
other happy warriors of the American Birth Control League."

1930

725. Birth Control International Information Centre, London.
"Round the World for Birth Control/with Margaret Sanger
and Edith How-Martyn, an Account of an International Tour
under the Auspices of Birth Control International Information Centre, London." London: The Centre, 193?, 56 p.
(OCLC: 2462884) Not Seen.

726. Robinson, Caroline Hadley. Seventy Birth Control Clinics:
A Survey and Analysis Including the General Effects of
Control on Size and Quality of Population. New York:
Arno Press and the New York Times, 1972: 351 p.
(Reprint of: Baltimore: The Williams & Wilkins Co., 1930)
Foreword by Robert Latou Dickinson pp. v-viii. Bibliog-
raphy. Index. (OCLC: 379147)
A guide to the "nature, extent, and status" of the world-
wide birth control movement, and a survey of seventy birth
control clinics.

727. Inman, Mary Louise. "The National Birth Control Conference."
Eugenics, 3 Jan. 1930: pp. 12-17.
Contrasts the early struggles of M.S. with the present so-
cial acceptance of birth control.

728. "Birth Control Unit Plans $100,000 Fund: Committee on Legis-
     lation Will Conduct Drive for Money to Push Its Bills."
     New York Times, 11 Jan. 1930: p. 9 col. 4.
     Plans were announced by the eastern division of the
     National Committee on Federal Legislation for Birth Control for
     a campaign to raise $100,000 to promote legislation "which
     would allow physicians to give contraceptive advice and to aid
     the further dissemination of birth control information."

729. "Birth Control Body Protests Radio Ban: Members of American
     League Score N.B.C. for Attitude Toward National Conven-
     tion." New York Times, 17 Jan. 1930: p. 18 col. 4.

730. "Honors Vendor of Paper: Birth Control Group to Fete Woman
     Who Sold Journal More Than 13 Years." New York Times,
     10 Feb. 1930: p. 27 col. 1.
     Kitty Marion, who sold the Birth Control Review in New
     York City for thirteen years, was given a retirement dinner at
     the Town Hall Club.

731. "Luncheon for Miss Marion: Birth Control League Honors
     Woman Who Sold Its Journal." New York Times, 12 Feb.
     1930: p. 21 col. 5.
     "The recent decision of the American Birth Control League
     to stop selling the Birth Control Review on street corners ...
     marks the end of the most radical phase of the birth control
     movement, Dr. James F. Cooper, medical director of the
     League, said yesterday."

732. "From Propaganda to Program." Survey, 64.2 15 April 1930:
     pp. 68-69.
     A touching tribute to Kitty Marion, radical feminist who
     sold copies of the Birth Control Review on the streets of New
     York.

733. "5 Leaders Honored By Town Hall Club: Members Elect Them
     for 1930 Honor Roll." New York Times, 20 April 1930: p.
     21 col. 1.
     M.S. is one.

734. "Mrs. Sanger Tells of Trip: Says Many Physicians in West
     Are Backing Birth Control Movement." New York Times,
     25 April 1930: p. 51 col. 1.

735. Corrigan, Jones I., S.J. "Birth Control a Social Menace."
     Catholic Mind, 28.11 8 June 1930: pp. 213-21.
     A "radio address delivered during the 'Catholic Truth
     Period' on Station WNAC, Boston." Presenting the Catholic
     position, Corrigan equates birth control with atheism and im-
     morality.

736. Smith, Helena Huntington. "They Were Eleven." New Yorker,
     6.20 5 July 1930: pp. 22-25.
     Extremely interesting "profile" of M.S.

737. "A Broadening View Point." Law Notes, 34 Nov. 1930: p.
     144.
     Comments approvingly on the Slee v. Internal Revenue Com-
     missioner decision.

738. Stone, Hannah M. "The 7th International Conference." Birth Control Review, 14.11 Nov. 1930: pp. 317-19.
     Dr. Stone reports on the Seventh International Birth Control Conference (Zurich, Sept. 1-5, 1930).

739. Jones, Eleanor Dwight. "News Notes: United States." Birth Control Review, 14.12 Dec. 1930: p. 359.
     Reprint of a letter from the president of the American Birth Control League to all its members. The American Birth Control League disclaims all connection with the National Committee on Federal Legislation for Birth Control, chaired by M.S.

1931

740. Sanger, Margaret. My Fight for Birth Control. New York: Farrar & Rinehart, 1931: 360 p. (OCLC: 350988) No Index.
     M.S.'s first autobiography. Reviewed by Amidon, Beulah. "I Would Be Heard." New Republic, 68.884 11 Nov. 1931: p. 357; Beard, Mary R. "An Indomitable Woman." Saturday Review of Literature, 8.18 21 Nov. 1931: p. 312; Booklist 28 Nov. 1931: p. 102; Hankins, Frank H. "Book Reviews." Birth Control Review, 15.11 Nov. 1931: pp. 322-325. (See item 748 for M.S. reply); Kelly, Florence Finch. "Margaret Sanger's Story of Her Fight for Birth Control." New York Times, 4 Oct. 1931: Sect. 4 p. 4 col. 2-5--p. 14 col. 2-3; Loveman, Amy. "Books for Christmas." Saturday Review of Literature, 8.21 12 Dec. 1931: p. 380; "Mrs. Sanger's Book Tells of Her Fight." New York Times, 28 Sept. 1931: p. 26 col. 1; Ross, Mary. "Accomplished by Faith." Books (New York Herald Tribune), 8.3 27 Sept. 1931: p. 1; Ross, Mary. "She Would Be Heard." Survey, 67.1 1 Oct. 1931: pp. 45-46.

741. _____ and Stone, Hannah M., M.D., eds. The Practice of Contraception; An Introductory Symposium and Survey. Baltimore: Williams & Wilkins Co., 1931. From the Proceedings of the Seventh International Birth Control Conference. Zurich, Switzerland, September, 1930: 316 p. With a Foreword by Robert L. Dickinson, M.D. Authors' Index. (OCLC: 1986726)
     An introduction by M.S. traces the history of the birth control conference. Papers deal with technical methods of contraception. Clinic reports are given for England, Germany, Russia, Austria, Holland, Denmark, India, China, and Japan. Dr. Stone reports on the Birth Control Clinical Research Bureau. Reviewed by Hankins, F. H. "Book Reviews." Birth Control Review, 16.7/8 July-Aug. 1932: p. 210.

742. Sanger, Margaret; Landis, J. M.; Skinner, Clarence R. "Shall the Citizens of Boston Be Allowed to Discuss Changing Their Laws?" in A Free Pulpit in Action. Clarence R. Skinner, ed. New York: Macmillan, 1931. pp. 164-85. (OCLC: 1433799)

In a meeting at the Community Church of Boston, M.S.,
J. M. Landis, and Clarence R. Skinner discussed state and
federal laws concerning birth control and answered questions
concerning birth control in European countries, the influence
of physicians, and the suppression of birth control information in Massachusetts.

743. Sanger, Margaret. "Comments on the Pope's Encyclical."
Birth Control Review, 15.1 Jan. 1931: pp. 40-41.
M.S. attacks Pope Pius XI's encyclical on birth control.

744. _____. "Birth Control Steps Out: A Note on the Senate
Hearing." People, 1 April 1931: pp. 27-28.
A summary of M.S.'s views as presented in her testimony
during hearings for the Gillett Bill (s.4582) on February 13,
1931.

745. _____. "Committee on Federal Legislation for Birth Con-
trol--Margaret Sanger," in "Should Legal Barriers Against
Birth Control Be Removed?" Congressional Digest, 10.4
April 1931: pp. 106-08. (See item 766.)

746. _____. "Book Reviews." Birth Control Review, 15.9 Sept.
1931: p. 261.
M.S. reviews Pregnant Woman in a Lean Age, a book of
poetry by Ralph Cheyney. New York: William Faro, Inc.,
1931.

747. _____. "A Public Nuisance." Birth Control Review, 15.10
Oct. 1931: pp. 277-280.
M.S.'s account of the first birth control clinic and of her
arrest and trial. Excerpt taken from My Fight for Birth
Control (see item 740).

748. _____. "Mrs. Sanger in Rebuttal." Birth Control Review,
15.11 Nov. 1931: p. 331.
In a letter to the editor, M.S. attacks Frank Hankins'
review of My Fight for Birth Control (see item 740).

749. Field, James Alfred. Essays on Population; and Other Papers.
Port Washington, New York: Kennikat Press, 1967: 440 p.
Index. (OCLC: 914295) (A reissue of the work first published by the University of Chicago Press, 1931).
This collection of Professor Field's essays on population
problems includes a treatment of the propaganda of birth control and the prosecution of M.S.

750. Goldman, Emma. Living My Life. 2 vols. New York: Alfred
A. Knopf, 1931: 993 p. Index. (OCLC: 638529)
A valuable autobiography, rich with comments about birth
control. Although M.S.'s name does not appear in the index,
the following notes are of interest: p. 559, the struggles of
Margaret and William Sanger; pp. 590-91, silence of M.S. to
legal problems of others in the birth control movement; p. 553,
M.S.'s contribution to birth control; p. 691, M.S. plans reception for Emma Goldman after Goldman's release from prison.

751. Guchteneere, R. de., M.D. Judgment on Birth Control. London: Sheed & Ward, 1931: 223 p. No Index. No
Bibliography. (OCLC: 5001925)

Attacks Malthusianism, neo-Malthusianism, eugenics, and the birth control movement. Presents anti-birth control, Catholic-oriented arguments. (For M.S. see: pp. 14, 42, 44-50, 78, 84, 116, 131, 146.)

752. Himes, Norman E. "The Truth about Birth Control." New York: The John Day Company, 1931: (The John Day Pamphlets, No. 4) 28 p. Bibliography. (OCLC: 6905637) An interesting account of the history of birth control and of the situation as it is seen in 1931.

753. Moore, Edward Roberts. The Case Against Birth Control. New York: The Century Co., 1931: (Introduction by Patrick Cardinal Hayes, Archbishop of New York), 311 p. Index. Bibliography. (OCLC: 2046661) Moore was chairman of the Committee on Population Decline and Related Problems for the National Conference of Catholic Charities. He sets forth arguments against birth control, presents the Catholic position, and stresses fears caused by the declining birth rate.

754. Stopes, Marie Carmichael. Contraception: Its Theory, History and Practice. 3rd ed. London: G. P. Putnam's Sons, 1931: 487 p. Index. (OCLC: 6156946) In this third edition, Stopes omits the criticism of M.S. noted in the first edition but adds a critical comment regarding M.S.'s methods of establishing a birth control clinic (see item 543 for first edition).

755. U.S. Congress. Senate. Judiciary Committee. "Birth Control Hearings Before a Subcommittee of the Committee on the Judiciary United States Senate." 71st Congress, 3rd Session on S.4582, Feb. 13 and 14, 1931. Washington, D.C. U.S.G.P.O., 1931: 84 p. Subcommittee on S.4582 consisted of Frederick Gillett, chairman, from Massachusetts; William Borah, from Idaho; and Sam Bratton, from New Mexico. "Statement of Mrs. Margaret Sanger" (pp. 2-7) is a plea to amend the Comstock laws. M.S. closes the hearings with a rebuttal of the anti-birth control testimony (pp. 76-83).

756. "Editorial." Birth Control Review, 15.1 Jan. 1931: p. 4. American Birth Control League clarifies its position. Although supporting "the bill sponsored by Mrs. Sanger's Committee," the league feels there is more important work to be done.

757. "News Notes: United States." Birth Control Review, 15.1 Jan. 1931: p. 26. Prints the text of a bill being introduced to the Senate for the National Committee on Federal Legislation for Birth Control.

758. "Assails Encyclical Views: Margaret Sanger Declares It Quotes from Ancient Theorists." New York Times, 13 Jan. 1931: p. 3 col. 3.

759. "Bill to Legalize the Importation and Dissemination of Contraceptive Literature and Devices." Commonweal, 13 4 Mar. 1931: p. 479.

Article presents a Roman Catholic view of the Gillett measure in Congress--"perhaps it should be named the Mrs. Margaret Sanger measure...."

760. "Comment Is Varied over Birth Control." New York Times 21 Mar. 1931: p. 13 col. 2-3.

Article reports Federal Council of Churches of Christ reactions to the announcement on birth control. Statement of M.S. is included.

761. "Council of Churches Holds Birth Control Morally Justified." New York Times, 21 Mar. 1931: p. 1 col. 6--p. 13 col. 4-5.

Reports that Federal Council of Churches of Christ in America has given "guarded" approval to birth control.

762. "Doctors Assailed over Birth Control; Mrs. Sanger Sees Catholic Groups Trying to Thwart Science Through Religion." New York Times, 24 Mar. 1931: p. 9 col. 3.

M.S. attacks Catholic physicians who "condemned the position taken by the Federal Council of Churches of Christ." Rev. Ignatius W. Cox replies to M.S.

763. "200 Hear Mrs. Sanger; She Discusses Birth Control Clinic Before Social Workers." New York Times, 26 Mar. 1931: p. 56 col. 5-6.

M.S. and Hannah M. Stone speak at Birth Control Clinical Research Bureau.

764. "Birth Control: Protestant View; Full Text of the Federal Council Report." Current History, 34 April 1931: pp. 97-100.

The text of the report issued by the Federal Council of the Churches of Christ in America, an organization representing twenty-seven Protestant denominations.

A majority of the committee accepts "the careful and restrained use of contraceptives by married people...."

765. "Chronology of Birth Control Agitation Throughout World." Congressional Digest, 10.4 April 1931: pp. 97-99.

Lists important birth control activities (1798-1931).

766. "Should Legal Barriers Against Birth Control Be Removed?" Congressional Digest, 10.4 April 1931: pp. 102-16.

Pro and con arguments are given by physicians, community groups, and Catholic, Protestant, and Jewish leaders. M.S. makes a statement on behalf of the Committee on Federal Legislation for Birth Control (see item 745).

767. "What Congress Has Done to Date about Birth Control Legislation." Congressional Digest, 10.4 April 1931: pp. 100-01.

Traces congressional legislation on birth control (1873 to 1931) listing M.S.'s part in the legislation. Gives the text of the Gillett Bill (S.4582, 1931), known as the "doctor's only" bill.

768. "Federal Council on Birth Control; An Editorial." Outlook and Independent, 157 1 April 1931: pp. 458-59.

Praises the statement issued by Federal Council of Churches of Christ, which represents twenty-seven Protestant denominations. In its statement made public on March 20, 1931, the council approved birth control. M.S. said, "Today is the most significant one in the history of the birth control movement."

769. "More Shooting at the Stork." Literary Digest, 109.2 11 April 1931: pp. 18-19.
Discusses the efforts to justify birth control on moral, medical, and economic grounds and airs the pros and cons of these efforts.

770. "Hails Church Move for Birth Control; Mrs. Sanger Tells Audience It Signalizes the 'Biological Emancipation' of Women." New York Times, 15 April 1931: p. 56 col. 2.
M.S. and Henry Pratt Fairchild speak in praise of position of Federal Council of Churches of Christ.

771. "Mrs. Sanger Asks Aid for Clinic." New York Times, 1 May 1931: p. 28 col. 3.
M.S.'s request for donations for the Birth Control Clinical Research Bureau is sparked by a "marked increase" in the number of women who are asking for help.

772. "Ten Women Named As Greatest Living; John Haynes Holmes Declares They Are Proof That There Is No Sex in Genius." New York Times, 18 May 1931: p. 19 col. 6.
John Haynes Holmes, Community Church pastor, includes M.S. on his list of "ten greatest women of today."

773. Bromley, Dorothy Dunbar. "Birth Control: Yes or No?" The Woman's Journal, N.S. 16 June 1931: pp. 20-21, 38.
This article attempts to summarize arguments for and against birth control; the article touches on the work both of M.S. and of the Clinical Research Bureau.

774. "Will Advise the Married; Mrs. Sanger Plans Medical Bureau to Give General Health Data." New York Times, 29 Sept. 1931: p. 9 col. 2.
M.S. announces "an information bureau" at the Birth Control Clinical Research Bureau that will give marital, as well as birth control advice.

775. "Editorial." Birth Control Review, 15.10 Oct. 1931: p. 275.
An editorial salute to M.S.

776. Goldwater, A. L., M.D. "The Pioneer of the Modern Birth Control Movement in America." Birth Control Review, 15.11 Nov. 1931: pp. 331-32.
This letter to the editor denies that M.S. originated the American birth control movement. Goldwater credits Dr. William J. Robinson with that role.

777. "News Notes: New York." Birth Control Review, 15.11 Nov. 1931: p. 329.
Reports that "M.S. has opened a bureau for advice on premarital and post-marital problems ... in conjunction with the regular work of the Clinical Research Bureau."

778. "Editorial." Birth Control Review, 15.12 Dec. 1931: p. 339.
Praises M.S. on her being selected as the first recipient of the American Woman's Association Award.

779. "News Notes: Texas." Birth Control Review, 15.12 Dec. 1931:
     p. 360.
     Reports that M.S.'s announced appearance in Houston,
     Texas, created debate in the Houston press. Over twenty-
     five hundred people heard her speak.
780. Williams, Michael. "The Religion of Death." Commonweal, 15
     30 Dec. 1931: pp. 234-36.
     This Catholic view sees birth control not as a movement, but
     as a revolution--with M.S. as its leader. Included is an inter-
     esting description of one of these revolutionaries, the woman
     sees the world from a completely "feminist" viewpoint.

1932

781. Sanger, Margaret H. "The Pope's Position on Birth Control."
     Nation, 134.3473 27 Jan. 1932: pp. 102-04.
     Author's analysis of the Pope's statements in his encyclical
     letter "Of Chaste Marriage."
782. _____. "A News Letter from Margaret Sanger." Birth
     Control Review, 16.4 April 1932: pp. 122-23.
     M.S. tells of the Catholic Church's interference during her
     speaking tour.
783. _____. "A Plan for Peace." Birth Control Review, 16.4
     April 1932: pp. 107-08.
     Summary of an address given on January 17, 1932 in New
     York City before the New History Society.
784. Allen, Devere, ed. Adventurous Americans. New York:
     Farrar & Rinehart, 1932: 346 p. No index. (OCLC:
     645516)
     This book contains twenty-four sketches of "radical" per-
     sonalities; the sketches have been written by anonymous close
     acquaintances. M.S. is included in a chapter entitled "Every
     Child a Wanted Child."
785. Dickinson, Robert L. and Bryant, Louise Stevens. Control
     of Conception: An Illustrated Medical Manual. Baltimore:
     Williams & Wilkins, 1932: 290 p. Index. Bibliography.
     (OCLC: 3268354) (Volume in "Medical Aspects of Human
     Fertility Series" issued by the National Committee on
     Maternal Health, Inc.)
     An illustrated compilation of the known means and medical
     indications for control of conception. The text includes a
     legal summary by Ms. Bryant.
786. Fishbein, Morris, M.D. Fads and Quackery in Healing. New
     York: Covici, Friede, 1932: 384 p. Index. (OCLC:
     1435559)
     In this work, Chapter 17 is devoted to "The Problem of
     Birth Control." The chief birth control advocates of the time
     are mentioned.
787. U.S. Congress. House. Committee on Ways and Means.
     Birth Control. Hearing Before the Committee on Ways and

Means House of Representatives. 72nd Congress, 1st session on H.R. 11082. May 19 and 20, 1932, Washington,
D.C., U.S.G.P.O., 1932: 149 p.
Includes statements and testimony of M.S. in her position
as national chairman of the Committee on Federal Legislation
for Birth Control. Documents also submitted by M.S. (pp.
6-26; 137-43).

788. U.S. Congress. House. Committee on Ways and Means.
72nd Congress, 1st session. Report No. 1435. Amend the
Tariff Act of 1930 and the Criminal Code. U.S.G.P.O.,
1932: 2 p. in serial vol. 3:9493.
An "adverse report" to accompany H.R. 11082 (Hancock
Bill).

789. U.S. Congress. Senate. Judiciary Committee. Birth Control.
Hearings Before a Subcommittee of the Committee on the
Judiciary United States Senate. 72nd Congress, 1st ses-
sion on S.4436. May 12, 19, and 20, 1932. Washington,
D.C.: U.S.G.P.O., 1932: 151 p.
Subcommittee consisted of Daniel Hastings (Delaware) and
Warren Austin (Vermont). "Statement of Mrs. Margaret
Sanger, National Chairman, Committee on Federal Legislation
for Birth Control." Pages 6-12 include statement, as well as
M.S.'s answers to questions posed by Senator Hastings.
Hearings include testimony for and against birth control.
"Statement of Mrs. Margaret Sanger--continued" (pp. 135-43).
M.S. answers anti-birth control testimony.

790. U.S. Congress. Senate. Committee on the Judiciary.
(Confidential) "Birth Control. Hearings Before a Subcommittee of the Committee on the Judiciary United States
Senate." 72nd Congress, 1st Session on S.4436. June 24
and 30, 1932. Washington, D.C.: U.S.G.P.O., 1933:
35 p. Subcommittee Daniel Hastings, Del. and Warren
Austin, Vermont.
On June 24 M.S. answers questions on available contraceptives (pp. 1-3). Testimony includes remarks by M.S.
(pp. 6-15). Contains a letter from M.S. to Senator Austin
(p. 35). Testimony given on June 30 is anti-birth control.

791. "Urges Cut in Birth Rate; Mrs. Sanger Says It Would Help to
Establish World Peace." New York Times, 18 Jan. 1932:
p. 6 col. 2.
M.S. lectured "under the sponsorship of the New History
Society."

792. Allen, Robert S. "Congress and Birth Control." Nation,
134.3473 27 Jan. 1932: pp. 104-05.
Allen describes M.S.'s educational effort in Congress, as
well as the responses of congressmen to the birth control
issue.

793. Ernst, Morris L. "How We Nullify." Nation, 134.3473 27 Jan.
1932: pp. 113-14.
Ernst discusses court cases that have been important to
birth control and predicts that birth control laws will be nul-
lified by the courts long before they are repealed.

794. "Future of Birth Control." Nation, 134.3473 27 Jan. 1932:
p. 89.
Editors support the efforts of M.S., Mary Ware Dennett,
and others in the birth control movement.

795. Parsons, Wilfrid, S.J. "The Great Birth-Control Plot."
America, 46 6 Feb. 1932: pp. 427-29.
The author, a priest, comments on M.S.'s article in the
Nation (see item 781). Several other articles are cited by the
author to give evidence of what he feels is a "birth-control
plot" against the Catholic Church. Morris L. Ernst is also
singled out due to his article, "How We Nullify" (see item 793).

796. Himes, Norman E. "Birth Control in Historical and Clinical
Perspective." American Academy of Political and Social
Science. Annals (of), 160 Mar. 1932: pp. 49-65.
After involving herself for some years in specialized study,
N. Himes presents statements that document the historical and
clinical aspects of birth control.

797. Holmes, S. J. "Will Birth Control Lead to Extinction?"
Scientific Monthly, 34 Mar. 1932: pp. 247-51.
Stresses the eugenic dangers of birth control and suggests
"that the race is at present tending to breed out its brains."
Emphasizes the declining birth rate.

798. "Sanger Talk Barred in School." New York Times, 7 Mar.
1932: p. 5 col. 7.
Reports that M.S. was denied permission to speak at the
Troup Junior High School in New Haven, Connecticut and that
she will use a local theater instead.

799. "Grants Sanger Permit in New Haven." New York Times, 8
Mar. 1932: p. 3 col. 2.
M.S. is given a permit to speak in New Haven, Connecticut
at the Fox College Theatre.

800. "Editorial." Birth Control Review, 16.4 April 1932: p. 100.
Praises the stand taken by Yale University to support
M.S. when she was barred from speaking in New Haven.

801. "House Gets Sanger Bill; It Would Aid Spreading of Data to
Doctors on Birth Control." New York Times, 5 April 1932:
p. 2 col. 5.
Reports M.S.'s "first success in getting a birth control
measure introduced in the House."

802. "Headline Footnotes; A Gentle Crusader." New York Times,
10 April 1932: Sect. 9 p. 2 col. 8.
Editorial praise of M.S.

803. "Mrs. Sanger Receives Gold Medal at Dinner; Birth Control
Leader Honored by Women's Association--Wells Sends a
Tribute." New York Times, 21 April 1932: p. 23 col. 3.
M.S. receives the American Women's Association Award.
H.G. Wells is among those sending tributes.

804. "News Notes." Birth Control Review, 16.5 May 1932: p. 151.
Reports on the introduction of a birth control bill (H.R.
11082) by Rep. Frank W. Hancock and lists the reasons why
M.S. "urges legislative action."

805. "News Notes." Birth Control Review, 16.5 May 1932: pp. 151-52.

Reports on a dinner, presided over by John Dewey, during which M.S. was presented with the American Women's Association medal.

806. "Editorial Paragraphs." Nation, 134.3487 4 May 1932: p. 500.

M.S. receives American Women's Association's gold medal, given at dinner April 20, 1932 in New York City.

807. Clyde, Ethel. "Birth Control Bill." New Republic, 70 11 May 1932: p. 355.

Ethel Clyde, chair of the American Birth Control League, urges supporters of M.S. to help Sanger in her efforts to pass two bills: (1) Sanger's birth control bill (S.4436), introduced by Senator Henry D. Hatfield of West Virginia; and (2) Sanger's bill (H.R. 11082), introduced by Congressman Frank W. Hancock of North Carolina.

808. "Urge Birth Control to Conserve Race; Margaret Sanger and Others Tell Senate Committee It Would Help Check Illiteracy." New York Times, 13 May 1932: p. 40 col. 5-6.

809. "Birth Control Act Scored and Upheld; Both Sides Give Views to House Committee as Foes of Lifting Ban Argue Before Senators; Mrs. Sanger Urges Change." New York Times, 20 May 1932: p. 3 col. 5.

Reports on House and Senate birth control bill testimony.

810. "Birth Control Bill Loses; House Committee Votes Unfavorable Report on the Hancock Measure." New York Times, 25 May 1932: p. 11 col. 5.

811. Stone, Hannah M., M.D. "Birth Control in America." Birth Control Review, 16.6 June 1932: pp. 188-89.

Dr. Stone discusses "the change of temper" toward birth control during past two years, especially in regard to the medical profession. Much credit is given to M.S.

812. Dennett, Mary Ware. "The Hatfield Bill and Criminal Obscenity." New Republic, 71 1 June 1932: p. 76.

At the "Hatfield (birth control) Bill" hearing, Mary Ware Dennett (chairman of the National Council, Voluntary Parenthood League) comments on M.S.'s statements.

813. "The Birth Control Racket." Commonweal, 16.6 8 June 1932: pp. 141-42.

An editorialized account aimed against M.S.'s efforts toward getting the Hancock bill passed (at the hearing before the Congressional Ways and Means Committee). The article calls for a return to "Christian moral principles."

814. "Editorial Comment." Catholic World, 135 July 1932: pp. 480-87.

A Catholic attack refers to birth control as "race suicide." Criticizes Catholic members of the American Women's Association who did not take "radical action" when that organization presented M.S. with a medal.

815. Osborn, Henry Fairfield. "Birth Selection vs. Birth Control." Forum, 88.2 Aug. 1932: pp. 79-83.

A call by a eugenist to "increase breeding in the desirable racial element," to have "not more, but better Americans." In the hands of M.S., birth control is a danger to the "evolution of the human race."

816. Riegel, Robert E. and Eager, Lawrence. "The Birth Control Controversy." Current History, 36 Aug. 1932: pp. 563-68.
A brief but interesting history of the birth control movement in the United States. The roles played by M.S. and Mary Ware Dennett are emphasized.

817. Osborn, Henry Fairfield. "Birth Selection Versus Birth Control." Science, 76.1965 26 Aug. 1932: pp. 173-79.
An address given at the Third International Congress of Eugenics, New York, August 22, 1932. In the address the aims of the birth control movement are attacked as being against the aims of eugenic "birth selection." What is needed is "positive eugenics," which would "increase breeding in the desirable racial element."

818. Kamperman, George, M.D. "The Birth Control Movement." Michigan State Medical Society." Journal, 31.9 Sept. 1932: pp. 577-82.
Kamperman traces the history of eugenic thought and of the attempts to control overpopulation. He remarks on M.S.'s part in the birth control movement and calls on physicians to take on a stronger role.

819. "Margaret Sanger Is Back; Reports Stay in Italy Without Interference by Mussolini." New York Times, 22 Sept. 1932: p. 23 col. 2.
Reports that M.S. is back after several months in Europe.

820. Wheatley, C. S., Jr. "Some Legal Aspects of Birth Control." Law Notes (Northport, N.Y.), 36 Oct. 1932: pp. 45-47.
Discussion includes interesting interpretations of People v. Byrne, People v. Sanger, Slee v. Internal Revenue Commissioner, etc.

821. "Catholics Assail Puerto Rico Report; Federation Demands Hoover Admonish Governor to Cease Advocating Birth Control." New York Times, 7 Oct. 1932: p. 6 col. 3-5.
National Catholic Alumni Federation protests to President Hoover "against the advocacy by Governor James R. Beverley of Puerto Rico of birth control as a solution to the overpopulation problem in that island...."

822. "Mrs. Sanger Aids Beverley; Protests to Hoover on Criticism of Birth Control Proposal." New York Times, 9 Oct. 1932: Sect. 1 p. 9 col. 2.
Quotes the text of a telegram sent to President Hoover by M.S. in which Sanger defends Governor James R. Beverley of Puerto Rico against opposition from the National Catholic Alumni Federation.

823. "Worse Than a Crime; It's a Blunder." Literary Digest, 114 10 Dec. 1932: p. 18.
Gives the opinion of Dr. Raymond Pearl of Johns Hopkins

University that the birth control movement has decreased the
birthrate among the "better classes" and increased it in the
Black and laboring classes, thus defeating eugenist aims.

1933

824. Sanger, Margaret H. "An Open Letter to Social Workers."
Birth Control Review, 17.6 June 1933: pp. 140-41.
This letter to the National Conference of Social Work urges
social workers to work for birth control.

825. _____. "Editorial." Birth Control Review, 1.3 N.S. Dec.
1933: p. 17 (1).
An excerpt from a speech given at the World Fellowship
of Faiths, Chicago, September 3, 1933.

826. Dell, Floyd. Homecoming: An Autobiography. New York:
Farrar & Rinehart, Inc., 1933: 368 p. No index. No
Bibliography. (OCLC: 1205737) No Index.
While he was associate editor of The Masses, Dell turned
thousands of letters requesting birth control information over
to those who illegally provided the information. The letters
came in response to articles appearing in The Masses that
defended Margaret and William Sanger (pp. 252-53).

827. Fyfe, Hamilton. Revolt of Women. London: Rich & Cowan,
Ltd. 1933: 275 p. No index. No Bibliography. (OCLC:
1935564) No Index.
This philosophical, historical essay on population asserts
that the first French advances in birth control were made in
a nonpolitical, nonfeminist manner. This state of affairs
contrasts with the "agitation" required by Marie Stopes in
England and by Margaret Sanger in America (M.S.: pp. 82,
110, 173-74, 199).

828. Irwin, Inez Haynes. Angels and Amazons: A Hundred Years
of American Women. Garden City, New York: Doubleday,
Doran, & Co., 1933: 531 p. Index. (OCLC: 592135)
Includes a brief treatment of M.S. in the chapter on medicine.

829. Maude, Aylmer. Marie Stopes: Her Work and Play. New York:
G. P. Putnam's Sons, 1933: 299 p. Index. No Bibliography. (OCLC: 1445668)
A biography of Marie Stopes, the English birth control
pioneer. Notes that Stopes spoke in New York at Town Hall
"a couple of weeks" before M.S. was stopped from speaking
there.

830. Thompson, Warren S. and Whelpton, P. K. "The Population
of the Nation." in: Recent Social Trends in the United
States: Report of the President's Research Committee on
Social Trends. Vol. 1. New York: McGraw-Hill Book
Company, Inc., 1933: pp. 1-58. (OCLC: 928920)
This report on population in the United States suggests
that had not legislation restricted the spread of birth control

information and interfered with the work of clinics, the birth rate decline would have "spread more evenly through social classes" with the poor showing a decline closer to that shown by "the well-to-do."

831. "Emphasis in Propaganda Henceforth on Birth Selection." Nation, 136.3526 1 Feb. 1933: p. 106.
A report of the decision given by the leaders of the American Birth Control League at the league's twelfth annual convention "that the emphasis in its propaganda would henceforth be laid upon 'birth selection' [eugenics], and that it would campaign for sterilization laws in states where they are needed."

832. "Mrs. Sanger Assails Birth Control Ideas: Condemns Theory Advanced by Dr. Latz as Lacking in Scientific Support." New York Times, 7 Feb. 1933: p. 3 col. 3.
M.S. held that the book, The Rhythm, by Leo J. Latz, advanced theories based on "folklore."

833. "The Birth Control Bill." The World Tomorrow, 16 15 Feb. 1933: p. 149.
An editorial plea for the passage of the "doctor's only bill" (S.4436) backed by M.S. (Hatfield bill).

834. "Mrs. Sanger Disputes Some of Mr. Caravati's Statements." New York Times, 10 May 1933: p. 16 col. 5.
Letter from M.S. to the editor is an attempt to correct several statements made by Henry L. Caravati of the National Council of Catholic Men.

835. Boyd, Mary Sumner; Little, C. C.; Ross, Edward A.; Burch, Guy Irving; and Hankins, Frank H. "Hail and Farewell from the Editorial Board of the Review." Birth Control Review, 17.7 July 1933: pp. 168-71.
The members of the editorial board of the Birth Control Review comment on the passing of the periodical.

836. Jones, Eleanor Dwight. "To Readers of the Birth Control Review." Birth Control Review, 17.7 July 1933.
The president of the American Birth Control League announces that the Birth Control Review in its present form will be discontinued as "a propaganda vehicle for birth control is no longer needed." The Review will continue as a "monthly news bulletin."

837. Adams, Mildred. "Crusader." Delineator, 123 Sept. 1933: pp. 15, 46, 48-9.
This well-written portrait of M.S. offers some interesting anecdotes in an attempt to reveal the private woman as well as the public one. The portrait seems to have been based on interviews with M.S. Article is reprinted in Woman of the Future (see item 842).

838. "News from Everywhere." Birth Control Review, 1.2 N.S. Nov. 1933: p. 14 (6).
Reports that the National Committee on Federal Legislation for Birth Control--M.S., chair--will hold a conference in Washington (January 15-17, 1934).

839. Yasuda, Tokutaro. "Birth Control in Japan." Contemporary
     Japan, 2 Dec. 1933: pp. 473-79.
     Yasuda recalls a meeting with M.S. in Japan (1922) that
     helped spark the Japanese birth control movement. In
     western Japan birth control became allied with the labor move-
     ment. The discussion includes the part played by Senji
     Yamamoto (the labor leader who translated M.S.'s Family
     Limitation into Japanese).
840. "An American Conference on Birth Contorl." Literary Digest,
     116.25 16 Dec. 1933: p. 21. "An Effort Will Be Made at
     the January Meeting to Link National Recovery with the
     Aims of Those Who Advocate Restricting the Size of Fami-
     lies." (subtitle)
     This editorial attacks birth control advocates for citing the
     declining birth rate. It advocates, instead, "equalizing the
     riches of the earth."

                                1934

841. Sanger, Margaret H., ed. American Conference on Birth Con-
     trol and National Recovery. Biological and Medical Aspects
     of Contraception. Washington, D.C.: Committee on Federal
     Legislation for Birth Control, 1934: 135 p. (OCLC:
     8770676) Not seen.
842. _____. "Woman of the Future." London: Birth Control In-
     ternational Information Centre, 1934: 32 p. (OCLC:
     6928013)
     Includes a reprint of an article by Mildred Adams (see item
     837) and a foreword by Michael Fielding.
     M.S. declares that woman will never be emancipated until
     she is in control of childbearing. Sanger calls for birth con-
     trol to end abortion and blames war on overpopulation.
843. _____. "The Case for Birth Control." The Crisis, 41.6
     June 1934: pp. 176-77.
     M.S. calls for a change in the laws and denounces the
     "arrogance" of the "church."
844. _____. "Catholics and Birth Control." New Republic,
     79.1019 13 June 1934: p. 129.
     In this letter, M.S. discusses the book, Rhythm, by Dr.
     Latz, which explicates the "safe period" and has the approval
     of the Roman Catholic Church. Moreover, Sanger points out,
     Rhythm can be mailed, whereas Contraceptive Practices (by
     Dr. Hannah M. Stone) cannot. Except for methods, she tells
     us, finally, both authors share the same principles.
845. _____. "Birth Control." State Government, 7 Sept. 1934:
     pp. 187-90.
     As chair of the National Committee on Federal Legislation
     for Birth Control, M.S. attacks the Comstock Law and dis-
     cusses the proposed amendment to the code--the "doctor's
     only" bill.

846. Breckinridge, Sophonisba P. The Family and the State: Selected Documents. Chicago: University of Chicago Press, 1934: 565 p. Index. Bibliography. (OCLC: 1894236)

   "The documents in this volume have been collected in an attempt to provide material for illustration and discussion of the problems presenting themselves in relation to marriage relationship and the institution of the family." (Preface)

   Pages 149-52 contain "The Movement to Secure the Right to Exercise Birth Control" from Laws Concerning Birth Control in the United States, published (1929) by Committee on Federal Legislation for Birth Control, Margaret Sanger, chairman (see item 675).

847. Bromley, Dorothy Dunbar. Birth Control; Its Use and Misuse. With an introduction by Robert Latou Dickinson, M.D. New York: Harper & Brothers, 1934: 304 p. Index. Bibliography. (OCLC: 2769588)

   In this work aimed at the lay reader, Bromley discusses various methods of contraception. Throughout the book credit is given to M.S. Appendix contains chart giving the status of state birth control laws in 1934 as well as the number of state birth control clinics in existence.

848. "For Legalized Birth Control: With an Introduction by Margaret Sanger." New York: The New Republic, 134: 34 p. (intro. pp. 3-6).

   This pamphlet contains reprints of two articles that appeared in The New Republic. Elizabeth H. Garrett's "Birth Control's Business Baby" (see item 858) and Helena Huntington Smith's "Wasting Women's Lives" (see item 867). An introduction by M.S. pleads for public recognition of the need for birth control legislation.

849. Kopp, Marie E. Birth Control in Practice: Analysis of Ten Thousand Case Histories of the Birth Control Clinical Research Bureau. New York: Robert M. McBride & Co., 1934: 290 p. Index. (OCLC: 5719070)

   A statistical report and analysis of 10,000 cases handled by M.S.'s clinic between January 1925 and July 1929. The methods used by the clinic are also discussed.

850. Oldenburger, Teunis. Birth Control for Saints and Sinners: A Critical Consideration of the Birth Control Movement As Influenced by Science and Revelation. Grand Rapids, Michigan: Calvin Press, 1934: 330 p. Index (incomplete). No Bibliography. (OCLC: 3689736)

   The author presents the history of birth control and the arguments of its proponents. Using the Bible and Revelations, then refutes these arguments and calls upon Christians to oppose the birth control movement (M.S. pp. 18-20, 24, 40, 43, 53, 55, 75, 85-86, 94, 97-98, 109-110, 112, 116, 131, 150-52, 184-85, 219, 247-48, 311).

851. Smith, Mortimer Brewster. Evangels of Reform. New York: Round Table Press, Inc., 1934: 241 p. No index. Bibliography. (OCLC: 1597614)

Pages 211-41 contain a sensitive sketch of the first twenty
years of M.S.'s activities for birth control--her most poignant
moment, perhaps, was her speech before a Senate committee
in Washington.

852. U.S. Congress. House. Committee on the Judiciary. Birth
Control. Hearings on H.R. 5978, 73rd Congress, 2nd
Session, Jan. 18, 19, 1934, U.S.G.P.O., 1934:   245 p.
(Pierce Bill).
Records the efforts to change the provisions of five sec-
tions of the U.S. Penal Code concerning the circulation of
contraceptive knowledge and dealing with the importation of
any articles or information of a contraceptive nature.   M.S.'s
statements as a witness are given (pp. 6-9, 230-239).

853. U.S. Congress. Senate. Committee on the Judiciary. Birth
Control. Hearings Before a Subcommittee on the Judiciary,
United States Senate. 73rd Congress, 2nd Session, on
S.1842. March 1, 20, and 27, 1934. Washington, D.C.:
U.S.G.P.O., 1934:   175 p.
Subcommittee: M. N. Neely, West Virginia and Daniel
Hastings, Delaware. (Hastings Bill)
Pro and con statements on birth control. M.S. makes final
rebuttal statement and includes letters and other materials sent
to her in support of her position (pp. 149-75).

854. Stix, Regine K., M.D. and Notestein, Frank W. "Effectiveness
of Birth Control: A Study of Contraceptive.Practice in a
Selected Group of New York Women." Milbank Memorial
Fund Quarterly, 12 Jan. 1934: pp. 57-68.
Studies the records of 714 women who went to the Birth
Control Clinical Research Bureau in 1931 (see item 887).

855. "Will Link Recovery with Birth Control: 500 Leaders in
Medicine, Education and Religion Will Confer at Capital
January 15-17." New York Times, 7 Jan. 1934: p. 21 col.
4.
Article lists those leaders expected to attend the American
Conference on Birth Control and National Recovery to be held
in Washington, D.C., January 15-17, under the auspices of
the National Committee on Federal Legislation for Birth Control
(M.S., president).

856. "See Birth Control as Recovery Need: Speakers at Washington
Conference Hold Job Claimants Must Be Reduced." New
York Times, 16 Jan. 1934: p. 6 col. 6.
At the American Conference on Birth Control and National
Recovery called by M.S., some addresses pointed to the rela-
tionship between birth control and national "well-being."

857. "500 Doctors Appeal for Birth Control: Washington Conference
Urges Law Allowing Physicians to Give Information." New
York Times, 17 Jan. 1934: p. 2 col. 1.
Resolutions adopted by doctors at a closed session of the
American Conference on Birth Control and National Recovery
urge endorsement of bills introduced by Senator Hastings and
Representative Pierce of Oregon "to authorize the dissemination

of contraceptive information and advice by recognized medical authorities."

858. Garrett, Elizabeth H. "Birth Control's Business Baby." New Republic, 77.998 17 Jan. 1934: pp. 269-72.

(Reply: New Republic, 77.1001 7 Feb. 1934: p. 367) (See item 848 for reprint.)

Author decries widespread availability of unsafe contraceptives and feels some share of the responsibility must be borne by the birth control movement. She describes the series of events that led M.S. to form a National Committee on Federal Legislation for Birth Control and talks of Sanger's hope that the control of contraceptive methods and products would revert from the commercial interests to the doctors.

859. "Ask Roosevelt Aid for Birth Control: Delegates to National Meeting Leave Resolutions with the President's Secretary." New York Times, 18 Jan. 1934: p. 23 col. 5.

M.S. heads the delegation that delivers resolutions urging President Roosevelt to advise Congress "of the importance of amending the criminal code to permit dissemination of birth control information."

860. "Birth Control and National Recovery." America, 50.16 20 Jan. 1934: p. 366.

This editorial reports on the Birth Control and National Recovery Conference held by the National Committee on Federal Legislation for Birth Control, Inc. It calls on Catholics to contact their congressmen in order to defeat H.R. 5978, introduced by Senator Hastings.

861. "Birth Control: Capital Has Bill to Repeal Comstock Law." News-Week, 3 27 Jan. 1934: pp. 28-29.

To oppose the Comstock Law, M.S. called "her American Conference on Birth Control into session in Washington." Speaking for birth control were Amelia Earhart and Mrs. Thomas N. Hepburn. Speaking against birth control at the hearing was, among others, Father Charles E. Coughlin. A representative of the International Federation of Catholic Alumni "made the startling charge that Mrs. Sanger and her associates were motivated by stock interests in contraceptive manufacturing concerns."

862. Hanau, Stella. "Birth-Control Conference, Washington, January 15-17, 1934." Nation, 138.3578 31 Jan. 1934: pp. 129-30.

Ms. Hanau summarized the work of the American Conference on Birth Control and National Recovery. Some highlights were the following: M.S. made a plea for the "forgotten woman." W. S. Thompson, director of the Scripps Foundation for Research in Population Problems, used Japan to illustrate that population pressure is a disturber of world peace. "The American Medical Association placed itself on record as refusing to study one of the four major problems affecting women of America."

863. Thorning, Joseph F. "The Birth Controllers at Washington." America, 50.18 3 Feb. 1934: pp. 418-19.

Reports on hearings held in the House on the "doctor's only bill" introduced by Rep. Walter Pierce of Oregon. The article is "Catholic oriented"; it singles out Margaret Sanger and Mrs. Thomas N. Hepburn for attack.

864. Stubbs, George. "Profits in Birth Control." New Republic, 77.1001 7 Feb. 1934: p. 367.

One of the manufacturers who sells contraceptives reacts to Garrett's article "Birth Control's Business Baby" (see item 858).

865. "Birth Control Advocates Champion Their Cause." Literary Digest, 117 10 Feb. 1934: p. 15.

"Mrs. Margaret Sanger and Mrs. Thomas Hepburn, Mother of the Movie Actress, Plead for Congressional Bill While Many Religious Organizations Offer Bitter Opposition." (sub-title) This editorial (opposing birth control) reports on testimony given for and against the Pierce Bill.

866. Stone, Hannah M., M.D. "The Federal Hearing." Birth Control Review, 1.6 N.S. Mar. 1934: pp. 42-43 (2-3).

Dr. Stone reports on the American Conference on Birth Control and National Recovery held in Washington (January 15-17). She notes that M.S. called "accusations of commercialism made against her ... unfounded," and claimed that M.S. had refused an offer of a quarter of a million dollars to appear on a radio program sponsoring "a certain chemical preparation...."

867. Smith, Helena Huntington. "Wasting Women's Lives." New Republic, 78 28 Mar. 1934: pp. 178-80.

This article reveals the results of several studies conducted on abortion in the U.S. during the early 1930's, including the studies of Dr. Marie E. Kopp at the Clinical Research Bureau (see item 848 for reprint).

868. Ryan, John A. "Fallacious Arguments of the Birth Controllers." Catholic Action, 16.4 April 1934: pp. 9-11, 23.

Monsignor Ryan rebuts the arguments of the birth controllers and is critical of a remark of M.S.'s attacking the celibacy of priests, which was spoken during her testimony on January 19, 1934 at a congressional hearing.

869. "Paradox of Birth Control." Nation, 139 11 July 1934: pp. 33-34.

A witty plea for Congress to pass the birth control bill. The article compares the Roman Catholic version of birth control with the M.S. version.

870. "Birth Control Policies of State and Nation Conflict." American City, 49 Oct. 1934: pp. 79, 81.

Reports on the article M.S. wrote for the journal State Government (see item 845).

871. Bromley, Dorothy Dunbar. "Birth Control and the Depression." Harper's Magazine, 169 Oct. 1934: pp. 563-74.

A plea to allow birth control information to be given to the victims of the depression. The article calls on doctors to supply needed contraceptives. Confusing state laws and

Catholic Church opposition are said to have an adverse psychological effect and are blamed for the inactivity of the medical profession.

872. "Church to Retain Canon on Divorce: Episcopal Convention Acts Despite Report Admitting 'Premium on Collusion': Waiving of 3-Day Notice Is Favored--Birth Control Also Before Bishops." New York Times, 16 Oct. 1934: p. 28 col. 2.

Birth control literature printed by the National Committee on Federal Legislation for Birth Control, of which M.S. is president, was distributed at the general convention of the Protestant Episcopal Church held at Atlantic City, October 15, 1934.

1935

873. Sanger, Margaret. "National Security and Birth Control." Forum and Century, 93.3 Mar. 1935: pp. 139-41.

Author summarizes the status of federal legislation concerning contraception. Secondly, she warns against "commercial" contraceptives that are overpriced and may be ineffective. And, thirdly, she discusses family planning in relation to national security.

874. _____. "Birth Control in Soviet Russia." Birth Control Review, 2.9 N.S. June 1935: p. 139 (3).

M.S. reports on a "brief tour" she made of Russia. She found the contraceptive materials used in clinics to be of "very poor" quality but admires the absence of legal and religious restrictions against birth control.

875. Ishimoto, Shidzué. Facing Two Ways: The Story of My Life. New York: Farrar & Rinehart, 1935: 373 p. Index. (OCLC: 2772668)

Autobiography of the first Japanese to stress planned parenthood as the answer to overpopulation. In Tokyo, Ishimoto established the first Japanese birth control clinic.

876. Maier, Walter A. For Better, Not for Worse: A Manual of Christian Matrimony. Saint Louis: Concordia Publishing House, 1935: 504 p. No index. No Bibliography. (OCLC: 2783650)

In a book devoted to Christian marriage from a Lutheran perspective, the author quotes M.S. mainly to show disagreement with her views.

877. U.S. Congress. House. Committee on the Post Office and Post Roads. Offenses Against the Postal Service. Hearings Before Subcommittee No. 8 of the Committee on the Post Office and Post Roads House of Representatives. 74th Congress, 1st Session on H.R. 154 ... H.R. 5370. March 8, April 4, and April 10, 1935: Washington, D.C.: U.S.G.P.O., 1935: 113 p.

M.S. testifies against H.R. 5370 "providing a Penalty for

anyone who shall knowingly cause obscene matter to be delivered by mail or to be delivered at the place at which it is
directed to be delivered." She testifies for an amendment to
the bill; the amendment which exclude doctors from prosecution (pp. 45-49, 95-101).

878. Brentano, Lowell. "Between Covers,-1." Forum and Century,
93.1 Jan. 1935: pp. 6-7.
Publisher recalls his meeting with M.S. and the publication
of her Woman and the New Race.

879. "To Hail Birth Control; Proponents Will Celebrate in Capital
Feb. 12 its 21st Birthday." New York Times, 2 Jan. 1935:
p. 23 col. 2.
Announces a "Birth-Control Comes of Age" dinner to celebrate the twenty-first birthday of the birth control movement.

880. "Birth Control Bill Shelved in House; Mrs. Sanger Declares
Fight Will Go On." New York Times, 6 Feb. 1935: p. 15
col. 3-4.
House Judiciary Committee shelves Pierce Bill.

881. "Birth Control Attains Majority." Literary Digest, 119.6 9
Feb. 1935: p. 28.
Notes the twenty-first birthday (Tuesday, February 12,
1935) of the birth control movement and reports a celebration
held in the Hotel Mayflower, Washington, D.C.

882. "Undiscouraged." New York Times, 10 Feb. 1935: Sect. 4
p. 2 col. 5.
Picture of M.S., with short caption.

883. "Will Honor Mrs. Sanger; Prominent Persons to Mark Anniversary of Birth Control Drive." New York Times, 10 Feb.
1935: Sect. 2 p. 4 col. 6.
Lists some of the "prominent" people expected at the
"Birth-Control Comes of Age" dinner.

884. "New Drive Mapped for Birth Control; 1,000,000 Signatures
Sought for Plea to President, Mrs. Sanger Says at Dinner."
New York Times, 13 Feb. 1935: p. 8 col. 4.
Reports on the twenty-first birthday dinner in Washington,
D.C. Quotes from speeches by M.S. and Pearl Buck.

885. Kennedy, Anne. "History of the Development of Contraceptive Materials in the United States." American Medicine,
41 Mar. 1935: pp. 159-61.
Written by the former executive secretary of the American
Birth Control League, this article cites the arrangements made
by M.S. for Dr. James F. Cooper to teach other United States
doctors the techniques of contraception as practiced in Europe.
Some details of Dr. Cooper's work are noted--for example, his
attempt to develop suitable vaginal jellies for use with the
diaphragm.

886. Himes, Norman E. "The Vital Revolution." Survey Graphic,
24 April 1935: pp. 171-73+.
Himes traces the history of the birth control movement and
calls for an equalization of information among all classes.

887. Stix, Regine K., M.D. and Notestein, Frank W. "Effectiveness

of Birth Control: A Second Study of Contraceptive Prac-
tice in a Selected Group of New York Women." <u>Milbank
Memorial Fund Quarterly</u>, 13 April 1935: pp. 162-78.
Expands the first study of the records of the Birth Control
Clinical Research Bureau (up from 714 to 991 cases through
June, 1932). (See also item 854.)

888. Turano, Anthony M. "Birth Control and the Law." <u>American
Mercury</u>, 34.136 April 1935: pp. 466-72.
Concentrates on the horrors endured by such American
women as M.S. and Ethel Byrne. The essay attributes these
horrors to Anthony Comstock's version of "law and order."

889. Swing, Raymond Gram. "Birth Control and Obscenity."
<u>Nation</u>, 140.3647 29 May 1935: pp. 621-22.
An examination of "the Post Office Bill." M.S.'s testimony
before the House committee is quoted.

890. Palmer, Gretta. "Birth Control Goes Suave." <u>Today</u>, 4 20
July 1935: pp. 14-15, 20.
A rather tongue-in-cheek report of the connection between
M.S., the birth control movement, and the moneyed classes.
"...The birth control advocates have acquired the support of
social leaders and adopted the effective tactics of experienced
lobbyists."

891. Charles, Enid. "Parenthood in Decline." <u>New Republic</u>,
84.1082 28 Aug. 1935: pp. 63-65.
This article presents a brilliant critique of the "birth control propagandists." Some sound reasons are given for a re-
versal of the decline in the birth rate (from a circa 1935
vantage point).

892. "Mrs. Sanger Going to India." <u>New York Times</u>, 18 Sept.
1935: p. 25 col. 3.
Short announcement of forthcoming trip.

893. "Events of the Month." <u>Birth Control Review</u>, 3.2 N.S.
Oct. 1935: p. 3.
Announces that M.S. will be the principal speaker at the
All India Women's Conference in December, 1935. She will
also visit China, Japan, and Hawaii.

894. "Mrs. Margaret Sanger Sails." <u>New York Times</u>, 24 Oct.
1935: p. 3 col. 2.
Begins trip to England, India, China, Japan, and Hawaii.

895. "Birth-Control Debate Renewed." <u>Literary Digest</u>, 120.24
14 Dec. 1935: p. 18.
Reviews the twenty-first year of the birth control movement, looking back to a time when Emma Goldman and Margaret
Sanger were co-supporters; the article notes that now "It is
not difficult ... for the movement to have a hearing."

896. "The Gods of the Machine." <u>Commonweal</u>, 23.9 27 Dec. 1935:
pp. 225-26.
This article reports on a sermon of Cardinal Hayes that
was given in response to a "mass meeting in Carnegie Hall,
held under the auspices of the American Birth Control
League." Birth control is attacked as Malthusianism and as a
tool of "mechanized, materialistic industry."

897. "Mrs. Sanger Saw Gandhi; Spent Two Days in India Discussing
     Birth Control with Leader." New York Times, 29 Dec. 1935:
     Sect. 1 p. 12 col. 3.

                              1936

898. Himes, Norman E. Medical History of Contraception. Balti-
     more: Williams & Wilkins, 1936. 521 p. (OCLC: 2831089)
     This scholarly work, issued by the National Committee on
     Maternal Health as part of its "Medical Aspects of Human Fer-
     tility Series," deals briefly with the "medical aspects" of M.S.'s
     career (pp. 314-17).
899. Luhan, Mabel Dodge. Movers and Shakers (Vol. 3 of Intimate
     Memories). New York: Harcourt, Brace and Company,
     1936. 542 p. Index. (OCLC: 1013941)
     Contains a short but valuable portrait of M.S.'s influence
     in introducing the New York "radical group" both to birth
     control and to the possibilities for "sex expression."
900. Palmer, Lynn Rachel and Greenberg, Sarah K. Facts and
     Frauds in Woman's Hygiene: A Medical Guide Against Mis-
     leading Claims and Dangerous Products. New York: Van-
     guard Press, 1936. 311 p. Index. Bibliography. (OCLC:
     551507)
     An excellent, frank discussion of the problems peculiar to
     a woman's body. M.S.'s individual contributions are noted.
901. Sutherland, Halliday. Laws of Life. New York: Sheed and
     Ward, 1936. 270 p. No Index. No Bibliography. (OCLC:
     3963783)
     Sutherland, who was sued for libel by Marie Stopes, dis-
     cusses the libel trial, attacks the eugenics and neo-Malthusian
     movements and, giving detailed charts, advocates the rhythm
     method as the only "natural method" of birth control. M.S.'s
     New York birth control clinic is discussed briefly. M.S. is
     mentioned as an illustration of "revolutionary social change."
902. "Birth Control Foe Replies to Critics; Dr. Moore Warns a
     Utilitarian Code Would Justify 'Mercy Killing' of Unemployed."
     New York Times, 1 Jan. 1936: p. 16 col. 1-6.
     Rev. Edward Roberts Moore, a Catholic spokesman, attacks
     the birth control movement and condemns M.S. for advocating
     the need for a "permit for parenthood."
903. "U.S. Loses in Test on Birth Control, Importation of Contra-
     ceptive Devices Upheld If They Are Not for Illegal Use."
     New York Times, 7 Jan. 1936: p. 24 col. 5.
     Reports decision of Judge Grover Moscowitz.
904. DeMello, F. M. "Birth Control Stirs India; Lectures by Mrs.
     Sanger Inaugurate a Debate upon Family Limitation."
     New York Times, 26 Jan. 1936: Sect. 9 p. 13 col. 6-7.
     Reports on the birth control situation in India.
905. "Margaret Sanger Ill in China." New York Times, 2 Mar.
     1936: p. 14 col. 8.

906. Tyson, Helen Glenn. "Social Work and Birth Control."
      Survey, 72.5 May 1936: pp. 137-38.
      Calls on social workers to do more to bring birth control
      information to the poor and notes that "The American Birth
      Control League can hardly keep up with the increasing demand
      for help in organizing clinics...."
907. "Mrs. Sanger Urges the Gassaway Bill; Declares Birth Control
      May Become National Issue If Measure Is Defeated; Reports
      on World Tour." New York Times, 5 May 1936: p. 19
      col. 1.
      M.S. endorses bill introduced by Rep. Percy L. Gassaway
      (U.S.).
908. "Well-Organized Propaganda." America, 55 23 May 1936: p.
      149.
      This editorial reports that M.S.'s attempts to interest
      Mahatma Gandhi in the birth control movement have failed and
      that M.S. has "misreported" the outcome.
909. Dick, Dorothy Hamilton. "Unaccustomed As I Am." Harper's
      Magazine, 173 July 1936: pp. 207-14.
      Dick was one of the upper-class advocates of birth control.
      This interesting firsthand account tells of her experiences as
      a public speaker for the cause.
910. Parkhurst, Genevieve. "Children Wanted." North American
      Review, 242.1 Autumn 1936: 92-104.
      Thoughtful short biography of M.S. Author tells of her
      1916 interview with M.S.
911. "Gandhi and Mrs. Sanger Debate Birth Control." Asia, 36
      Nov. 1936: pp. 698-703.
      Although Gandhi thought highly of M.S.'s reasons for teach-
      ing birth control, he chose continence for himself and for
      India.
912. "Mrs. Sanger Gets Town Hall Award." New York Times, 11
      Nov. 1936: p. 32 col. 8.
      Reports that M.S. will receive the annual Award of Honor
      from the Town Hall Club.
913. "People and Things." Survey, 72.12 Dec. 1936: p. 378.
      Notes that M.S. "received the annual Award of Honor
      given by New York's Town Hall Club...."
914. "A Way Out." Sign, 16 Dec. 1936: p. 260.
      This Catholic editorial comments on M.S.'s receiving the
      Town Hall Club's annual award.
915. "Physician Upheld on Birth Control; Court Rules Contracep-
      tives May Be Imported for Use under Doctor's Direction;
      Mailing Them Is Legal; Margaret Sanger Hails Decision as
      Clarifying Law That Blocked Medical Advice." New York
      Times, 8 Dec. 1936: p. 9 col. 1-3.
916. "Town Hall Club Honors Dishonor." Ave Maria, 44 19 Dec.
      1936: pp. 791-92.
      This Catholic editorial links M.S. with the declining birth
      rate and ridicules her being given the Town Hall Club annual
      award of honor.

917. "Sanger Milestone." Time, 28 21 Dec. 1936: p. 24.
    Reports on the U.S. Circuit Court of Appeals upholding of
    Judge Grover M. Moscowitz's decision (U.S. v. One Package).
918. "Birth Control Aid Received by 56,000; Mrs. Sanger Reports
    Clinical Work Nearly 100% Effective but Urges Wider Scope."
    New York Times, 30 Dec. 1936: p. 10 col. 5.
    Reports on speech given by M.S. at the Conference on
    Control Research and Clinical Practice in New York.

                            1937

919. Sanger, Margaret. "In Perspective." in "A New Day Dawns
    for Birth Control: Summary of Seven Years Which Led to
    Legalization and Cleared the Way for an Epoch-Making
    Advance." New York: National Committee on Federal
    Legislation for Birth Control, Inc., July 1937. (OCLC:
    5363768)
    In an introductory statement (pp. 7-13) to this report by
    the committee (following the victory of the U.S. vs. One
    Package decision), M.S. looks at the long struggle to change
    the Comstock Law. She discusses the rationale that converted
    her from lawbreaker to law changer. She thanks and names
    many of those who helped and she calls for more clinics and
    for the control of venereal disease (see also item 922).
920. _____. "The Future of Contraception." Journal of Contra-
    ception, 2.1 Jan. 1937: pp. 3-4.
    The opening address given at the Conference on Contracep-
    tive Research and Clinical Practice held in New York on
    December 29-30, 1936.
    M.S. speaks on behalf of the Birth Control Clinical Research
    Bureau and briefly reflects on the success of the movement.
921. Groves, Ernest R. The American Woman: The Feminine Side
    of a Masculine Civilization. New York: Greenberg, 1937.
    438 p. Index. Footnotes. (OCLC: 1007157)
    As stated in the preface, "this book traces woman's ad-
    vance in status in a setting of masculine dominance."
922. "A New Day Dawns for Birth Control: Summary of Seven
    Years Which Led to Legalization and Cleared the Way for an
    Epoch-Making Advance." New York: National Committee on
    Federal Legislation for Birth Control, Inc., July 1937:
    47 p. (OCLC: 5363768)
    Summarizes the work of the National Committee on Federal
    Legislation for Birth Control in its fight for the legalization
    of physician-prescribed contraceptives. The committee formed
    in 1929 and attempted, unsuccessfully, to pass a series of
    "doctor's only" bills. It dissolved in 1936 following Judge
    Grover M. Moscowitz's favorable U.S. vs. One Package deci-
    sion. This pamphlet also contains a statement by M.S. called
    "In Perspective" (see item 919).
923. "Court Upholds Clinic Program." Birth Control Review, 4.5
    N.S. Jan. 1937: pp. 3-5.

Praises the decision of the U.S. Circuit Court of Appeals in the U.S. vs. One Package case as well as the work done by M.S. to gain this victory.

924. "Birth Control Today." Nation, 144.2 9 Jan. 1937: p. 34.
Article notes the emergence of the birth control movement "into the bright light of scientific acceptance and friendly publicity." Credit for this status is given to Morris L. Ernst for his successful court fights, to M.S., to Dr. H. M. Stone, and to the thirteen years of work of the Birth Control Clinical Research Bureau.

925. "Mrs. Sanger Gets Town Hall Medal; Birth Control Leader Praises U.S. Court for Ruling Liberalizing Law; Federal Help Is Urged; Rabbi S. E. Goldstein Says the Nation Must Take Over Work--Others Pay Tribute." New York Times, 16 Jan. 1937: p. 15 col. 5.

926. Stone, Hannah M. "Birth Control Wins." Nation 144.3 16 Jan. 1937: pp. 70-71.
Dr. Stone speaks of M.S.'s and Morris L. Ernst's work to "nullify" the Comstock Laws of 1873 in 1935 and 1936 court cases. Mainly, this effort achieved the goals of the National Committee on Federal Legislation for Birth Control--that is, it freed the medical profession from existing legal restrictions and prohibitions, established contraception as a recognized part of medical practice, and removed legal barriers to the dissemination of contraceptive information.
Dr. Stone also reported the success of the Conference on Contraceptive Research and Clinical Practice held in New York on December 29-30, 1936. It marked a turning point, she said, "for the removal of birth control from the field of controversy to that of scientific consideration--from the platform and the pulpit to the laboratory and the clinic" (see item 942.5).

927. "Urges Birth Control to Keep World Peace; Mrs. Sanger Sees Menace in Rising Populations of Italy, Germany, and Japan." New York Times, 18 Jan. 1937: p. 20 col. 5.
Speech given at Washington (D.C.) Town Hall.

928. "Path Held Cleared for Birth Control; Ernst Says Court Decision Has Removed Last Barrier to Program of League; New Responsibility Seen; Matsner Calls on Doctors to Make Information Available to All Who Want It." New York Times, 29 Jan. 1937: p. 7 col. 4.
Reports on statements of Morris L. Ernst, Dr. Eric M. Matsner, Dr. C. C. Little, and M.S. regarding U.S. vs. One Package decision.

929. "Editorial." Birth Control Review, 4.6 N.S. Feb.-Mar. 1937: pp. 1-2.
Reports on the annual meeting of the American Birth Control League, where M.S. was guest of honor. Sanger announced that she planned to visit China in the autumn.

930. "Margaret Sanger Receives Award." Birth Control Review, 4.6 N.S. Feb.-Mar. 1937: p. 8.

The Town Hall Club medal was awarded to M.S. by Henry Pratt Fairchild on January 15, 1937.

931. "Gaining Ground." Survey, 73.2 Feb. 1937: p. 48.

Reports on the victory of the National Committee on Federal Legislation for Birth Control in the U.S. vs. One Package decision. Gives remarks made by Morris Ernst, "attorney for the birth control interests."

932. North, Wallace W. "Volunteers Venture." Survey, 73.2 Feb. 1937: pp. 39-40.

An interesting account of the way in which a local clinic was established with advice from M.S. and the American Birth Control League.

933. McLaughlin, Kathleen. "Drop in Population Feared for Nation; Birth Control Move May Push Census to 75,000,000, Life Insurance Man Says; Favors Spacing Children; Mrs. Sanger, However, Says Parents of Smaller Families Are More Responsible." New York Times, 28 Mar. 1937: Sect. 6 p. 6 col. 1.

Louis I. Dublin predicts a dangerous population decline; M.S. responds.

934. "Mrs. Sanger on Speaking Tour." Birth Control Review, 4.7 N.S. April 1937: pp. 6-7.

M.S. will make a speaking tour for the Pennsylvania Birth Control Federation. A speech given by her in February "proved invaluable" in aiding the work of the Illinois Birth Control League.

935. "Contraceptive Advice, Devices and Preparations Still Contraband." Journal of the American Medical Association, 108.14 3 April 1937: pp. 1179-80.

This editorial denies that the U.S. vs. One Package decision has legalized birth control. It warns physicians that they are still extremely vulnerable on this matter and advises them to ignore the interpretations of the National Committee on Federal Legislation for Birth Control, Inc. (for replies, see items 937 and 938).

936. Mayer, Herbert E. "Comstock Act--Admissibility of Contraceptive Devices." Columbia Law Review, 37 May 1937: pp. 854-56.

Reports the decision in United States vs. One Package, 86F(2d) 737, and concludes that the Comstock Act "has been almost emasculated by judicial nullification."

937. Ballard, Frederick A.; Ernst, Morris L.; Dick, Alexander C.; Tweed, Harrison; Scribner, Charles E. "Correspondence: Contraceptive Advice, Devices and Preparations." Journal of the American Medical Association, 108.21 22 May 1937: pp. 1819-20.

This letter from the legal advisory committee of the National Committee on Federal Legislation for Birth Control, Inc. attacks the April 3, 1937 editorial (see item 935 "Contraceptive Advice") and upholds the importance of the U.S. vs. One Package decision (see item 938 for further comment).

938. Woodward, W. C., M.D. "Correspondence: Contraceptive Advice, Devices and Preparations." Journal of the American Medical Association, 108.21 22 May 1937: p. 1820.
    Written by the director of the Bureau of Legal Medicine, this letter supports the editorial of April 3, 1937 (see item 935 "Contraceptive Advice") and replies to the letter from the Legal Advisory Committee of the National Committee on Federal Legislation for Birth Control, Inc. (see item 937).

939. "Birth Control Council of America." Birth Control Review, 4.9 N.S. June 1937: p. 5.
    Announces the formation of the Birth Control Council of America to coordinate the activities of the American Birth Control League and the Birth Control Clinical Research Bureau. M.S. will serve as chair.

940. "Mrs. Sanger Aids Bermuda Program." Birth Control Review, 4.9 N.S. June 1937: p. 3.
    M.S. spoke before the House of Assembly and made two public speeches in Bermuda. She praised the birth control work being done there.

941. Laurence, William L. "Birth Control Is Accepted by American Medical Body; Association Backs Doctors in Use of 'Legal Rights' on Contraceptive Advice--Hearing Today on Public Health Issue." New York Times, 9 June 1937: p. 1 col. 2-3--p. 26 col. 1-3.
    Reports on the official acceptance of birth control by the American Medical Association.

942. "Catholics to Fight Birth Control Aid; Father Cox to Urge Doctors of Faith to Back Opposition to Contraceptives' Use; Assails 'Pagan' Doctrine; Sees Sterilization and Killing of Insane Next--Mrs. Sanger Asks Federal Action." New York Times, 10 June 1937: p. 25 col. 5.
    Catholic reaction by Rev. Ignatius Cox--to AMA decision.

942.5 Stone, Hannah M. "Birth Control Wins." Eugenics Review, 29 July 1937, pp. 113-15.
    Reprinted from the Nation (see item 926). Dr. Stone reports on two significant events that mark the victory of the birth control movement. The first was the decision of the U.S. Circuit Court of Appeals in the case of the Japanese pessaries. (U.S. vs. One Package). The second was the meeting of the Conference on Contraceptive Research and Clinical Practice (1936) during which research for new contraceptive methods was discussed.

943. "Birth Controllers Demobilized." Time, 30.2 12 July 1937: p. 47.
    Article contains portrait captioned "Margaret Sanger: Her battle won, she left the field." Notes that in the previous week M.S. had dissolved the National Committee on Federal Legislation for Birth Control, Inc., and states that Sanger plans to "intensify the work of the Birth Control Clinical Research Bureau in Manhattan...."

944. "More Clinics Urged for Birth Control; Increase to 3,000 to

Aid All Mothers in United States Is Mrs. Sanger's Aim."
New York Times, 19 July 1937: p. 13 col. 8.
In a report on seven years' work of the National Committee
on Federal Legislation for Birth Control, M.S. recommends more
clinics as well as a visiting nurse service to teach birth control.

945. Wood, Mabel Travis. "Birth Control's Big Year." Current
History, 46.5 Aug. 1937: pp. 55-59.
The U.S. vs. One Package decision and the American
Medical Association's "recognition of birth control" are seen as
turning points in the birth control movement. This article
also traces the history and growth of the birth control clinics.
It sees the Catholic Church as "the only organized opposition
remaining...."

946. "Medical News: General." Journal of the American Medical
Association, 109.6 7 Aug. 1937: p. 440.
Announces the formation of the Birth Control Council of
America "to coordinate the activities of the American Birth
Control League and the Birth Control Clinical Research Bureau."
M.S. will chair the new council.

947. "Birth Control: Pro (and) Con." Literary Digest, 124 14
Aug. 1937: pp. 20-21.
Gives brief statements by those for and against birth con-
trol. M.S. is included.

948. "We Lead in Birth Control." Literary Digest, 124 21 Aug.
1937: p. 6.
Reports that the U.S. has more birth control clinics than
any other country, 320, but that M.S. feels 3000 more clinics
are needed "at once." The article also reports on police raids
made against seven clinics in Massachusetts.

949. "Birth Control." Survey, 73.9 Sept. 1937: pp. 294-95.
Some interesting news notes relating to the birth control
movement: National Committee on Federal Legislation for Birth
Control is dissolved. Supporters are asked to join the new
Birth Control Council of America--M.S., chairman. M.S. sailed
for China "in response to appeals of prominent Chinese medical
men for assistance in developing birth control...." M.S. calls
for an increase to 3000 clinics and suggests "educational cara-
vans to carry contraceptive information to remote places."

950. "Mrs. Sanger Assails 'Population' Nations; She Cites Japan as
a Present Aggressor That Has Refused to Limit Its Births."
New York Times, 23 Sept. 1937: p. 28 col. 2.

951. "World News." Birth Control Review, 22.1 Oct. 1937: p. 5.
M.S.'s "tour of the Orient" interrupted by "Sino-Japanese
hostilities.... She is returning to the U.S."

1938

952. Sanger, Margaret. Margaret Sanger: An Autobiography.
New York: W. W. Norton, 1938. 504 p. Index. No
Bibliography. (OCLC: 700090)

Kennedy, D. M. (p. 277) calls this a "campaign" biography --says it was "ghost-written." (See item 1165.) Reviewed by Amidon, Beulah. "Crusaders." New Republic, 97 7 Dec. 1938: p. 152; Booklist, 35 1 Dec. 1938: p. 116; Elting, M. L. "The Book Forum." Forum and Century, 1006 Dec. 1938: p. v; Feld, Rose C. "A Life Story That Is the Biography of a Cause: Margaret Sanger's Description of Her Long Fight for Birth Control Is an Important Sociological Document." New York Times Book Review, 13 Nov. 1938: Sect. 4 p. 9 col. 1; Himes, Norman E. "Books." Birth Control Review, 23.3 Dec. 1938: pp. 146-47; New Yorker, 14 5 Nov. 1938: p. 72; Pruette, Lorine. "A Serious Feminine Crusader." Books (New York Herald Tribune), 27 Nov. 1938: p. 2; "Sanger Saga." Time, 32.20 14 Nov. 1938: p. 83; Wallace, Margaret. "Personal History of a Pioneer." Saturday Review of Literature, 19.3 12 Nov. 1938: p. 6.

953. _____. Margaret Sanger: An Autobiography. With a new preface by Dr. Alan F. Guttmacher, M.D., Elmsford, New York: Maxwell Reprint Co., 1970. 504 p. Index. (OCLC: 894700)

Reprint of item 952 with the addition of Dr. Guttmacher's preface, which is a posthumous assessment of M.S.'s influence on the birth control movement.

954. _____. "Status of Birth Control: 1938." New Republic, 94 20 April 1938: pp. 324-26.

M.S. discusses the role of the National Committee on Federal Legislation for Birth Control, Inc. in the fight against the Comstock laws. She emphasizes the importance of the U.S. vs. One Package decision and thanks Hannah M. Stone and Morris L. Ernst for their part in it. She also emphasizes the importance of the approval of birth control by the American Medical Association in June 1937. She sees the next objective of the birth control movement as "the inclusion of birth-control service in local, state and national health programs."

955. Hersey, Harold Brainerd. Birth Control Pioneer; The Biography of Margaret Sanger. New York: Sovereign House, 1938: 337 p. (OCLC: 29193)

Not Seen. Work was never published. Author's copy held by the New York Public Library.

956. Himes, Norman E. Practical Birth-Control Methods. New York Modern Age Books, 1938. 254 p. Illustrations. Index. Bibliography. (OCLC: 7097502) With the medical collaboration of Abraham Stone, M.D. Introduction by Robert L. Dickinson, M.D. Foreword by Havelock Ellis. Illustrations by Irving Geis.

Himes presents an authoritative practical guide to birth control. Several pages are devoted to M.S.'s work. For revised edition see Stone, A. Planned Parenthood (item 1058).

957. Noll, John Francis. "Catechism of Birth Control." Huntington, Indiana: Our Sunday Visitor Press, 1938: 62 p. No Bibliography. No Index. (OCLC: 6749471)

Using a question and answer method, the author gives what
"others" may call "the Catholic case." In an effort to support
the argument that M.S. had communist support, the author
links M.S. with Emma Goldman, Ben Reitman, and Rose Pastor
Stokes.

958. Stone, Hannah M. "Birth Control and Population." in
      America Now; An Inquiry into Civilization in the United
      States. ed. by Harold E. Stearns. New York: The
      Literary Guild of America, Inc., 1938. Index. (OCLC:
      420233)
      Dr. Stone includes M.S. in this short history of birth con-
      trol. She also discusses eugenics and the declining birth rate
      (pp. 456-68).

959. Benjamin, Hazel C. "Lobbying for Birth Control." Public
      Opinion Quarterly, 2 Jan. 1938: pp. 48-60.
      Benjamin was librarian for the National Committee on
      Federal Legislation for Birth Control and in charge of its
      records. She discusses the tactics used by M.S., her reasons
      for pursuing "doctor's only" legislation, her use of social and
      professional leaders, and her propaganda techniques. M.S.
      considered the U.S. vs. One Package decision the culmination
      of eight years of lobbying.

960. "The Accident of Birth: A $250,000,000 Industry is Scrutinized
      for Social Responsibility and Is Found to Be in Need of
      Some Drastic Legislation--One Way or the Other." Fortune,
      17.2 Feb. 1938: pp. 83-86+.
      This excellent article reports on the state of the contracep-
      tive industry, describes ineffective and dangerous products
      sold, and calls for legislative reform.

961. Clarke, Elbert H. "Birth Control and Prosperity." Forum
      and Century, 99.2 Feb. 1938: pp. 107-11.
      Clarke suggests that, historically, the "most revolutionary
      thing" since W.W. I is the declining birth rate. The historian
      of the year 2000 will be very interested in "the activities of
      a woman named Margaret Sanger."

962. Shih, Hu. "To Have Not and Want to Have." in Annals of the
      American Academy of Political and Social Science, 198 July
      1938: pp. 59-64.
      Japan, Italy, and Germany blame aggressive military action
      on population pressure but refuse to limit their populations.
      Japan prohibits birth control information and "repeatedly re-
      fuses to permit Mrs. Margaret Sanger to land in Japan."

963. "News from the States: District of Columbia." Birth Control
      Review, 23.2 Nov. 1938: p. 134.
      M.S. was one of the speakers at a meeting of the Mother's
      Health Association of the District of Columbia (October 5,
      1938).

964. Shryock, Richard H. "Freedom and Interference in Medicine."
      Annals of the American Academy of Political and Social
      Science, 200 Nov. 1938: pp. 32-59.
      Dr. Shryock considers many aspects of medical history.

M.S.'s "aggressive lay leadership" in birth control is briefly described.

965. "Mrs. Sanger Alarmed by Low Birth Rate; She Favors Subsidies to Those Who Desire Children." New York Times, 13 Nov. 1938: Sect. 1 p. 6 col. 2.
M.S. suggests "subsidies" for "healthy and intelligent couples" who want children.

966. "Toward United Action." Birth Control Review, 23.3 Dec. 1938: p. 138.
A joint committee of the American Birth Control League and the Clinical Research Bureau is attempting to develop a "program of united action." M.S. is a member of the committee.

1939

967. Sanger, Margaret. "Doors to a New World." Birth Control Review, 23.5-6 Feb.-Mar. 1939: pp. 165-68.
The address given at the annual meeting of the American Birth Control League on January 19, 1939. M.S. thanks all those who helped form the new Birth Control Federation of America.

968. _____. "Tribute." Birth Control Review, 24.1 Nov. 1939: p. 5.
A short tribute to Havelock Ellis after his death.

969. _____. "Editorial." Birth Control Review, 24.2 Dec. 1939: p. 22.
A Christmas message from M.S. calling for a return of "peace and prosperity" to a troubled world.

970. Bartlett, Robert Merrill. They Did Something about It. New York: Association Press, 1939. 146 p. No Index. (OCLC: 2624199)
Pages 126-44 contain a brief, charmingly written "life sketch" of M.S. entitled "A Promise to Keep."

971. Ellis, Havelock. My Life: Autobiography of Havelock Ellis. Boston: Houghton Mifflin Co., 1939. 647 p. Index. (OCLC: 363141)
Ellis does not mention M.S.'s name but describes his friendship with her--and Edith Ellis' jealousy, which was sparked by that friendship. Letters between Havelock and Edith (pp. 520-84) refers to Sanger as "M."

972. Hapgood, Hutchins. Victorian in the Modern World. New York: Harcourt, Brace and Company, 1939. 604 p. Index. (OCLC: 289175)
In his autobiography, Hutchins recalls meeting M.S. (a friend at that time of Emma Goldman's). Hutchins presents brief but interesting opinions about M.S.'s entrance into the American birth control movement.

973. Stone, Hannah M. and Stone, Abraham. A Marriage Manual: A Practical Guide-Book to Sex and Marriage. Rev. ed.

New York: Simon and Schuster, 1939. 334 p. Index.
(OCLC: 4355332)
Guidebook written by Hannah Stone, doctor at M.S.'s birth
control clinic.

974. "Birth Control Rift Ended by Merger; Rival Factions Join and
Map Plans to Widen Health and Welfare Program; Mrs.
Sanger an Officer; Dr. R. N. Pierson Selected as President
of Federation--Both Acclaim Organization." New York Times,
19 Jan. 1939: p. 15 col. 5.
American Birth Control League and Birth Control Clinical
Research Bureau merge into Birth Control Federation of
America.

975. "Aid to Peace Seen in Birth Control; Mrs. Sanger Says Population Rate Must be Adjusted." New York Times, 20 Jan.
1939: p. 10 col. 4.
Speech given before the newly formed Birth Control Federation of America.

976. "Departmental Functions of the Federation." Birth Control Re-
view, 23.5-6 Feb.-Mar. 1939: p. 164.
Outlines the organizational setup of the new Birth Control
Federation of America.

977. "Eighteenth Annual Meeting." Birth Control Review, 23.5-6
Feb.-Mar. 1939: pp. 163-64.
Reports on the annual meeting of the American Birth Con-
trol League. M.S. was one of the principal speakers.

978. "Forward under One Banner." Birth Control Review, 23.5-6
Feb.-Mar. 1939: pp. 162-63.
Announces a merger of the American Birth Control League
with the Birth Control Clinical Research Bureau to form the
Birth Control Federation of America. M.S. will serve as
honorary chair and as a member of the board of directors.

979. "Contraceptives and the Law." University of Chicago Law
Review, 6.2 Feb. 1939: pp. 260-69.
This short article appears in "Notes" and discusses the
history of legal problems in regard to contraceptive techniques.
The major legal actions are included in the citations.

980. "News From the States: Texas." Birth Control Review,
23.7 April 1939: p. 198.
M.S. speaks in El Paso, Texas.

981. "Campaign Opened for Birth Control; Wide Distribution of
Scientific Knowledge Urged at Dinner of Group Seeking
$310,876; Aldrich Endorses Drive; Banker Sends Cable
Message--Mrs. Sanger Says Abortion Rings Menace Women."
New York Times, 11 April 1939: p. 17 col. 1.
Birth Control Federation of America fund-raising campaign
opened. M.S. attacks "abortion rings."

982. "Creating the World of Tomorrow." Birth Control Review,
23.8 May 1939: pp. 204-05.
Reports on statements made at a dinner held by the
Citizens Committee for Planned Parenthood in New York City
on April 10, 1939. Excerpts from M.S.'s speech are included.

983. "For Planned Parenthood; Mrs. Sanger Says Birth Control
     Will Reduce Abortion Rate." New York Times, 1 May 1939:
     p. 30 col. 8.

984. "Recall for Mrs. Sanger." Ave Maria, 49 6 May 1939: p.
     569.
     Editorial effort to remind M.S. of her First Holy Communion
     and that she was once a Catholic.

985. "News from the States: California." Birth Control Review,
     23.9 June 1939: p. 224.
     M.S. speaks in California.

986. Lindeman, Edward C. "The Responsibilities of Birth Control."
     Atlantic Monthly, 164.1 July 1939: pp. 22-28.
     Author calls on leaders of the birth control movement,
     "and especially the undaunted M.S.," to formulate educational
     plans to expel the new fears concerning birth control that
     have replaced some old fears.

987. "Worse Than Any 'Ism'." The Catholic World, 149 Aug. 1939:
     pp. 513-16.
     This "editorial comment" views birth control as "race
     suicide." It attacks the "Sangerites" and implies that Eleanor
     Roosevelt supports them.

988. Wharton, Don. "Birth Control: The Case for the State."
     Atlantic Monthly, 164.4 Oct. 1939: pp. 463-67.
     Author recalls the efforts of Dr. George M. Cooper to
     bring birth control to North Carolina after M.S. won the fight
     for doctors' use of contraceptives. The effort of nurse Roberta
     Pratt led to a donation--for a year's financing--by Dr. Clarence
     J. Gamble.

1940

989. Sanger, Margaret. "Birth Control Through the Ages."
     Twice A Year, Fall-Winter 1940, Spring-Summer 1941,
     Double Number 5/6: pp. 429-40.
     M.S. presents a chronological history of the birth control
     movement, with a year-by-year description of key events.

990. Clarke, Helen I. Social Legislation: American Laws Dealing
     with Family, Child, and Dependent. New York: Appleton-
     Century-Crofts, Inc., 1940. 655 p. Index. (OCLC:
     2084517)
     "This book summarizes American legislation on selected sub-
     jects, makes frequent reference to judicial decisions, and at-
     tempts to set both legislation and judicial opinion in an
     historical matrix." One of the subjects treated is birth
     control.

991. Ernst, Morris L. and Lindey, Alexander. The Censor Marches
     On; Recent Milestones in the Administration of the Obscenity
     Law in the United States. New York: Doubleday, Doran
     and Co., Inc., 1940. 346 p. Index. (OCLC: 1355045)
     A "bird's eye view" of censorship during the first few

decades of the twentieth century. Included are insights into
the cases dealing with M.S.'s Family Limitation as well as with
the New York City Birth Control Clinic. The text of the court
decision of the Japanese Pessaries (U.S. vs. One Package)
case involving Dr. Hannah M. Stone is given in Appendix A.

992. Women of Achievement. New York: House of Field, Inc.
     Publishers, 1940. 213 p. Index. Illustrations. (OCLC:
     1432492)
     This biographical reference work includes a one-page ac-
count of M.S., with portrait.

993. "Films." Birth Control Review, 24.3 Jan. 1940: p. 42.
     A "slide-film dramatization for the lay audience" entitled
"Why Let Them Die?" will be shown at the New York State
Birth Control Federation Annual Meeting. M.S., among others,
is seen and heard in the film.

994. "Public Information Program." Birth Control Review, 24.3
     Jan. 1940: p. 47.
     Announces that the Birth Control Review is suspending
publication and outlines a new form of publication program for
"carrying forward the movement."

995. "Leaders Aid Drive for Birth Control; 1,000 Named on Com-
     mittee to Sponsor a Campaign Throughout Nation; Mrs.
     Sanger is Chairman; Action Launched at Meeting at Which
     Mother of the President is Guest." New York Times, 25
     Jan. 1940: p. 23 col. 1.
     M.S. will chair the National Committee for Planned Parent-
hood.

996. "Wider Drive Set for Birth Control; Sponsors Will Seek to Make
     Plan an 'Integral Part' of Public Health Service." New York
     Times, 26 Jan. 1940: p. 15 col. 3.
     Reports on annual meeting of the Birth Control Federation
of America.

997. "Rise of Birth Control: Centers Operate in 42 States, New
     York Convention Reveals." Newsweek, 15 5 Feb. 1940:
     p. 29.
     Reports on the meeting held in New York by the Birth
Control Federation of America. M.S. was reelected honorary
chairman.

998. "Cancels Exhibit on Birth Control; Negro Exposition in Chica-
     go Says Catholic Organizations Protested Against It; Mrs.
     Sanger Indignant." New York Times, 8 July 1940: p. 18
     col. 4.

999. "Mrs. Sanger Wins." Catholic Digest, 4 Sept. 1940: pp. 32-
     33.
     M.S. is labeled "meddler with nature" and is congratulated
for the declining population and "on her rapid elimination of
our race."

1000. Decotte, Ben E. "Six Arguments Against Sangerism." Ave
      Maria, 52 28 Sept. 1940: pp. 391-94. Same article in
      Catholic Digest, 5 Nov. 1940: pp. 51-54.
      This Catholic father presents his six arguments against
"Sangerism"--his six children.

1001.   Himes, Norman E.   "A Decade of Progress in Birth Control."
        Annals of the American Academy of Political and Social
        Sciences, 212 Nov. 1940:   pp. 88-96.
        In the words of this specialist on the history of contra-
        ception, "in this article we are concerned mainly with the
        progress of opinion in favor of birth control, with the growth
        of clinics, with recent changes in legislation, and with major
        shifts in emphasis and important social trends in the field of
        birth control in the last decade."
        Mentioned is the founding in 1935 by M.S. of the Journal
        of Contraception (in February 1940, the periodical became
        known as Human Fertility).

1002.   "Mrs. Sanger Retreats."   Ave Maria, 52 9 Nov. 1940:   p.
        581.
        This editorial commends the officers of the First Congre-
        gational Church of Holyoke, Mass. for refusing M.S. the use
        of their building.

1941

1003.   Cargill, Oscar.   Intellectual America; Ideas on the March.
        New York: Cooper Square Publishers, Inc., 1968 (re-
        print of: New York: Macmillan Co., 1941).   777 p.
        Index.   No Bibliography.   (OCLC: 1968)
        In this sweeping study of European ideologies in American
        history, Cargill praises M.S.'s work and links her to the
        changing sexual morality of the 1920's.

1004.   "New Drive Planned for Birth Control; Chief Aim of National
        Group in 1941 Is to Add It to More Public Health Ser-
        vices."   New York Times, 31 Jan. 1941:   p. 21 col. 6.

1005.   "Appeasement in Holyoke--A Story with a Strange Ending."
        Protestant Digest, 3.10 Easter, 1941:   pp. 72-74.
        Describes the events that took place in Holyoke, Mass.
        in 1940 when M.S. was scheduled to speak on behalf of the
        initiative petition, which was designed to allow physicians to
        provide contraceptive information for reasons of health.
        Economic pressure from the Catholic Church caused the First
        Congregational Church to cancel the meeting.   The meeting
        was finally held at the Skinner's Local Textile Workers Union,
        C.I.O.

1006.   Schmiedeler, Edgar.   "Are American Women Shirkers?"
        Catholic World, 153 July 1941:   pp. 426-29.
        An attack on the "woman's movement," generally, and the
        birth control movement, specifically, accusing both of creat-
        ing the declining birth rate.   M.S. is symbolized by her pub-
        lication The Rebel Woman.   According to the author, even
        Catholic women have joined the "shirkers."

1007.   "Bars Birth Control Exhibit."   New York Times, 22 Aug.
        1941:   p. 17 col. 3.
        Poletti bans birth control at the Syracuse Fair.

1008. "Poletti Assailed on Birth Control; Planned Parenthood So-
ciety Defends Exhibit Barred from Syracuse Fair." New
York Times, 26 Aug. 1941: p. 21 col. 6.
New York State Federation for Planned Parenthood.

1009. "Mrs. Poletti Aids Stand on Exhibit; Declines to See Birth
Control Display Barred by Husband from State Fair."
New York Times, 27 Aug. 1941: p. 21 col. 5.
New York State Fair at Syracuse.

1010. "Mineola Fair Bars Birth Control Unit; Officials Follow Lead
of Lieutenant Governor Poletti Who Banned Exhibit at
Syracuse." New York Times, 29 Aug. 1941: p. 11 col.
4.
Birth control exhibit banned at Mineola Fair. M.S. protests.

1011. "Poletti Upholds Fair Exhibit Ban; He Tells Women Law Made
It Improper to Advocate Birth Control at State's Show."
New York Times, 29 Aug. 1941: p. 11 col. 1.

1012. "Progress Hailed in Birth Control; Mrs. Sanger Guest at
Dinner Marking Anniversary of Clinic She Founded; Other
Cities Celebrate; Poletti's Ban on Fair Exhibit Is Strongly
Condemned at Meeting Here." New York Times, 17 Oct.
1941: p. 18 col. 8.

1013. "M-Day for Birth Control." Newsweek, 18 20 Oct. 1941:
pp. 65-66.
This reports on celebration dinners throughout the country
to mark the twenty-fifth anniversary of the opening of the
Brownsville Clinic by M.S. and Ethel Byrne.

1014. "From Birth Control to Fertility." Time, 38.17 27 Oct. 1941:
p. 74.
Article contains portrait of M.S. captioned "Fertilitarian
Sanger: She Celebrated 30 Days on Blackwell's Island."
Notes the change of emphasis of the birth controllers from the
cry of "limited" families to the urging of "U.S. parents to
have as many babies as they can afford, to 'space' them two
years apart." Changed title of Journal of Contraception to
Human Fertility.

1015. Daniels, Jonathan. "A Native at Large: Birth Control and
Democracy." Nation, 153.18 1 Nov. 1941: p. 429.
Notes the twenty-fifth anniversary of M.S.'s first trip to
jail and the efforts of the Massachusetts Mothers' Health
Council to change the laws.

1016. "Birth Controllers Celebrate." Ave Maria, 54 8 Nov. 1941:
p. 581.
This short editorial comments on the twenty-fifth anniversary of the opening of M.S.'s Brooklyn clinic and laments the
declining birthrate.

1017. Belisle, Eugene L. "Birth Control in Massachusetts." New
Republic, 105.23 8 Dec. 1941: pp. 759-60.
In this article, which details Catholic political action,
author notes the organized efforts by the faculty of Holy
Cross College to prevent M.S. from speaking in Worcester.

"An even more violent attack upon her right to speak in Holyoke gained her many new adherents all over the state." Author suggests that "lay Catholic reaction to hierarchical fascism in the Margaret Sanger-Holyoke affair" may have furthered the cause of the birth control movement in Massachusetts.

1943

1018. Schmiedeler, Edgar. Twenty-Five Years of Uncontrol. Huntington, Ind.: Our Sunday Visitor Press, 1943. 189 p. No Index. No Bibliography. (OCLC: 4823975) This is a fascinating anti-birth control, Catholic look at both the birth control movement and M.S.'s career. M.S.: pp. 5-6, 20-21, 23, 46, 52, 61-73, 77, 81-88, 90-91, 99, 105, 110-11, 114-15, 118-21, 131, 140, 143, 151-54, 170-72.

1019. _____. "Putting Birth Control Over." Catholic Mind, 41 April 1943: pp. 34-44. This strong attack on M.S. outlines methods of propaganda used in the birth control movement. The article stresses M.S.'s communist connections ("Red Comrades") and her "Anarchist Philosophy."

1020. "Mrs. Sanger on Mother's Day." America, 69 22 May 1943: pp. 170-71. This editorial pokes fun at M.S.'s "Mother's Day card, which contains the story of 'Mimi'--a girl who thinks that she is being unpatriotic in taking time off from her defense job to have a baby."

1021. Coogan, J. E. "What Is the Pope Looking At?" America, 69 10 July 1943: p. 377. A personal attack on M.S., giving the Catholic viewpoint.

1022. Fairchild, Henry Pitt. "Family Limitation and the War." American Annals of the Academy of Political and Social Science, 229 Sept. 1943: pp. 79-86. Article contains a discussion of the contribution of the birth control movement to world peace, the progress of the movement, and the movement's opposition.

1944

1023. Sutherland, Halliday, M.D. Control of Life. London: Burns, Oates and Washbourne, Ltd., 1944. 276 p. Index. (OCLC: 2320124) This work is an anti-birth control presentation by an English doctor. It gives the Catholic position and supplies intricate charts for using the rhythm method. Sutherland praises those in the United States who testified against the Gillett Bill and gives some short quotes from their statements.

1024. Stone, Abraham and Pilpel, Harriet F. "The Social and Legal

Status of Contraception." North Carolina Law Review, 22
April 1944: pp. 212-25.
In two separate parts, each author outlines the legal and
social gains achieved by the birth control movement.

1025. Buckman, Rilma. "Social Engineering: A Study of the Birth
Control Movement." Social Forces, 22.4 May 1944: pp.
420-28.
Focusing on the work of M.S., this article reviews the
history of the birth control movement and the methods it has
employed. The birth control movement is used to illustrate
the successful process of "social engineering."

1026. O'Neill, J. M. "Birth Control Debate." New Republic, 111
11 Dec. 1944: pp. 785, 788-91.
A reasoned appeal from a Catholic professor calling for
an intelligent investigation of the birth control issue.
O'Neill denies that Catholics are necessarily in favor of re-
strictive laws (for rebuttal, see item 1029). For further
comments by O'Neill see also: New Republic, 111 25 Dec.
1944: p. 872 and New Republic, 112 30 April 1945: pp.
587-89.

1945

1027. Ernst, Morris L. The Best Is Yet.... New York: Harper
& Brothers Publishers, 1945: 291 p. No Index. No
Bibliography. Has table of contents. (OCLC: 310274)
These are the fascinating ramblings of the great "censor-
ship" lawyer. Included are a few interesting observations
of M.S. and the suggestion that Sanger be given the Nobel
Peace Prize (pp. 81, 144, 252-55).

1028. Goldstein, David. Suicide Bent: Sangerizing Mankind. St.
Paul, Minn., Radio Replies Press, 1945. 244 p. Index.
(OCLC: 191088)
Speaking as a former socialist, the author names M.S. as
the major proponent of "race suicide." Many religious points
of view are brought forth in this anti-Sanger exposition.

1029. Trowbridge, Cornelius P. "Catholicism Fights Birth Control."
New Republic, 112 22 Jan. 1945: pp. 106-09.
This article was written in response to the one written by
J. M. O'Neill (see item 1026).
Trowbridge attacks O'Neill's contention that Catholics are
not necessarily opposed to birth control and gives illustra-
tions of anti-birth control tactics used by Catholics.

1030. "Lasker Awards." New York Times, 24 June 1945: Sect. 4
p. 9 col. 5.
Reports that the Albert and Mary Lasker Awards have been
given to M.S. and to Dr. Hannah M. Stone.

1946

1031. Delisle, Françoise. Friendship's Odyssey. London: William
       Heinemann, Ltd., 1946. 495 p. No Index. (OCLC:
       1973058)
       This autobiography details Françoise Cyon's (Delisle is a
       pseudonym) life with Havelock Ellis. Mentioned is Sanger and
       Ellis' friendship and a yearly financial allowance given to the
       two by M.S. (pp. 405, 436-40, 454, 456, 485).
1032. "Mrs. Sanger to Sweden; Birth-Control Advocate Flies to Sex
       Education Conference." New York Times, 21 Aug. 1946:
       p. 24 col. 4.
       M.S. to attend International Sex Education Conference.

1947

1033. "Mrs. Sanger's Plan Opposed by Britons." New York Times,
       4 July 1947: p. 10 col. 7.
       Reports opposition to M.S.'s proposal that Britain and
       "other hungry countries" adopt a ten-year "moratorium on
       babies."
1034. "Pope Hits Birth Control; Indirectly Attacks Proposal for
       10-Year Birth Moratorium." New York Times, 9 July 1947:
       p. 3 col. 4.
1035. "People: Domestic Issues." Time, 50.2 14 July 1947: p. 42.
       Article contains portrait captioned "Margaret Sanger Slee:
       A ten-year plan." M.S. "advised Europe and Asia to stop
       having babies for ten years."
1036. "Unwelcome Visitor." Ave Maria, 66 23 Aug. 1947: p. 226.
       Brief article relates the negative reaction of the British
       press to the statements made by M.S. during her visit to
       England to attend a conference.

1948

1037. Sanger, Margaret. "Address by Mrs. Margaret Sanger." in
       International Congress on Population and World Resources
       in Relation to the Family. Proceedings. Aug. 1948,
       Cheltenham, England. London: H. K. Lewis and Co.,
       Ltd., N.D. pp. 85-95.
       In this fascinating speech, M.S. recalls her work in the
       birth control movement, her journey around the world, and
       the people she has met. Sanger looks toward a time in the
       future when a better means of contraception will be found.
       She mentions that, although she has coined the term "birth
       control," she can accept the term "Family Planning" and
       especially likes the phrase "planned parenthood." She also
       pays tribute to Marie Stopes. (For Proceedings entry see
       item 1040.)

1038. Friede, Donald. The Mechanical Angel: His Adventures and Enterprises in the Glittering 1920's. New York: Alfred A. Knopf, 1948. 246+ p. Index. (OCLC: 1523027)

In a text that offers many insights into the American publishing world of the 1920's, the author gives a firsthand account of M.S. putting adhesive tape over her mouth at the Ford Hall in Boston while someone read the speech she had wanted to deliver (p. 146).

1039. Friends of the Smith College Library. "Sixth Annual Report." Northhampton, Mass.: Smith College Library, Mar. 1948: 43 p. (Prepared by Margaret Stous Grierson)

Pages 20-21 contain a description of M.S.'s and Anne Kennedy's gifts to the Smith College Library.

1040. International Congress on Population and World Resources in Relation to The Family. Proceedings. Aug. 1948, Cheltenham, England. London: H. K. Lewis and Co., Ltd. Published for the Family Planning Association of Great Britain, N.D. 246 p. No Index. No Bibliography.

These are the proceedings of the congress held in Cheltenham, England on August 23-27, 1948 and sponsored by the Family Planning Association of Great Britain "with a generous financial guarantee from Mrs. Margaret Sanger." Among the participants were Dr. C. P. Blacker, Margaret Sanger (see item 1037), Dr. Abraham Stone, Dr. John Rock, Mrs. Elise Ottesen-Jensen, and Dr. Helena Wright.

1041. Ike, Nobutaka. "Birth Control in Japan." Far Eastern Survey, 17.23 8 Dec. 1948: pp. 271-74.

This article recounts the growth of birth control in Japan and suggests that the attempt to bar M.S. from Japan in 1921 caused publicity that helped "increase public curiosity and interest."

1949

1042. Blanshard, Paul. American Freedom and Catholic Power. Boston: Beacon Press, 1949. 350 p. Bibliography. Notes. Index. (OCLC: 7416552)

Looks at the Catholic Church's stand against birth control--a few mentions of M.S.

1043. Rock, John, M.D. and David Loth. Voluntary Parenthood. New York: Random House, 1949. 308 p. Index. No Bibliography. (OCLC: 510055)

This book is aimed at the lay reader. It gives a brief history of birth control, attempts to point out available medical help, and discusses economic and ethical aspects of birth control.

1044. Rogers, Agnes. Women Are Here to Stay: The Durable Sex in Its Infinite Variety Through Half a Century of American Life. New York: Harper & Brothers Publishers, 1949. 220 p. Index. Illustrations. (OCLC: 324541)

A portrait of M.S. and brief biographical note (p. 57) appear in this interesting pictorial history of the American woman.

1045. "Smith Class Urged to Aid Democracy." New York Times, 7 June 1949: p. 25 col. 7.
M.S. is awarded an honorary degree by Smith College.

1046. "Life Congratulates ... Margaret Sanger." Life, 26.26 27 June 1949: p. 34.
Picture, with short caption, shows M.S. at Smith College to receive an honorary LL.D. degree.

1950

1047. Stone, Irving, and Richard Kennedy, eds. We Speak For Ourselves: A Self-Portrait of America. Garden City, New York: Doubleday, 1950. 462 p. No Index. (OCLC: 1392392)
Pages 456-62 contain a brief excerpt from M.S.'s Autobiography.

1048. "Planned Parenthood Honors Its Pioneers." New York Times, 2 Feb. 1950: p. 25 col. 1.
M.S. is among those honored by the Planned Parenthood Federation of America. She spoke at the Palmer House in Chicago.

1049. "Sanger at 66." Newsweek, 35 6 Feb. 1950: p. 48.
Brief article reports M.S.'s appearance at the Palmer House in Chicago, notes her background in the birth control movement, and quotes her efforts to find "a ready simple, good, and harmless contraceptive."

1050. "Mrs. Sanger Barred by MacArthur from Birth Control Talks in Japan." New York Times, 13 Feb. 1950: p. 1 col. 2-2--p. 5 col. 3-4.

1051. "Mrs. Sanger Not Wanted." Ave Maria, 70 4 Mar. 1950: p. 259.
General Douglas MacArthur's directive denying M.S. permission to deliver a series of lectures in Japan is applauded.

1052. Naismith, Grace. "The Racket in Contraceptives." The American Mercury, 71.319 July 1950: pp. 3-13.
This article reports on a variety of worthless contraceptives, many advertised under the guise of "feminine hygiene." Douches, rhythm techniques, and various devices are discussed. The diaphragm (as used by the Margaret Sanger Research Bureau) is recommended until a better method is found.

1053. "1950 Planned Parenthood Awards to Go to Mrs. Sanger and Dr. Moses; Leader in the Birth-Control Movement Since 1914 and Baltimore Obstetrician Are First Women to Get Foundation's Prize." New York Times, 19 Oct. 1950: p. 14 col. 4-5.
M.S. and Dr. Bessie L. Moses will receive the Albert and Mary Lasker Foundation Awards.

1054. "Mrs. Sanger Urges U.S. Sterility Plan; Sponsorship of
    Government is Sought to Curb Diseased and the Feeble-
    Minded." New York Times, 26 Oct. 1950: p. 26 col. 3.
    Message given by M.S. when receiving Lasker Award
    (accepted by son: Dr. Grant Sanger).
1055. "Lasker Planned Parenthood Award to Mrs. Sanger." Science
    News Letter, 58 28 Oct. 1950: p. 281.
    Notice of Lasker Foundation Awards given to M.S. and to
    Dr. Bessie L. Moses, obstetrician and medical director of the
    Bureau for Contraceptive Advice. The two were the first
    women recipients of the award.
1056. Loth, David. "Planned Parenthood." Annals of the American
    Academy of Political and Social Science, 272 Nov. 1950:
    pp. 95-101.
    Written by a director of public information for the Planned
    Parenthood Federation of America, this article contains a
    description of M.S.'s efforts to foster a health program and
    to continue and expand that program as "planned parenthood."
1057. "People: The Mixture As Before." Time, 56:19 6 Nov. 1950:
    p. 43.
    Article includes portrait of M.S. at sixty-seven and notes
    that the $1,000 winner of the Lasker Award for planned par-
    enthood suggested a government program to sterilize "the
    feeble-minded and victims of transmissible congenital dis-
    eases." She announced that she would donate her award
    money to the women of Japan "to control and guide their own
    biological destiny."

1951

1058. Stone, Abraham, M.D. and Himes, Norman E. Planned Par-
    enthood: A Practical Guide to Birth Control Methods.
    New York: Viking Press, 1951. 221 p. Index. (OCLC:
    1070455) (Introduction by Robert L. Dickinson, M.D.)
    A revised edition of Norman E. Himes' Practical Birth Con-
    trol Methods (see item 956). The book discusses methods of
    contraception, the history of birth control, and the state of
    the movement in 1950.
1059. Miller, Lois Mattox. "Margaret Sanger: Mother of Planned
    Parenthood." Reader's Digest, 59 July 1951: pp. 27-31.
    Brief biography of M.S. with focus on her efforts to gain
    acceptance of birth control in the U.S. and throughout the
    world.
1060. "Mrs. Sanger Decries British Baby Subsidy." New York
    Times, 28 Sept. 1951: p. 25 col. 3-5.
    M.S. denounces the payment of government subsidies to
    large families in Britain.
1061. Murphey, Douglas J. "The Catholic Case Against Margaret
    Sanger." Reader's Digest, 59 Dec. 1951: pp. 139-42.
    Gives Catholic criticism of M.S. and of birth control.

1062. "Mrs. Sanger Plans Japan Lecture Tour." New York Times, 11 Dec. 1951: p. 46 col. 8.

1952

1063. Sanger, Margaret. "The Humanity of Family Planning." in: Third International Conference on Planned Parenthood. Report of the Proceedings 24-29 November, 1952. Bombay, India. Bombay: Family Planning Association of India, N.D.
M.S. cites the problems of overpopulation, calls for abortion to be replaced by birth control, and asks that governments control births with sterilization when necessary. With eugenic implications, she states that "Parenthood should be considered a privilege, not a right." Also, she briefly discusses her meeting with Mahatma Gandhi in 1936 (pp. 53-55) (see item 1071).

1064. _____. "Japan Wants Birth Control." Nation, 175.24 13 Dec. 1952: pp. 553-55.
M.S. discusses her visits to Japan in 1922 and 1952 and details the advances made there for the birth control movement. She urges an educational program that will stress contraception and eliminate the need for abortion.

1065. Harmsen, Hans, M.D. "Reports from Countries: W. Germany." in: Third International Conference on Planned Parenthood. Report of the Proceedings 24-29 November, 1952. Bombay, India. Bombay: Family Planning Association of India, N.D.
Dr. Harmsen, president of the German Committee on Planned Parenthood, discusses the history of birth control in Germany (including M.S.'s visit to Berlin in 1929). An interesting look at the National Socialist attempt to increase the population during World War II is also included pp. 209-213. (For complete Proceedings entry see item 1071.)

1066. Kato, Shidzué. "Reports from Countries: Japan; 1. History of the Birth Control Movement in Japan." in: Third International Conference on Planned Parenthood. Report of the Proceedings 24-29 November, 1952. Bombay, India. Bombay: Family Planning Association of India, N.D.
Senator Kato, known as the Margaret Sanger of Japan, outlines the history of birth control in Japan and strongly emphasizes M.S.'s influence pp. 232-34. (For complete Proceedings entry see item 1071.)

1067. King, Gordon. "Reports from Countries: Hong Kong." in: Third International Conference on Planned Parenthood. Report of the Proceedings 24-29 November, 1952. Bombay, India. Bombay: Family Planning Association of India, N.D.
As president of the Family Planning Association of Hong Kong, Professor King recounts the history of the birth control

movement in Hong Kong. M.S.'s visit to Hong Kong in 1936 is credited with helping to initiate the Hong Kong Eugenics League (pp. 215-18). (For complete Proceedings entry, see item 1071.)

1068. Levine, Lena, M.D. "Group Treatment in Problems of Sex and Reproduction." in: Third International Conference on Planned Parenthood. Report of the Proceedings 24-29 November, 1952. Bombay, India. Bombay: Family Planning Association of India, N.D.

As associate medical director of the Margaret Sanger Research Bureau, New York, Levine tells of the bureau's use of group therapy for marriage counseling and for infertility pp. 166-171. (For complete Proceedings entry, see item 1071.)

1069. Raina, (Lt. Col.) B. L. "Reports from Countries: India; History of the Movement in India." in: Third International Conference on Planned Parenthood. Report of the Proceedings 24-29 November, 1952. Bombay, India. Bombay: Family Planning Association of India, N.D.

An extract from Raina's speech given at the public meeting. It lists attempts made to achieve birth control in India. M.S.'s visit to India (1935-36) is credited with "stimulating the interest in family planning" pp. 218-19. (For complete Proceedings entry, see item 1071.)

1070. Stone, Abraham, M.D. "Research in Contraception: A Review and Preview." in: Third International Conference on Planned Parenthood. Report of the Proceedings 24-29 November, 1952. Bombay, India. Bombay: Family Planning Association of India, N.D.

Speaking as director of the Margaret Sanger Research Bureau, New York, Stone gives a brief history of the development of contraceptive techniques pp. 96-103. (For complete Proceedings entry, see item 1071.)

1071. Third International Conference on Planned Parenthood. Report of the Proceedings 24-29 November, 1952. Bombay, India. Bombay: Family Planning Association of India, N.D. 247 p. No Index.

These are the papers submitted at the Third International Conference on Planned Parenthood. There is a short foreword by M.S. Some of these papers have been included in this bibliography. (See items 1063, 1065, 1066, 1067, 1068, 1069, 1070, 1072.)

1072. Vogt, William. "Reports from Countries: United States of America." in: Third International Conference on Planned Parenthood. Report of the Proceedings 24-29 November, 1952. Bombay, India. Bombay: Family Planning Association of India, N.D.

The National Director of the Planned Parenthood Federation of America recounts the history of the birth control movement in the U.S. and describes the work of the federation pp. 241-45. (For complete Proceedings entry, see item 1071.)

1073. "Personalities and Projects." Survey, 88 Feb. 1952: pp. 86-
87.
The article profiles Dr. Abraham Stone's government-
sponsored visits to India and Ceylon; the visits were made in
connection with family-planning programs.

1074. Bliven, Bruce. "Birth Control in India." New Republic, 126
18 Feb. 1952: pp. 14-15.
With the full support of Prime Minister Nehru, Dr. Abraham
Stone, member of the faculty of New York University Medical
College and scientific director for the Margaret Sanger Re-
search Bureau, traveled to India to teach contraceptive meth-
ods. His trip was made under the auspices of the U.N.
World Health Organization at the invitation of the Indian
Health Minister, Rujkumari Amrit Kaur.

1075. Taylor, Care E., M.D. "Will India Accept Birth Control?"
Atlantic Monthly, 190.3 Sept. 1952: pp. 51-53.
Dr. Taylor was a medical missionary in India. This article, "which won first prize in the Essay Contest sponsored
by the Planned Parenthood League of Massachusetts, evalu-
ates the cultural factors that determine the reaction of In-
dians to birth control."

1076. "Mrs. Sanger's Visit Excites Japanese." New York Times,
10 Nov. 1952: p. 10 col. 1.

1077. "Margaret Sanger in Hong Kong." New York Times, 11 Nov.
1952: p. 8 col. 5.

1078. "World Unit Set Up for Birth Control; Association Created at
Parley in India--Margaret Sanger Named an Honorary
Head." New York Times, 30 Nov. 1952: Sect. 1 p. 1
col. 4--p. 4 col. 4-5.
Third International Conference on Planned Parenthood
forms the International Planned Parenthood Association.
M.S. and Lady Rama Rau are named as honorary presidents.

1079. "India: Planned Parenthood." Newsweek, 40 8 Dec. 1952:
p. 32.
The International Planned Parenthood Association is organized in Bombay, India. Margaret Sanger and Lady Rama
Rau are chosen to head the organization.

1080. "Mrs. Sanger Pleased by Reception in Asia." New York
Times, 14 Dec. 1952: Sect. 1 p. 72 col. 8.
M.S. comments on her trip to Japan and India.

1953

1081. Sanger, Margaret. "Address to the Japanese People." in:
The Population Problems Research Council. "Family Plan-
ning Movement in Japan." Tokyo: The Population Prob-
lems Research Council, The Mainichi Newspapers, 1953.
This speech, dated October 1952, praises Japan's heritage,
warns against Japanese population growth, and offers "Some
Suggestions for Japan's Future Population Studies" pp. 4-18.
(See also item 1084.)

1082. Beard, Mary R. The Force of Women in Japanese History.
Washington, D.C.: Public Affairs Press, 1953. 196 p.
No Index. (OCLC: 137017)
Touches upon M.S.'s influence on Shidzué Ishimoto, the
founder of the Japanese birth control movement (pp. 168-69,
172).

1083. Ditzion, Sidney. Marriage, Morals, and Sex in America: A
History of Ideas. New York: Bookman Associates, 1953.
440 p. Index. (OCLC: 259465)
Short discussion of M.S.'s radical connections.

1084. The Population Problems Research Council. "Family Planning
Movement in Japan." Population Problems Series No. 9,
Tokyo: The Population Problems Research Council, The
Mainichi Newspapers, 1953. 46 p. (OCLC: 4293670)
Include M.S.'s "Address to the Japanese People" (see
item 1081) and M.S.'s itinerary in Japan from October 30 to
November 9, 1952. Also includes a prizewinning essay by
Shoichi Arai, a Japanese student.

1085. Gilman, Mildred. "Margaret Sanger Back from India."
Nation, 176.8 21 Feb. 1953: pp. 169-70.
An interview with M.S. after her global trip for birth con-
trol. Her experiences in Japan and India are discussed.

1086. "Mrs. Sanger Elected Head of World Group." New York
Times, 22 Aug. 1953: p. 3 col. 6.
M.S. elected president of the International Federation of
Planned Parenthood at the Fourth International Conference on
Planned Parenthood which took place in Sweden.

1954

1087. Sanger, Margaret. "When Children Are Wanted." in: This
I Believe: 2, written by Edward R. Murrow, Raymond
Swing, ed. New York: Simon and Schuster, 1954.
(OCLC: 2785919)
This brief "personal philosophy" was written for Edward
R. Murrow's radio series "This I Believe" (pp. 130-31).

1088. Stone, Abraham. "The Control of Fertility." Scientific
American, 190.4 April 1954: pp. 31-33.
Discussed are a number of studies that were aided by
grants from the Planned Parenthood Federation. The studies
concerned the effectiveness of progesterone and allied
steroids in controlling fertility.

1089. "Mrs. Sanger Talks to Japanese Diet; Tells Legislators That
Birth Control Could Solve Vital Overpopulation Problem."
New York Times, 16 April 1954: p. 5 col. 6.

1090. Lyon, Jean. "'Safe Days' and 'Baby Days'; India Tries
Birth Control." Reporter, 11.4 14 Sept. 1954: pp. 18-20.
A fascinating look at the overpopulation problem in India.
Dr. Abraham Stone, under the auspices of the World Health
Organization, made a study in 1951; on the basis of his re-

sults, Stone advocated the rhythm method as being the most feasible birth control procedure. The Lyon article describes the problems involved in the use of the rhythm method.

1955

1091. Huth, Mary Josephine. "The Birth Control Movement in the United States." Diss. Saint Louis University, 1955: 759 p. Bibliography. (OCLC: 920391) Not available from University Microfilms.

This interesting dissertation sees the birth control movement as a "genuine social movement." But the author rejects the movement's goals and views the movement and its leaders from a Catholic viewpoint.

1092. Amano, Fumiko Y. "Family Planning Movement in Japan." Contemporary Japan, 23.10-12 1955: pp. 752-65.

Written by one of the movers of the Japanese birth control movement, this article sketches the history of the movement in Japan from the 1920's through the 1950's. M.S.'s visits to Japan--and her significance to the movement--are cited.

1093. "Margaret Sanger in Hospital." New York Times, 27 July 1955: p. 7 col. 2.

M.S. admitted to Cedars of Lebanon Hospital in Los Angeles "with a heart ailment."

1094. "Red China to Attend Birth Control Talk." New York Times, 21 Oct. 1955: p. 3 col. 6.

M.S. announces that Communist China has been invited to attend the Fifth International Conference on Planned Parenthood to be held in Tokyo.

1095. "Red Shun Parenthood Parley." New York Times, 24 Oct. 1955: p. 12 col. 4.

M.S. announces Communist Chinese have declined to attend the international conference.

1096. Trumbull, Robert. "Overpopulation Held War Peril." New York Times, 25 Oct. 1955: p. 16 col. 6.

Reports on proceedings at the Fifth International Conference on Planned Parenthood held in Tokyo.

1097. "Mrs. Sanger Honored; Birth Control Leader Is Cited by Japanese Government." New York Times, 8 Nov. 1955: p. 14 col. 4.

M.S. receives scroll and silver plates from Japanese Government.

1956

1098. Sanger, Margaret. "Asia Discovers Birth Control." Reader's Digest, 69 July 1956: pp. 36-38.

As president of the International Planned Parenthood Federation, M.S. outlines the state of birth control in Japan, China, and India. She also gives her views on abortion.

1099. Triviere, Leon. "Birth Control in China." Contemporary China, 2 1956/57: pp. 94-99.

The author sees three phases in the Chinese birth control movement. The first followed the revolution of 1911 and focused on the emancipation of women. The second dealt with the problem of overpopulation that existed in the 1930's. The third was adopted by the government in 1954 and provided both contraceptive and abortion information. M.S. is shown as having launched a strong campaign in 1922 in China. She is seen, however, as having been "too early for the majority of Chinese women."

1100. Deverall, Richard L-G. "Japan's A-Bomb: Population." America, 95 28 April 1956: pp. 102-04.

A concise presentation of Japan's population problem and of M.S.'s efforts to establish birth control before and after World War II.

1101. Gilman, Mildred. "Japan's Birth-Rate War." Nation, 182.23 9 June 1956: pp. 491-92.

The need to limit Japan's population has resulted in a battle of choice between abortion and contraceptive methods. M.S. is credited with having created publicity for Japan's birth control movement.

1957

1102. Sanger, Margaret. "A Summing Up." Humanist, 38 July 1978: p. 62.

Brief segment from the response M.S. gave when she was named 1957 Humanist of the Year. Gives her Great Truth: that children must be born by choice and not by chance.

1103. Holbrook, Stewart H. Dreamers of the American Dream. Garden City, New York: Doubleday and Co., Inc., 1957. 369 p. Index. (OCLC: 185935)

In an interesting section, "The Rights of Woman," Holbrook suggests that because of their need to remain "respectable" the suffrage workers did not help M.S. in her causes.

1104. Underwood, Kenneth Wilson. Protestants and Catholics; Religious and Social Interaction in Our Industrial Community. Boston: Beacon Press, 1957. 484 p. Index. Bibliography. Notes. (OCLC: 227839)

In 1940, because of Roman Catholic pressure, M.S. was refused permission to speak in the First Congregational Church of Holyoke, Mass. against the Massachusetts birth control law. Underwood uses this incident as a springboard to study the interactions of the churches with the community. Most of the information is taken from firsthand accounts.

1105. "TV Interview in Doubt; Mrs. Sanger Says Wallace Canceled Her Appearance." New York Times, 6 Sept. 1957: p. 41 col. 2.

1106. "Mrs. Sanger Quizzed." New York Times, 23 Sept. 1957:
p. 50 col. 3.
M.S. appears on Mike Wallace show.

1958

1107. Taeuber, Irene B. The Population of Japan. Princeton:
Princeton University Press, 1958. 461 p. Bibliography.
Index. (OCLC: 169702)
In what must be a landmark of demographic analysis, this
study includes extensive background material on the family
planning movement in Japan and includes some footnotes regarding M.S.'s influence and activities.
1108. "At 71, Mrs. Sanger Scores Dr. Jacobs; U.S. Birth Control
Pioneer Marks Birthday Today--Calls Ban 'Disgraceful'."
New York Times, 14 Sept. 1958: Sect. 1 p. 59 col. 3-6.
M.S. attacks New York City hospitals' policy of banning
birth control. She blames Dr. Morris A. Jacobs, commissioner of hospitals.

1959

1109. Sanger, Margaret. "Inaugural Speeches: Mrs. Margaret
Sanger." in: Sixth International Conference on Planned
Parenthood. Report of the Proceedings 14-21 February,
1959. Vigyan Bhavan, New Delhi, India. London: Inter-
national Planned Parenthood Federation, N.D.
As president of the International Planned Parenthood
Federation, M.S. explains the aims of the federation (pp. 10-
11). (For complete Proceedings entry, see item 1118.)
1110. Calder-Marshall, Arthur. Sage of Sex; A Life of Havelock
Ellis. New York: G. P. Putnam's Sons, 1959. 292 p.
Index. (OCLC: 1149463)
Relates Ellis' friendship with M.S. and discusses its effect on Ellis' wife, Edith.
1111. Guttmacher, Alan F., M.D. Babies by Choice or by Chance.
Garden City, New York: Doubleday and Co., 1959. 289
p. Index. Bibliography. (OCLC: 1437469)
As the author points out (p. 10), the focus of this book
"is on the control of conception, both positive and negative."
He also states that doctors can now use the results of scien-
tific studies of contraception due to the efforts and courage
of pioneers Margaret Sanger, Hannah Stone, and others.
1112. Huxley, Julian. "Population Planning and Quality of Life."
in: Sixth International Conference on Planned Parenthood.
Report of the Proceedings 14-21 February, 1959, Vigyan
Bhavan, New Delhi, India. London: International Planned
Parenthood Federation, N.D.
Huxley sees birth control as a way to "secure an improve-

ment in the quality of life." He stresses the dangers of overpopulation and calls for as much financial support for birth
control as exists for "death control" (pp. 21-26). (For complete Proceedings entry, see item 1118.)

1113.   Kitaoka, Juitsu. "How Japan Halved Her Birth Rate in Ten
        Years." in: Sixth International Conference on Planned
        Parenthood. Report of the Proceedings 14-21 February,
        1959. Vigyan Bhavan, New Delhi, India. London: Inter-
        national Planned Parenthood Federation, N.D.
        The amazing decrease in the Japanese birth rate is shown
        in charts. Despite widespread support for contraceptive use,
        most of the decrease has been due to abortion. Much of the
        credit for the birth control movement in Japan is given to
        Shidzué Kato, "the Margaret Sanger made in Japan" (pp. 27-
        30). (For complete Proceedings entry, see item 1118.)

1114.   May, Henry F. The End of American Innocence: A Study of
        the First Years of Our Own Time 1912-1917. New York:
        Alfred A. Knopf, 1959. 413 p. Index. (OCLC: 419291)
        In this history of the "cultural revolution," May makes
        brief mention of M.S.

1115.   Nehru, Jawaharlal. "Inaugural Speeches: Shri Jawaharlal
        Nehru." in: Sixth International Conference on Planned
        Parenthood. Report of the Proceedings 14-21 February,
        1959. Vigyan Bhavan, New Delhi, India. London: Inter-
        national Planned Parenthood Federation, N.D.
        Prime Minister Nehru expresses the belief that birth con-
        trol must be linked with economic improvement and educational
        advance if it is to be effective (pp. 7-10). (For complete
        Proceedings entry, see item 1118.)

1116.   Pincus, Gregory; Rock, John; Garcia, Celso R. "Field Trials
        with Norethynodrel as an Oral Contraceptive." in: Sixth
        International Conference on Planned Parenthood. Report
        of the Proceedings 14-21 February, 1959. Vigyan Bhavan,
        New Delhi, India. London: International Planned Parent-
        hood Federation, N.D.
        Reports on research on the birth control pill done on
        women in Puerto Rico and Haiti. Although there were some
        "side reactions," the pill was found "safe for use over a
        considerable number of months" (pp. 216-30). (For complete
        Proceedings, see item 1118.)

1117.   Rock, John; Garcia, Celso-Ramon; Pincus, Gregory. "Clini-
        cal Studies with Potential Oral Contraceptives." in: Sixth
        International Conference on Planned Parenthood. Report
        of the Proceedings 14-21 February, 1959. Vigyan Bhavan,
        New Delhi, India. London: International Planned Parent-
        hood Federation, N.D.
        This article reports on birth control-pill research (pp. 212-
        14.) (For complete Proceedings, see item 1118.)

1118.   Sixth International Conference on Planned Parenthood. Re-
        port of the Proceedings 14-21 February, 1959. Vigyan
        Bhavan, New Delhi, India. London: International Planned

Parenthood Federation, N.D. 374 p. Index. Theme: Family Planning: Motivations, and Methods.

These are the papers that were presented at the Sixth International Conference on Planned Parenthood, which was sponsored by the International Planned Parenthood Federation. A short introduction by M.S. Some of the papers are included in this bibliography. (See items 1109, 1112, 1113, 1115, 1116, 1117, 1119.)

1119. Stone, Abraham, M.D. "The Premarital Consultation." in: Sixth International Conference on Planned Parenthood. Report of the Proceedings 14-21 February, 1959, Vigyan Bhavan, New Delhi, India. London: International Planned Parenthood Federation, N.D.

Dr. Stone, medical director of the Margaret Sanger Research Bureau, New York, discusses the process of premarital consultation (pp. 195-99). (For complete Proceedings, see item 1118.)

1120. Sulloway, Alvah W. Birth Control and Catholic Doctrine. Boston: Beacon Press, 1959. 257 p. Index. Bibliography. Notes. Bibliographic Notes. (OCLC: 407220) Preface by Aldous Huxley.

Sulloway gives the history of the Roman Catholic view of birth control and criticizes Catholic arguments. He sees M.S. making the "new morality" a part of "a militant feminism," and credits her early "radicalism" with making the movement work. (For Catholic views of M.S., see index + p. 200, note 15.)

1121. Terao, Takuma. "Outline of Birth Control Movement in Japan with Some Remarks on the Controversial Points." Tokyo: Japanese National Commission for UNESCO, 1959: 51 p. No Index. No Bibliography.

This exceptional overview of birth control in Japan relates the problem of overpopulation to expansionism and war. Before WW II, militaristic aims--demanding large industrial and armed forces--were in opposition to the birth control movement. After the war the Eugenics Protection Law (1948) placed sterilization and abortion in the hands of the physicians. By 1951, a campaign against abortion emphasized contraception. In 1954 the Fifth International Conference on Planned Parenthood met in Tokyo, with M.S. present and advising.

1122. "Experts Advocate Sterilization Plan." New York Times, 21 Feb. 1959: p. 3 col. 4.

Sixth International Conference on Planned Parenthood in India advocates sterilization. Reports that M.S. will retire as president of the International Planned Parenthood Federation and be succeeded by Elise Ottesen-Jensen.

1960

1123. Sanger, Margaret. "Population Planning: Program of Birth

Control Viewed as Contributing to World Peace." New York Times, 3 Jan. 1960: Sect. 4 p. 8 col. 5-6.

A letter to the editor equating birth control with peace and asking President Eisenhower to rethink his "simply none of the Government's business" policy.

1124. _____. "My Fight for America's First Birth-Control Clinic." Reader's Digest, 76 Feb. 1960: pp. 49-54.

A condensed reprint. (See item 1124.5.)

1124.5 _____. "Why I Went to Jail." Together, 4.2 Feb. 1960: pp. 20-22.

M.S. gives her account of the opening of the Brownsville clinic in Brooklyn (October 1916). She also discusses her arrest and trial and her jail experience. (For Reader's Digest reprint, see item 1124.)

1125. Sinclair, Upton. My Lifetime in Letters. Columbia: University of Missouri Press, 1960. 412 p. Index. (OCLC: 287933)

Pages 148-50 contain two letters from M.S. spaced forty-three years apart.

1126. Kastner, Frederic F. X. "Sanger Views Challenged; No Link Seen Between World Peace and Smaller Population." New York Times, 10 Jan. 1960: Sect. 4 p. 12 col. 6.

Letter to editor disputes M.S. letter of January 3. (See item 1123.)

1127. Guttmacher, Alan F. "The Research Frontier ... Pills for Population Control?" Saturday Review, 43.6 6 Feb. 1960: pp. 50-51.

Guttmacher gives a short history of contraceptives, crediting M.S. with bringing the diaphragm to this country in 1913. He also discusses the newly developed birth control pill.

1128. Sulloway, Alvah W. "The Legal and Political Aspects of Population Control in the United States." Law and Contemporary Problems, 25 Summer 1960: pp. 593-613.

This interesting article emphasizes legal decisions made concerning the birth control movement and underlines the influence of the Roman Catholic Church. Sulloway discusses sterilization, abortion, and contraception.

1129. Dean, Joseph. "Planned Parenthood's Mounting Influence." Information; The Catholic Church in American Life, 74 Nov. 1960: pp. 16-27.

In an interesting know-your enemy article, Dean outlines the growth and influence of the Planned Parenthood Federation. M.S.'s background and work are emphasized.

1130. "Mrs. Sanger Staying; Anti-Kennedy Birth-Control Leader Delays Moving." New York Times, 10 Nov. 1960: p. 39 col. 6.

M.S. announces she will wait until the first year of the Kennedy Administration is over before leaving the country.

1961

1131. Drinnon, Richard. Rebel in Paradise: A Biography of Emma
      Goldman. Chicago: University of Chicago Press, 1961.
      349 p. Index. Bibliographic Essay. (OCLC: 266217)
      Briefly examines the influence of Emma Goldman--and the
      anarchists--on M.S.
1132. Lestapis, Stanislas De, S.J. Family Planning and Modern
      Problems: A Catholic Analysis. New York: Herder and
      Herder, 1961. 326 p. Index. No Bibliography. (OCLC:
      752161)
      This book contains a comprehensive survey of the world-
      wide arguments for contraceptive birth control. At the same
      time, it presents and teaches the Roman Catholic views of
      fertility regulation.
1133. "Birth-Control Pioneer: Margaret Sanger." New York Times,
      12 May 1961: p. 12 col. 1-2.
      Biographical sketch of M.S. on the occasion of being
      honored as an "international humanitarian" by the World Pop-
      ulation Emergency Campaign.
1134. "Population Issue Raised by Huxley." New York Times, 13
      May 1961: p. 12 col. 4-6.
      Reports that M.S. was honored by World Population Crisis
      Conference and presented with $100,000 "to further her
      work."
1135. "The Population Bomb." America, 105 27 May 1961: pp. 364-
      65.
      Although Catholics recognize the existence of a population
      problem, they cannot morally accept the position of those who
      would "Sangerize" the world. The Western world must not
      limit its population while the Communist world is continuing
      to grow.
1136. "Pioneers in Birth Control." Eugenics Review, 53.2 July
      1961: p. 69.
      This article notes two events that happened on May 12,
      1961. The first was a tribute paid to Marie Stopes by the
      placing of a plaque on the Marie Stopes Memorial Clinic in
      London. The second was a tribute to M.S. made by Julian
      Huxley (see item 1138).
1137. Houghton, Vera. "International Planned Parenthood Federa-
      tion (I.P.P.F.): Its History and Influence." The Eugenics
      Review 53.3 Oct. 1961: pp. 149-53.
      This history of the International Planned Parenthood Feder-
      ation focuses on the work of M.S., including the conference
      she organized and her travels--especially to Japan and India.
      The pioneer work of Marie Stopes in England and of Baroness
      Shidzué Ishimoto in Japan are also cited. (For conclusion of
      article, see item 1143.)
1138. Huxley, Sir Julian. "The Impending Crisis." Eugenics Re-
      view, 53.3 Oct. 1961: pp. 135-38.
      This speech was given at the Conference on the World Pop-

ulation Crisis, "held in conjunction with the World Tribute to
Margaret Sanger on May 11th and 12th, 1961 in New York
City."

Huxley praises M.S. and discusses the problem of overpopulation.

1962

1139. Bates, Marston. <u>The Prevalence of People</u>. New York:
Charles Scribner's Sons, 1962. 283 p. Notes. References.
Index. (OCLC: 5077946)
An exploration and interpretation of "the population problem." In Chapter 7 ("The Control of Reproduction"), Bates
discusses M.S.'s entrance (1912) into the birth control movement.

1140. Briant, Keith. <u>Marie Stopes: A Biography</u>. London:
Hogarth Press, 1962. 286 p. Index. (OCLC: 1194023)
Discusses the relationship between Marie Stopes and M.S.,
and attacks the validity of M.S.'s <u>Autobiography</u>.

1141. Briant, Keith. <u>Passionate Paradox; The Life of Marie Stopes</u>.
New York: W. W. Norton and Co., 1962. 286 p. Index.
(OCLC: 788479)
American edition of <u>Marie Stopes: A Biography</u>.

1142. Stycos, J. Mayone. "A Critique of the Traditional Planned
Parenthood Approach in Underdeveloped Areas." in:
<u>Research in Family Planning</u> edited by Clyde V. Kiser,
Princeton, New Jersey: Princeton University Press,
1962. (OCLC: 260504)
This paper (pp. 477-501) was presented at a conference
sponsored by the Milbank Memorial Fund and The Population
Council, Inc. (October 13-19, 1960, New York). It criticizes
the effectiveness of the planned-parenthood clinics in underdeveloped areas, blaming the clinics' lack of success on
"medical bias," "middle-class bias," and "feminist bias." Some
of the blame is placed on M.S. for advocating doctor-centered
clinics and for her dislike of abortion. Abortion, sterilization,
coitus interruptus, and the condom are recommended by the
author.

1143. Houghton, Vera. "International Planned Parenthood Federation (I.P.P.F.): Its History and Influence." <u>Eugenics
Review</u>, 53.4 Jan. 1962: pp. 201-207.
This is the concluding part of the history of the International Planned Parenthood Federation (see item 1137 for
part 1). The section focuses on the work of Elise Ottesen-
Jensen in Sweden, Japanese and Indian problems of overpopulation, and worldwide conferences held by the I.P.P.F.

1963

1144. Beam, Lura. <u>Bequest from a Life: A Biography of Louise</u>

Stevens Bryant. Baltimore, Maryland: Waverly Press
Inc., 1963. 194 p. No Index. (OCLC: 655546)
Describes the workings of the National Committee on
Maternal Health (pp. 88-95).

Beam, Lura. Bequest from a Life: A Biography of Louise
Stevens Bryant. (Privately Published, 1963)
Kennedy (p. 291) "shed some light on the role Dickinson's
secretary played in the long negotiations with Mrs. S."
(Robert Latou Dickinson--Committee on Maternal Health)

1145. Haller, Mark H. Eugenics: Hereditarian Attitudes in American Thought. New Brunswick, New Jersey: Rutgers University Press, 1963. 264 p. Index. Bibliographic Essay.
(OCLC: 529593)
The "eugenic coloring" of M.S.'s birth control movement
in the 1920's is part of this history of the American eugenics
movement.

1146. Proceedings. Seventh Conference of the International Planned
Parenthood Federation: February 10-16, 1963. Singapore.
Theme: "Changing Patterns in Fertility." International
Congress Series No. 72. Amsterdam: Exerpta Medica
Foundation, 1964. 748 p.
"Message from Margaret Sanger" (sent by telegram),
founder-president of the International Planned Parenthood
Federation (contained in p. 25).

1147. Rock, John, M.D. The Time Has Come: A Catholic Doctor's
Proposals to End the Battle over Birth Control. New
York: Alfred A. Knopf, 1963. 216 p. Index. (OCLC:
261086)
With a foreword by Christian A. Herter.
Dr. Rock, one of the developers of the birth control pill,
discusses birth control in historical, medical, and theological
aspects. He views the rhythm method as unreliable and pre-
sents the pill as an alternative that might be acceptable to
Catholic theologians.

1964

1148. Blacker, C. P., M.D. "The International Planned Parenthood
Federation: Aspects of Its History." Eugenics Review
56.3 Oct. 1964: pp. 135-42.
This paper was "presented at the Fourth Conference of the
International Planned Parenthood Federation, Western Hemis-
phere Region, San Juan, Puerto Rico, April 19-27, 1964."
Dr. Blacker was an administrative officer of the I.P.P.F. He
speaks of his meetings with Margaret Sanger, Abraham Stone,
Havelock Ellis, and others. He recounts the highlights of the
I.P.P.F. and of conferences beginning with the World Popula-
tion Conference (Geneva, 1927).

1149. Smith, Peter. "The History and Future of the Legal Battle
over Birth Control." Cornell Law Quarterly, 49 Winter
1964: pp. 275-303.

Review of "the legislative and judicial history of the birth control controversy in this country." Noted are the efforts of M.S.'s legislative committee and the Planned Parenthood Association to introduce birth control legislation in the federal and state courts.

1965

1150. Lasch, Christopher. The New Radicalism in America: 1889–1963. New York: Alfred A. Knopf, 1965. 349 p. Index. Footnotes. (OCLC: 256273)
Lasch includes a brief paragraph on M.S. in his chapter "Woman as Alien."

1151. Pincus, Gregory. The Control of Fertility. New York: Academic Press, 1965. 360 p. Index. Chapter References. (OCLC: 424347)
Dr. Pincus, pioneer of the birth control pill, has dedicated this scientific work to "Mrs. Stanley McCormick."

1152. Dowse, Robert E. and Peel, John. "The Politics of Birth-Control." Political Studies, 13.2 June 1965: pp. 179–97.
Covers the history of the positions taken by British political parties regarding birth control. One of the turning points in Labour Party history was the prosecution of Guy Aldred for selling M.S.'s Family Limitation.

1966

1153. Berelson, Bernard, et al. eds. Family Planning and Population Programs: A Review of World Developments. Chicago: University of Chicago Press, 1966. 848 p. Index. No Bibliography. (OCLC: 270835)
The International Conference on Family Planning Programs (Geneva, Switzerland, August 23–27, 1965). Sponsored by Ford Foundation and the Population Council, the conference had additional support from the Rockefeller Foundation. One of the tasks of the conference was to guide and expedite subsequent efforts by spreading information about family-planning programs from one geographic area to another and from one specialization area to another. This volume contains papers both on the major planning programs intact throughout the world in mid-1965 and on the major substantive problems confronting the specialists involved (from foreword). M.S.'s visit to India (1935-36) at the invitation of the All-India Women's Conference is mentioned on page 111. The debt owed by private planning agencies to M.S. is noted on page 260.

1154. Fryer, Peter. The Birth Controllers. New York: Stein & Day, 1966. 384 p. Bibliography. Index. (OCLC: 260861)

"This book gives an account of the chief pioneers of birth control, as family planning used to be called, showing the sort of opposition they encountered and describing their other public activities. It summarizes the various contraceptive methods they taught, and it charts the idea of family limitation which inspired them and which they fostered" (from preface, p. 11).

1155. Lader, Lawrence. Abortion. Boston: Beacon Press, 1966. 212 p. Index. Bibliography. Notes. (OCLC: 7086424)
Lader discusses the state of abortion (both legal and illegal) in the 1960's. He traces abortion history and law, and in a chapter dealing with abortion in Japan, relates M.S.'s attempts to introduce contraception.

1156. Noonan, John T., Jr. Contraception: A History of Its Treatment by the Catholic Theologians and Canonists. Cambridge, Mass.: Harvard University Press, 1966. 561 p. Index. No Bibliography. Footnotes. (OCLC: 711475)
This scholarly work traces the history "of the teaching of the theologians and canonists of the Catholic Church on contraception," and "attempts to discover the reasons for the positions taken."

1157. Samuel, T. J. "Population Control in Japan: Lessons for India." Eugenics Review, 58.1 Mar. 1966: pp. 15-22.
Recounts the success of birth control in Japan and suggests that the lessons learned there might be helpful in India. States that General Douglas MacArthur refused M.S. permission to enter Japan in 1949 because her visit "might be interpreted by the Japanese as an attempt to interfere in their population policy."

1158. Lader, Lawrence. "Three Men Who Made a Revolution." New York Times Magazine, 10 April 1966: pp. 8-9, 55, 58, 63, 66.
This article deals with the development of the birth control pill, the research then in progress, and the parts played by three key figures: Dr. Gregory Pincus, Dr. John Rock, and Dr. M. C. Chang. M.S. is credited with being the "impetus behind the pill."

1159. "Margaret Sanger Award Goes to a New Yorker." New York Times, 27 April 1966: p. 23 col. 1.
Dr. Carl G. Hartman received the first M.S. Award in Medicine.

1160. "Dr. Clarence J. Gamble Dies; Birth-Control Leader Was 72." New York Times, 18 July 1966: p. 27 col. 4-5.

Obituaries

1161. Blacker, C. P., M.D. "Obituary: Margaret Sanger." Eugenics Review, 58.4 Dec. 1966: pp. 179-81.
Dr. Blacker's words in remembrance of M.S. center mainly

on two of her major impacts. The first impact came as the
result of her work between 1912 and 1939 and was mainly felt
in the U.S. The second resulted from M.S.'s effort to make
Asia the center for an international birth control movement.
Cogley, John. "They Left Richer World; Margaret Sanger and
    Menninger Were Pioneers Against Formidable Obstacles."
    New York Times, 8 Sept. 1966: p. 40 col. 3-6.
    Tributes to M.S. and Dr. William Claire Menninger.
"Crusaders: Rebel With a Cause." Newsweek, 68 19 Sept.
    1966: pp. 34+.
"Every Child a Wanted Child." Time, 88.12 16 Sept. 1966:
    pp. 96+.
Illustrated London News, 249.6633 17 Sept. 1966: p. 10.
    Brief obituary with portrait.
"Margaret Sanger." New York Times, 11 Sept. 1966: Sect.
    4 p. 12 col. 2.
    Editorial tribute to M.S.
"Margaret Sanger." Publishers Weekly, 190.12 19 Sept. 1966:
    p. 48.
"Margaret Sanger Is Dead at 82; Led Campaign for Birth Con-
    trol." New York Times, 7 Sept. 1966: p. 1 col. 1-2--p.
    41 col. 2-6.
"Margaret Sanger; Nurse." Nursing Outlook, 14.10 Oct. 1966:
    p. 25.
"Milestones." Time, 88.12 16 Sept. 1966: p. 77.
"Mrs. Sanger Is Eulogized As a 'Good, Fighting Saint'." New
    York Times, 9 Sept. 1966: p. 45 col. 1.
    Reports on a memorial service in Tucson, Arizona.
"Planned Parenthood's First Lady Passes." Life, 61.12 16
    Sept. 1966: p. 49.
    Obituary of M.S. with portrait.
"Summa Cum Laude." Christian Century, 83.38 21 Sept.
    1966: p. 1139.
Tolchin, Martin. "Margaret Sanger's Legacy." New York
    Times, 11 Sept. 1966: Sect. 4 p. 7 col. 5.
    Tribute to M.S.

Major Biographies

1162.   Douglas, Emily Taft. Margaret Sanger: Pioneer of the Fu-
        ture. New York: Holt, Rinehart and Winston, 1970. 274
        p. Index. Bibliography. (OCLC: 53453)
        Comprehensive biography tracing M.S.'s life from childhood
to death. Reviewed by Alexander, John. "Margaret Sanger:
Pioneer of the Future." Saturday Evening Post, 249 May/
June, 1977: pp. 10-11+; Booklist, 66 1 May 1970: p. 1070;
Booklist, 66 1 May 1970: p. 1070; Booklist, 66 15 May 1970:
p. 1152; Boyer, Paul S. American Historical Review, 76.2
April 1971: pp. 566-67; Choice, 7 Sept. 1970: p. 890;
Christian Century, 87.3 21 Jan. 1970: p. 86; Gruening,

Ernest. "Rabbitry." Nation, 210 25 May 1970: pp. 633-34;
Harrison, Deborah W. Library Journal, 94 1 Oct. 1969: p.
3438; Marx, Paul. "Radical with Dignity." New Republic,
162.20 16 May 1970: pp. 22+; Reining, Priscilla. Science
Books & Films, 13 May 1977: p. 26; Reuss, Henry S. (U.S.
Representative, Wisconsin). New Leader, 53.7 30 Mar. 1970:
p. 17.

1163. Gordon, Linda. Woman's Body, Woman's Right: A Social
History of Birth Control in America. New York: Grossman
Publishers, 1976. 479 p. Index. Reference Notes.
(OCLC: 2331643)

Gordon underestimates M.S.'s place in the birth control
movement. Emphasizes the influences of the radicals and
socialists and closely connects M.S. with the eugenists. Re-
viewed by Banner, Lois W. Reviews in American History, 6
June 1978: pp. 155-62; Booklist, 73 1 Jan. 1977: p. 635;
Bridenthal, Renate. Science and Society, 42 Autumn 1978:
pp. 347-50; Choice, 13 Feb. 1977: p. 1667; David, Henry P.
Contemporary Psychology, 22.4 April 1977: p. 338; Eron,
Carol L. Book World (Washington Post), 30 Jan. 1977: p.
E8; Fee, Elizabeth and Wallace Michael. "The History and
Politics of Birth Control; A Review Essay." Feminist Studies,
5.1 Spring 1979: pp. 201-15 (see items 1167 and 1204); Fox-
Genovese, Elizabeth. "Comment on the Reviews of Woman's
Body, Woman's Right." Signs, 4 Summer 1979: pp. 804-08
(The writer's many comments about Gordon's critics and M.S.
make her reach for "higher" criticism worth reading.); Groat,
H. Theodore. Sociology: Reviews of New Books, 4 Jan.
1977: p. 38; Kane, Leslie. Library Journal, 101.21 1 Dec.
1976: p. 2484; Kennedy, David M. "Review." Journal of
American History, 64.3 Dec. 1977: pp. 823-24; Kirkus Re-
views, 44 1 Aug. 1976: p. 878; Kliatt Paperback Book Guide,
12 Spring 1978: p. 29; Lane, Ann J. "Review Essay: The
Politics of Birth Control." Marxist Perspectives, 2.3 Fall
1979: pp. 160-69; Law, Sylvia A. "Book Review: Woman's
Body, Woman's Right: A Social History of Birth Control in
America by Linda Gordon." (New York: Penguin Books,
1977) Women's Rights Law Reporter, 4.4 Summer 1978: pp.
263-65 (see item 1239); Leavitt, Judith Walzer. "Review."
Journal of Interdisciplinary History, 9.3 Winter 1979: pp.
579-81; Lemons, J. Stanley. "Review." American Historical
Review, 82.4 Oct. 1977: p. 1095; Lerner, Gerda. "Review
Essay: Motherhood in Historical Perspective." Journal of
Family History, 3.3 1978: pp. 297-301; Lindemann,
Constance. American Journal of Sociology, 83.6
May 1978: pp. 1562-64; Politics and Society, 7.4 1977:
p. 510; Progressive, 41.2 Feb. 1977: p. 61; Publisher's
Weekly, 212 17 Oct. 1977: p. 82; Riley, Glenda. Best
Sellers, 36 Feb. 1977: p. 364; Shorter, Edward. "Review."
Journal of Social History, 11.2 Winter 1977: pp. 269-74.

1164. Gray, Madeline. Margaret Sanger: A Biography of the

Champion of Birth Control. New York: Richard Marek
Publishers, 1979. 494 p. Index. No Bibliography.
(Several Pages of footnotes) (OCLC: 4194428)

Based on extensive research. Numerous interviews with
people who had known M.S. An exhaustive biography that
covers both personal and public life. Reviewed by American
Heritage, 30.5 Aug. 1979: p. 108; Booklist, 75 15 Mar.
1979: p. 1125; Cashman, William J. Best Sellers, 39 Aug.
1979: p. 176; Chesler, Ellen. "The Unknown Margaret
Sanger." Ms, 7.12 June 1979: pp. 39+ (see item 1184);
Choice, 16 Oct. 1979: p. 1086; Grambs, Jean D. Science
Books & Films, 15 Mar. 1980: p. 199; Hill, Christine M.
Library Journal, 104.6 15 Mar. 1979: p. 722; Kirkus Reviews, 47 15 Jan. 1979: p. 99; Kirkus Reviews, 47 1 Mar.
1979: p. 271; Milton, Joyce. Saturday Review, 6 14 April
1979: pp. 46-47; New Republic, 180.8 24 Feb. 1979: pp.
40-41; New Yorker, 55 21 May 1979: pp. 147-48; Park, Clara
Clairborne. "One Woman's Sexual Revolution." Book World
(Washington Post), 18 Mar. 1979: pp. E1-2; Publishers
Weekly, 215.5 29 Jan. 1979: p. 109.

1165. Kennedy, David M. Birth Control in America: The Career
of Margaret Sanger. New Haven: Yale University Press,
1970. 320 p. Index. Selected Bibliography. Bibliographical Essay. (OCLC: 78042)

This book originated as a doctoral dissertation. (See item
1232.)

Kennedy concentrates on M.S.'s public career as birth control leader and traces the movement's change from radicalism
to conservatism. His chapters "Birth Control and American
Medicine" and "Birth Control and the Law" are especially
valuable. They include descriptions of Robert L. Dickinson's
influence and of the work of the National Committee on Federal
Legislation for Birth Control ("doctor's only" legislation). Re-
viewed by Boyer, Paul S. American Historical Review, 76.2
April 1971: p. 566; Bremner, Robert H. Journal of American
History, 57.4 Mar. 1971: pp. 939-40; Choice, 7 Oct. 1970:
p. 1148; Conway, Jill K. "The Campaign for Contraception."
Science, 169 4 Sept. 1970: pp. 964-65; Fuller, Edmund.
"Margaret Sanger: Her Life and Hopes in Fact and Fiction."
Wall Street Journal, 175 29 June 1970: p. 12; Guttmacher,
Alan F. "Birth Control in America." New York Times, Book
Review, 19 April 1970: p. 6 col. 1--p. 22 col. 1; Harrison,
Deborah W. Library Journal, 95 Aug. 1970: p. 2663; Kolmer,
Elizabeth. "Review." America, 123.6 12 Sept. 1970: pp.
152-53; Lindemann, Constance. "Margaret Sanger and the
Birth Control Movement." Women and Health, 3.2 March-April
1978: pp. 12-13, 16-21; O'Neill, William L. "Birth Control in
America." Commonweal, 92.12 12 June 1970: pp. 299-300;
Publishers Weekly, 197.9 2 Mar. 1970: p. 74; Science Books:
A Quarterly Review, 6 Sept. 1970: p. 156; Tomalin, Claire.
"What Does a Woman Want?" New Statesman, 79.2050 26 June
1970: pp. 917-18.

1166. Lader, Lawrence. The Margaret Sanger Story and the Fight for Birth Control. Garden City, New York: Doubleday, 1955. 352 p. No Index. No Bibliography. (OCLC: 422978)

A well-written popularized biography of Margaret Sanger. Appendix 1: Acknowledgments and Sources Appendix 2: Planned Parenthood Federation of America with addresses of state leagues and local committees. Reviewed by Booklist, 51 1 May 1955: p. 365; Fairchild, Henry Pratt. "The Margaret Sanger Story and the Fight for Birth Control by Lawrence Lader." Nation, 180.19 7 May 1955: p. 406; Kirkus Reviews, 23 1 Feb. 1955: p. 113; Mills, C. Wright. "A Woman with a Mission." New York Times Book Review, 17 April 1955: p. 10 col. 4-5; New Yorker, 31 14 May 1955: pp. 176-77; Saturday Review, 38 30 April 1955: p. 22; Willis, Katherine Tappert. Library Journal, 80 15 Mar. 1955: p. 644; Witherspoon, Frances. "Crusader for Birth Control." New York Herald Tribune Book Review, 17 July 1955: p. 6.

1167. Reed, James. From Private Vice to Public Virtue: The Birth Control Movement and American Society since 1830. New York: Basic Books, Inc. 1978. 456 p. Bibliographical Essay. Index. (OCLC: 3205324)

Study focuses on those individuals whose actions represent innovation or change in the birth control movement. Those given status as "birth controllers" are M.S., Robert Dickinson, Clarence Gamble, and Gregory Pincus. (See 1261 for dissertation.) Reviewed in Bullough, Vern L. "Review." Journal of the History of Medicine and Allied Sciences, 33 Oct. 1978: pp. 565-66; Choice, 15 Sept. 1978: p. 958; Cott, Nancy F. "Abortion, Birth Control, and American Public Policy." Yale Review, 67.4 Summer 1978: pp. 600-05; Dual review with Abortion in America: The Origins & Evolution of National Policy, 1800-1900 by James C. Mohr, Oxford University Press, 1978; David, Henry P. "Historians Discover Birth Control." Contemporary Psychology, 23.7 July 1978: pp. 485-86; Dual review as above; Dooley, Eugene A. Best Sellers, 38 May 1978: p. 56; Drachman, Virginia G. Ohio History, 88 Winter 1979: pp. 111-12; Efthimion, Mary. Science Books & Films, 14 Mar. 1979: p. 205; Fee, Elizabeth and Wallace, Michael. "The History and Politics of Birth Control: A Review Essay." Feminist Studies, 5.1 Spring 1979: pp. 201-15 (see items 1163 and 1204); Filene, Peter G. "The Birth of Birth Control." New York Times Book Review, 26 Feb. 1978: pp. 11, 37; Garrison, Dee. "Review of: From Private Vice to Public Virtue: The Birth Control Movement and American Society since 1830 by James Reed." Journal of Social History, 12.4 Summer 1979: pp. 651-53; Heininger, Janet E. "Review." Wisconsin Magazine of History, 62 Spring 1979: pp. 252-53; Humphries, Drew. "Review." American Journal of Sociology, 85.3 November 1979:

pp. 712-13; Jackman, Norman. Contemporary Sociology, 8
May 1979: p. 458; Kennedy, David M. "Decrease and Stul-
tify: Contraception and Abortion in American Society." Reviews in American History, 7.1 Mar. 1979: pp. 18-25; Kett,
Joseph F. "The Acceptance of Contraception." Science,
200 12 May 1978: pp. 645-46; Kirkus Reviews, 45 1 Dec.
1977: p. 1312; Lane, Ann J. "Review Essay: The Politics
of Birth Control." Marxist Perspectives, 2.3 Fall 1979: pp.
160-69; McLaren, Angus. "Review." Queen's Quarterly,
86 Spring 1979: pp. 155-57; Mitchell, Sally. Library Journal,
103 1 Feb. 1978: p. 363; O'Reilly, Jane. "Abortion: The
Hidden Agenda." Nation, 226.14 15 April 1978: pp. 437-39;
Pickens, Donald K. "Review." American Historical Review,
83.5 Dec. 1978: pp. 1321-22; Pivar, David J. "Review."
Journal of American History, 65.4 Mar. 1979: pp. 1141-42;
Ryan, Mary P. "Reproduction in American History."
Journal of Interdisciplinary History, 10.2 Autumn 1979: pp.
319-32. Triple review with Abortion in America: The Origins
& Evolution of National Policy, 1800-1900 by James C. Mohr,
Oxford University Press, 1978 and American Midwives: 1860
to the Present by Judy B. Litoff, Greenwood, 1978; Savitt,
Todd L. "Review." Journal of Southern History, 44.4 Nov.
1978: pp. 649-50; Spengler, Joseph J. "Review." Annals
of the American Academy of Political and Social Science, 440
Nov. 1978: pp. 197-98; Virginia Quarterly Review, 54.4
Autumn 1978: p. 149.

1967-1984

1168. Andrist, Ralph K. "Paladin of Purity." American Heritage,
24.6 1973: pp. 4-7, 84-89.
Historical analysis of the hypocritical Victorian America is
presented, with Anthony Comstock as its self-appointed
chief censor. The author states, "one of his [Comstock's]
last great crusades was against birth control, and his special
target was Margaret Sanger."

1169. Anticaglia, Elizabeth. Twelve American Women. Chicago:
Nelson-Hall Co., 1975. 256 p. Bibliography.
The author includes the biography of M.S. (pp. 156-83),
one of the women who made a sociological change in American
history.

1170. Archer, Jules. Famous Young Rebels. New York: Julian
Messner, 1973. 191 p. Index. (OCLC: 514594)
Aimed at young adults, this book contains a biographical
sketch of M.S.

1171. Aul, Donald J. "Margaret Sanger Labeled 'Racist'." Ameri-
can Journal of Public Health, 71.1 Jan. 1981: p. 91.
In this letter to the editor, Mr. Aul denounces Dorothy
Wardell's article (see item 1293) as a glorification of M.S.
Aul labels M.S. a "racist" and an anti-Semite. (See item
1294 for Wardell's reply.)

1172. Banner, Lois W. Women in Modern America: A Brief History.
New York: Harcourt Brace Jovanovich, Inc., 1974. 276
p. Index. Bibliography. (OCLC: 980013)
In this interesting history of the modern American woman,
M.S. is depicted as a radical feminist.

1173. Bartleson, Henrietta Lorraine. "The American Birth Control
Movement: A Study in Collective Behavior with Especial
Reference to N. Smelser's Model of Norm-Oriented Movements." Syracuse University, 1974: 473 p. DAI 1975
36(1):544A (Ph.D. Dissertation) Order #AAD75-13961.
Not Seen; Abstract only. Examines and analyzes the birth
control movement, emphasizing the legislative and judicial
processes used.

1174. Baskin, Alex. "Margaret Sanger, The Woman Rebel and the
Rise of the Birth Control Movement in the United States."
in: Baskin, Alex, ed. Woman Rebel. New York: Archives of Social History, 1976: pp. i-xxii. (OCLC:
3796831)
One of the best available short biographies of M.S. (See
item 1175.)

1175. Baskin, Alex, Advisory Editor and Historical Consultant.
"Woman Rebel." New York: Archives of Social History,
1976. pp. xxii & 56. (OCLC: 3796831)
Reprints the issues of the Woman Rebel (1-7) and includes
an introductory essay by Professor Baskin. (See item 1174.)

1175.5 Berkman, Joyce Avrech. "Historical Styles of Contraceptive
Advocacy." in: Birth Control and Controlling Birth,
Women-Centered Perspectives. ed. by Helen B. Holmes,
Betty B. Hoskins, and Michael Gross. Clifton, New
Jersey: Humana Press, 1980: pp. 27-36. (OCLC:
6734812)
This paper was presented at a workshop held in 1979 at
Hampshire College. Berkman sees M.S.'s crusade as a "prac-
tical campaign for contraceptives," first emphasizing the
diaphragm and later the pill.

1175.55 Bishop, Mary F. "The Early Birth Controllers of B.C."
B.C. Studies (Canada), 61 Spring, 1984: pp. 64-84.
This excellent short history of birth control in Canada in-
cludes reference to the influence of M.S.

1176. Bodemer, C. W. "Concepts of Reproduction and Its Regula-
tion in the History of Western Civilization." Contraception, 13.4 April 1976: pp. 427-46.
An excellent concise history of contraception.

1177. Box, Muriel, ed. Birth Control and Libel: The Trial of
Marie Stopes. New York: A. S. Barnes and Company,
1968. 392 p. No Index. No Bibliography. (OCLC:
438380)
Contains the testimony given at the Marie Stopes vs. Dr.
Halliday Sutherland libel trial.

1178. Brecher, Edward M. The Sex Researchers. Boston: Little,
Brown and Company, 1969. 354 p. Index. (OCLC:
29348)

This "first history of sex research" includes, among others, Havelock Ellis in a chapter called "The First of the Yea-Sayers." M.S. is briefly mentioned.

1179. Bremner, William J., M.D. and DeKretser, David M., M.D. "The Prospects for New, Reversible Male Contraceptives." New England Journal of Medicine, 295.20 11 Nov. 1976: pp. 1111-17.

Reports on research being done on new methods of male contraception. Notes that much of the lag in the development of male contraceptives may have been due to M.S. and Katharine McCormick, who executed "feminist pressure" for a female-oriented oral contraceptive. This "pressure" led to the development of the birth control pill.

1180. Brin, Ruth F. Contributions of Women: Social Reform. Minneapolis, Minnesota. Dillon Press, 1977: 159 p. (OCLC: 3071619)

Pages 100-23 contain the life story of M.S.

1181. Campbell, Patricia J. Sex Education Books for Young Adults 1892-1979. New York: R. R. Bowker Company, 1979. 169 p. Index. (OCLC: 5499039)

In Chapter 4, "Two Trials," Campbell discusses the trials of M.S. in 1916 and of Mary Ware Dennett in 1929 and writes of their encounters with the Comstock Law. An interesting analysis of M.S.'s What Every Girl Should Know is included.

1182. Chang, M. C. "Development of the Oral Contraceptives." American Journal of Obstetrics and Gynecology, 132.2 15 Sept. 1978: pp. 217-19.

Chang gives an account of his work with Gregory Pincus on the development of the birth control pill.

1183. Chang, M. C. "Mammalian Sperm, Eggs, and Control of Fertility." Perspectives in Biology and Medicine, 11.3 Spring 1968: pp. 376-83.

Chang recounts his association with Gregory Pincus and the development of the birth control pill. He also recalls a 1950 meeting with M.S. and Katharine McCormick.

1184. Chesler, Ellen. "The Unknown Margaret Sanger." Ms, 7.12 June 1979: pp. 39+.

Rev. of Margaret Sanger: A Biography of the Champion of Birth Control by Madeline Gray. (See item 1164.)

Gray's book is called "competent but trivial." The review article is a tribute to Sanger's accomplishments and a call for "a full accounting" from "a future biographer."

1185. Cisler, Lucinda. "A Campaign to Repeal Legal Restrictions on Non-Prescription Contraceptives: The Case of New York." in: The Condom: Increasing Utilization in the United States. Myron H. Redford, et al., eds. San Francisco: San Francisco Press, Inc., 1974. (OCLC: 1415033)

Traces attempts through 1973 to appeal or change New York State's law on contraception. The article (pp. 83-108) concentrates on nonprescription contraceptives, especially condoms, and finds M.S. and the American Birth Control League "very deprecatory of nonprescription methods."

1186. Coigney, Virginia. Margaret Sanger: Rebel with a Cause.
      Garden City, New York: Doubleday, 1969: 185 p. No
      Index. Bibliography. (OCLC: 23025)
      Biography written for young people. Contains list of ma-
      jor dates pertinent to M.S.'s life as well as to the birth con-
      trol movement.
1187. Corea, Gena. The Hidden Malpractice: How American Medi-
      cine Treats Women as Patients and Professionals. New York:
      William Morrow and Co., 1977. 309 p. Index. Bibliog-
      raphy. (OCLC: 2597175)
      Contains a chapter, "History of the Birth-Control Move-
      ment," which focuses on M.S.'s struggle. Corea connects
      Sanger with the eugenics movement.
1188. Crittenden, Ann. "A Colloquy on the Sanger Spirit." New
      York Times, 18 Sept. 1979: Sect. B p. 8 col. 1.
      This colloquy celebrated the 100th anniversary of the birth
      of M.S.
1189. Cyrus, Virginia. "Margaret Sanger's Fight for the Right to
      Choose." Know News, 6.3 May 1975: p. 11.
      Briefly outlines M.S.'s career in the birth control move-
      ment and views the "Right to Choose campaign" as a legacy
      of her work.
1190. Dash, Joan. A Life of One's Own; Three Gifted Women and
      the Men They Married. New York: Harper & Row, Pub-
      lishers, 1973. 388 p. (Also includes Edna St. Vincent
      Millay and Maria Goeppert-Mayer.) (OCLC: 606211)
      Examines M.S.'s career as well as her relationships with
      her two husbands, William Sanger and J. Noah H. Slee (pp.
      1-113).
1191. Davis, Kenneth S. "The Story of the Pill." American Heri-
      tage, 29.5 1978: pp. 80-91. Illus.
      Subtitled "How a Crash Program Developed an Efficient
      Oral Contraception in Less Than a Decade," article includes
      the backgrounds of M.S., Mrs. Stanley (Katharine Dexter)
      McCormick, and Dr. Gregory Goodwin Pincus. These three
      had a crucial meeting in 1951 to determine whether a phys-
      iological contraceptive could be developed for mass use. In
      June 1960, the U.S. food and Drug Administration formally
      approved "the Pill" for use as an oral contraceptive.
1192. Demerath, Nicholas J. Birth Control and Foreign Policy:
      The Alternative to Family Planning. New York: Harper
      & Row, 1976. 228 p. Index. Bibliography. (OCLC:
      2020592)
      Demerath states that birth control "is now a foreign policy
      objective, a foreign policy program, and a foreign aid expen-
      diture." He seeks to show evidence that family planning as
      promulgated at present should be abandoned and that "socie-
      tal strategies" of fertility reduction should be adopted.
      Author includes a brief history of birth control and the
      "Family Planning Establishment." M.S.'s part in both are
      detailed.

1193. Dennis, Frances. "The IPPF: 21 Years of Achievement."
Journal of Biosocial Science, 5.4 Oct. 1973: pp. 413-19.
Dennis traces the history of the International Planned
Parenthood Federation. She sees the federation as a culmina-
tion of the work of "Margaret Sanger in the United States,
Marie Stopes and Edith How-Martyn in England, Lady Rama
Rau in India, Senator Shidzué Kato in Japan, and Elise
Ottesen-Jensen in Sweden."

1194. Diczfalusy, Egon. "Gregory Pincus and Steroidal Contraception: a New Departure in the History of Mankind."
Journal of Steroid Biochemistry, 11.1A July 1979: pp. 3-
11.
An interesting look at the history of the birth control pill.

1195. Dienes, C. Thomas. Law, Politics, and Birth Control. Ur-
bana, Illinois: University of Illinois Press, 1972: 374 p.
Index. Bibliography. (OCLC: 532132)
The author's study spans over one hundred years. It
focuses on the activities of such persons as Anthony Comstock,
Margaret Sanger, and others, examining how their activities
interrelated with politics and national and state laws. Central
to the study are the means and efforts by which the laws relating to birth control were first written and then later
changed. Also important are the social and legal processes by
which these changes were accomplished. Appendixes include:
Federal Legislation Relating to Birth Control, 1960; New York
Legislation Relating to Birth Control; Massachusetts Legislation Relating to Birth Control; Connecticut Legislation Relating to Birth Control.

1196. Dienes, C. Thomas. "Moral Beliefs and Legal Norms: Perspectives on Birth Control." St. Louis University Law
Journal, 11 Summer 1967: pp. 536-69.
Dienes examines Catholic legal thought as it has dealt
with the birth control issue.

1197. Diller, Lawrence, M.D. and Hembree, Wylie, M.D. "Male
Contraception and Family Planning: A Social and Historical Review." Fertility and Sterility, 28.12 Dec. 1977:
pp. 1271-79.
This paper calls for a greater emphasis on male contraception, citing the prevalence of the vasectomy to illustrate the
male concern for birth control. The "feminist influence" of
M.S. and Katharine McCormick is partially blamed for the
lack of research in a funding of male contraceptive methods.

1197.3 Dodd, Dianne. "The Hamilton Birth Control Clinic of the
1930's." Ontario History (Canada), 75.1 1983: pp. 71-86.
In 1933, M.S. was a visitor to the Hamilton clinic where
she was able to influence Mary Elizabeth Hawkins, a wealthy
American-born Vassar graduate, to employ certified medical
doctors to administer birth control materials and give advice.
Also noted was the instruction in birth control techniques
received by Dr. Elizabeth Bagshaw (Hamilton clinic) at New
York's Sanger Clinic.

1197.5 Dolan, Edward F., Jr. <u>Matters of Life and Death</u>. New
York: Franklin Watts, 1982. 119 p. Index. Bibliography. (OCLC: 8666981)
This book for young people contains a brief comparison
of the experiences M.S. and others underwent during the
current abortion struggle.

1198. "Dr. Pincus, Developer of Birth-Control Pill, Dies: Worcester
Foundation Chief Worked with Chang and Rock on Contra-
ceptive." <u>New York Times</u>, 23 Aug. 1967: p. 45 col. 1.
Dr. Gregory Goodwin Pincus, with Dr. M. C. Chang and
Dr. John Rock, developed the relatively safe and simple pill
that revolutionized birth control.

1199. Drill, Victor A. "History of the First Oral Contraceptive."
<u>Journal of Toxicology and Environmental Health</u>, 3.1-2
Sept. 1977: pp. 133-38.
Dr. Drill, who worked as director of biological research
at the G. D. Searle and Co. laboratories from 1953 to 1970,
discusses the development of the birth control pill.

1200. Dubofsky, Melvyn. <u>We Shall Be All: A History of the Industrial Workers of the World</u>. Chicago: Quadrangle Books,
1969. 557 p. Index. Notes (OCLC: 30286)
Brief mention of M.S.'s trip to Lawrence, Mass. to aid
children during I.W.W. strike of 1912.

1201. Duvall, Elizabeth S. "Hear Me for My Cause: Selected Letters of Margaret Sanger 1926-1927." Northampton, Mass.:
Smith College, April 1967: 32 p. (OCLC: 1188386)
Ms. Duvall, bibliographer of the Sophia Smith collection,
has selected for this pamphlet many letters M.S. wrote to her
second husband Noah Slee and also one she wrote to her son,
Grant. The letters to Mr. Slee concern M.S.'s preparations
in England for the World Population Conference held in Geneva, Switzerland in late 1927. Many of the letters contain
names of many current notables in the birth control movement.

1202. Dykeman, Wilma. <u>Too Many People, Too Little Love; Edna
Rankin McKinnon: Pioneer for Birth Control</u>. New York:
Holt, Rinehart and Winston, 1974. 276 p. No Index. No
Bibliography. (OCLC: 667024)
Fascinating biography of the lawyer Edna McKinnon.
Dykeman looks at McKinnon's work with Clarence Gamble, the
Birth Control Research Bureau, the Planned Parenthood Feder-
ation, and the Pathfinder Fund (M.S.: pp. 28-42, 65-66, 77,
98-99, 106, 267).

1203. Ehrenreich, Barbara and English, Deirdre. "Complaints and
Disorders: The Sexual Politics of Sickness." Old West-
bury, New York: The Feminist Press, 1973. 94 p.
No Index. Bibliography. (OCLC: 741018)
Traces "medical sexism" in nineteenth- and twentieth-
century American history. Depicts M.S. not as a feminist
but as an "uplifter" of the poor woman. "The fact that the
birth control movement took a racist and classist line makes
even the final victory a dubious one."

1204. Fee, Elizabeth and Wallace, Michael. "The History and Poli-
       tics of Birth Control: A Review Essay." Feminist Studies,
       5.1 Spring 1979: pp. 201-15.
       Reviews Linda Gordon's Woman's Body, Woman's Right
       (item 1163) and James Reed's From Private Vice to Public
       Virtue (item 1167) and compares the two. Gordon's book is
       seen as "a socialist-feminist analysis"; Reed's as "a liberal
       reformist perspective." Review favors Gordon's interpreta-
       tion.

1204.5 Field, Marilyn Jane. The Comparative Politics of Birth Con-
       trol: Determinants of Policy Variation and Change in the
       Developed Nations. New York: Praeger, 1983. 305 p.
       (OCLC: 9829009)
       This researcher details some of M.S.'s earlier visits to
       Europe, Sanger's adoption of medical supervision for birth
       control, and neo-Malthusian ideas.

1205. Flexner, Eleanor. Century of Struggle: The Woman's Rights
       Movement in the United States. Cambridge, Mass.:
       Belknap Press of Harvard University Press, rev. ed.,
       1975. 405 p. Index. Chapter Notes. (OCLC: 1724839)
       M.S.'s efforts in the field of population control are noted--
       also her early efforts for birth control.

1206. Foner, Philip S., ed. Helen Keller: Her Socialist Years,
       Writings and Speeches. New York: International Pub-
       lishers, 1967. 128 p. (OCLC: 1183838)
       The reprint of Helen Keller's article, "Birth Control,"
       which appeared in the New York Call, November 26, 1915,
       (see item 193) appears on pages 70-71. Article contains Ms.
       Keller's comments both on the William Sanger case and on the
       cause of Margaret Sanger.

1207. Garrison, Webb. "A Woman Who Changed Our History."
       Today's Health, 47 Jan. 1969: pp. 44-45+.
       Succinct, uncritical biography.

1208. Gaulard, Joan Marie. "Woman Rebel: The Rhetorical Control
       Movement, 1912 to 1938." Indiana University, 1978. DAI
       1979 39(9): 5207A. (Ph.D. Dissertation) 230 p. Bib-
       liography. (OCLC: 4787897)
       Not available from University Microfilms.
       Study provides an excellent review of M.S.'s use of lan-
       guage and action to achieve her goal. Supported by research
       of the unpublished materials on M.S., the author completes a
       design organized to show that M.S.'s defiant action was always
       part of a larger plan of agitation, education, organization, and
       legislation. As pointed out in the text, time and time again
       M.S. engaged in action and publication that invited repressive
       counteraction. Such actions finally, in 1938, culminated in a
       series of Supreme Court decisions regarding the availability
       and distribution of birth control information and materials.

1209. Gerson, Noel B. The Crusader: A Novel on the Life of
       Margaret Sanger. Boston: Little, Brown and Company,
       1970. 375 p. (OCLC: 67240)

The author's "Afterword" includes a discussion of the thin distinction "at times" between the "straight" biography and the biographical novel. Although Mr. Gerson tells us he is sticking to the facts, he nevertheless gives us a more dramatic view of M.S.'s relationship with others, especially with her father, by using this novelistic technique.

1210. Giffin, Frederick C., ed. Woman as Revolutionary. New York: New American Library, 1973. 256 p. No Index. No Bibliography. (OCLC: 1487097)

This anthology of writings by women includes an excerpt from M.S.'s Woman and the New Race.

1211. Gilfond, Henry. Heroines of America. New York: Fleet Press Corp., 1970. 136 p. Index. (OCLC: 120908)

A short biography of M.S. is one of many biographies included in this work meant for young people.

1212. Goldzieher, Joseph W., M.D. and Rudel, Harry W., M.D. "How the Oral Contraceptives Came to be Developed." American Medical Association. Journal, 230.3 21 Oct. 1974: pp. 421-25.

Despite the crucial roles played by M.S., Katharine McCormick, and Abraham Stone, the birth control pill "became a reality only because of ... developments in steroid chemistry, and because of vigorous advocates who overcome the hesitancy of the pharmaceutical industry to venture into such an emotionally charged arena."

1213. Goodart, Margaret Metcalf. "Contraception: The Secular Controversy, 1830-1937." University of California, Davis. 1975. 304 p. DAI 1975 36 (4):2363A (Dissertation) Order No. 75-22, 847. Not seen; abstract only.

Discusses birth control as a tool of "social reform."

1214. Gordon, Linda. "Birth Control and Social Revolution." in: A Heritage of Her Own; Toward a New Social History of American Women. ed. by Cott, Nancy F. and Pleck, Elizabeth H. New York: Simon and Schuster, 1979. (OCLC: 5310536)

This is an excerpt from Gordon's book, Woman's Body, Woman's Right (pp. 445-75). (See item 1163.)

1215. Gordon, Linda. "The Politics of Birth Control, 1920-1940: The Impact of Professionals." International Journal of Health Services, 5.2 1975: pp. 253-77.

Gordon outlines the feminist-oriented birth control movement's transition into a male-controlled planned parenthood campaign led by doctors and eugenists.

1216. Gordon, Linda. "The Politics of Population: Birth Control and the Eugenics Movement." Radical America, 8.4 1974: pp. 61-97.

Gordon views M.S.'s "personal-political transformation" as a "microcosm of the general transformation of the birth control campaign." Although it began with radical objectives, the birth control movement linked itself with eugenics and racism. It deteriorated completely when feminism was aban-

doned, when "birth control" became "family planning" and
was controlled by men. By the 1950's, feminist motives had
disappeared, and the movement had become a government-
motivated "population control" campaign.

1217.   Graebner, Alan. "Birth Control and the Lutherans: The
        Missouri Synod as a Case Study." Journal of Social His-
        tory, 2.4 Summer 1969: pp. 303-32.
        The Missouri Synod of the Lutheran Church is used as a
        case study to illustrate the changing Protestant attitude
        toward birth control. The Missouri Synod was anti-birth con-
        trol through the 1930's, reflecting its view of the inferior
        status of woman as well as its fear of "race suicide." Be-
        ginning in the 1940's there was a shift to a pro-birth control
        position.

1217.8 Green, Dorothy and Murduck, Mary Elizabeth, eds. "The
        Margaret Sanger Centennial Conference: November 13 &
        14, 1979." Northampton, Mass.: The Sophia Smith Col-
        lection, Smith College, 1982: 68 p. Bibliography.
        (OCLC: 11123651) (Comments by Anne Harper)
        Page 67 has a biographical chronology of M.S. The staff
        of the Sophia Smith Collection used the collection's resources
        to celebrate the centenary of M.S.'s birth. There were four
        conference sessions. One involved a panel that judged M.S.'s
        work and her legacy to the current advocates of reproductive
        control for women.

1218.   Green, Shirley. The Curious History of Contraception. Lon-
        don: Ebury Press, 1971. 210 p. Index. No Bibliography.
        (OCLC: 286769)
        A popularized history.

1218.3 Greer, Germaine. Sex and Destiny; The Politics of Human
        Fertility. New York: Harper & Row, 1984. 539 p. Index.
        Notes. (OCLC: 10020305)
        Greer includes chapters that deal with the history of con-
        traceptives and the eugenic movement. She stresses the
        hostility that existed between M.S. and Marie Stopes, finds
        the birth control movement primarily a eugenic movement, and
        sees M.S. as an egocentric who was motivated by "her desire
        for notoriety and admiration."

1218.5 Grosskurth, Phyllis. Havelock Ellis: A Biography. New
        York: Alfred A. Knopf, 1980. 492 p. Index. Bibliog-
        raphy. (OCLC: 5750054)
        This interesting biography of Ellis examines his relation-
        ship with Margaret Sanger.

1219.   Guttmacher, Alan F., M.D. "Contraception." in: Ethical
        Issues in Medicine: The Role of the Physician in Today's
        Society. E. Fuller Torrey, M.D., ed. Boston: Little,
        Brown and Company, 1968. (OCLC: 185196)
        Dr. Guttmacher was the president of Planned Parenthood-
        World Population. His essay (pp. 25-51) briefly traces the
        history of contraceptive methods and of the birth control
        movement. He stresses the problem of overpopulation, ex-

plains the uses of the birth control pill and intrauterine devices, and looks forward to new and better methods of contraception.

1220. Haberman, Clyde and Krebs, Albin. "'Cause Lady's' Biography." New York Times, 25 June 1979: Sect. C p. 12
col. 2. CBS begins production on a movie about M.S. that
will feature Bonnie Franklin in the starring role.

1221. Hahn, Emily. Mabel: A Biography of Mabel Dodge Luhan.
Boston: Houghton Mifflin Co., 1977. 228p. Index. No
Bibliography. (OCLC: 2934093)
This biography of Mabel Dodge Luhan, rebel socialite, men-
tions M.S. as one of the radicals who frequented Mabel's New
York salon.

1222. Hahn, Emily. Once upon a Pedestal. New York: Thomas Y.
Crowell Co., 1974. 279 p. Index. Biography. (OCLC:
866597)
This look at the history of the American woman includes
a short account of M.S.'s career.

1223. Hall, Ruth. Passionate Crusader: The Life of Marie Stopes.
New York: Harcourt Brace Jovanovich, 1977. 351 p.
Index. Bibliography. (OCLC: 2817903)
Ms. Hall's book is well documented. It presents the reader
with a good deal of material about England's birth control
movement in which Marie Stopes had a large part. The author
mentions the contraception information Sanger contributed to
Married Love, as well as the rivalry between the two birth
control advocates.

1224. Hardin, Garrett, comp. Population Evolution and Birth Con-
trol; a Collage of Controversial Ideas. 2nd edition. San
Francisco: W. H. Freeman and Company, 1969. 386 p.
Index. (OCLC: 23275)
This interesting collection includes an excerpt from M.S.'s
An Autobiography; the story of Jake Sachs and his wife that
inspired M.S.'s fight for birth control.

1224.5 Holtzman, Ellen Martha. Marriage, Sexuality, and Contraception in the British Middle Class 1918-1939: The Correspondence of Marie Stopes. Ann Arbor: University Microfilms Inc., 1982. 170 p. Bibliography. (OCLC:
10463008)
Author mentions that M.S. was a confidant of Marie Stopes
prior to the publication of Married Love. (See item 1223,
Ruth Hall, Passionate Crusader, p. 116.)

1225. Imber, Jonathan Bruce. "Strategies of Despair: Abortion in
America and in American Medicine." University of Pennsylvania, 1979: DAI 1980 40(10): 5617-18A.
In part of this thesis, Imber argues that M.S. and the
birth control movement "condemned abortion practice and pro-
moted the use of contraception." (From abstract only.)

1226. Ingle, Dwight J. "Gregory Goodwin Pincus, April 9, 1903-
August 22, 1967." National Academy of Sciences. Biographical Memoirs, 42 1971: pp. 229-70.

This tribute to Gregory Pincus includes a chronological
bibliography of his writings. It discusses Pincus' work, including his part in the development of the birth control pill.

1226.5 Isaacs, Stephen L. Population Law and Policy; Source Materials and Issues. New York: Human Sciences Press,
1981. 431 p. Index. (OCLC: 6862128)
This book incorporates all "the most important materials
and issues of population law and policy." In an interesting
chapter, "Contraception," Isaacs discusses the Comstock Laws
and the key court decisions involving birth control.

1227. Jaffe, Frederick S. "Knowledge, Perception, and Change:
Notes on a Fragment of Social History." Mount Sinai Journal of Medicine, 42.4 July-Aug. 1975: pp. 286-99.
This excellent article outlines the changes which took place
in the Planned Parenthood Federation of America from the
1950's to the 1970's. Technologically, there was a change
from the diaphragm to the birth control pill. Politically,
there was an end to "doctrinal arguments" with the Catholic
Church. Sociologically, there was a greater emphasis on
clinics for the poor.

1228. Jenness, Linda. "Margaret Sanger's Pioneering Role: How
Women Won the Right to Birth Control." The Militant, 37
16 Mar. 1973: p. 5.
A communist-oriented view of M.S.'s career.
The Militant is published by the Communist Party of the
U.S.A.

1229. Jensen, Joan M. "Archives: The Evolution of Margaret
Sanger's Family Limitation Pamphlet, 1914-1921." Signs,
6.3 Spring 1981: pp. 548-67.
This excellent article traces "the metamorphosis of Margaret Sanger's pamphlet from strategy paper for working-class
women to prescriptive manual for women in the middle class."
The first edition of Family Limitation is reprinted with notes
indicating changes made through the tenth edition.

1230. Johnson, R. Christian. "Feminism, Philanthropy and Science
in the Development of the Oral Contraceptive Pill."
Pharmacy in History, 19.2 1977: pp. 63-78.
For M.S., birth control meant feminist control of the body.
She persuaded another feminist, Katharine Dexter McCormick,
to financially support Gregory Pincus' search for an oral con-
traceptive. The development of the birth control pill was
M.S.'s final triumph.

1231. Kantner, John F. "From Here to 2000: A Look at the Popu-
lation Problem." Johns Hopkins Medical Journal, 144.1
Jan. 1979: pp. 18-24.
An excellent overview of the efforts of Planned Parenthood
Federation and other organizations to reduce fertility.

1232. Kennedy, David M. "Birth Control: Its Heroine and Its
History in America, The Career of Margaret Sanger."
Yale University, 1968. 424 p. (Ph.D. Dissertation)
Order #AAD69-08372 (Ann Arbor, Michigan: University

Microfilms, 1973) Bibliography. Bibliographic Essay.
(OCLC: 4705433)
After undergoing minor changes, Kennedy's dissertation
was published in book form. (See item 1165.)

1233. Ketchum, Richard M. Faces from the Past. New York:
American Heritage Press, 1970. (OCLC: 89926)
Brief biography of M.S. Recounts her court cases and
remarks on the continued importance of birth control (pp.
98-101).
Ketchum, Richard M. "Faces from the Past." American
Heritage, 21.4 June 1970: pp. 52-53.
Brief biography of M.S. Recounts her court cases. Re-
marks on continued importance of birth control. (Same as
above.)

1234. Kostman, Samuel. Twentieth Century Women of Achievement.
New York: Richard Rosen Press, 1976. 178 p. No Index.
(OCLC: 1733509)
Pages 34-55 contain the major facts of M.S.'s life and
career as seen from a "current" viewpoint.

1235. Kulkin, Mary-Ellen. Her Way: Biographies of Women for
Young People. Chicago: American Library Assoc., 1976.
449 p. Index. (OCLC: 2347033)
As the title implies, this work is a guide to biographies
written for children. Included are some "young adult" titles.

1236. Lader, Lawrence. Abortion II: Making the Revolution.
Boston: Beacon Press, 1973. 242 p. Index. Bibliographic Notes. (OCLC: 600259)
Lader traces the development of the abortion movement
from 1965 to the Supreme Court decision of January 22, 1973
(Roe V. Wade). He credits his part in it to the inspiration
of M.S. An interesting segment describes Lader's interviews
with M.S.

1237. Lader, Lawrence. Breeding Ourselves to Death. New York:
Ballantine Books, 1971. 120 p. Illus. Index. (OCLC:
145310) (With a foreword by Dr. Paul R. Ehrlich)
In hard-hitting fashion, this slim text details the impact
on the birth control movement after Hugh Moore and the Hugh
Moore Fund contributed huge sums of money and executive
ability to M.S.'s International Planned Parenthood Federation
and to its continuation as the Planned Parenthood-World Population.

1238. Lader, Lawrence and Milton Meltzer. Margaret Sanger: Pi-
oneer of Birth Control. New York: Thomas Y. Crowell
Co., 1969. 174 p. Index. Bibliography. Illustrated with
Photographs. (OCLC: 49918)
A volume in the "Women of America" series, edited by
Milton Meltzer. A biography of M.S. for young readers.

1239. Law, Sylvia A. "Book Review: Woman's Body, Woman's Right:
A Social History of Birth Control in America by Linda
Gordon (New York: Penguin Books, 1977)." Women's
Rights Law Reporter, 4.4 Summer 1978: pp. 263-65.

Although this is basically a review of Gordon's book, (see item 1163), Law relates the birth control struggle to the current struggle over abortion. She holds M.S. responsible for turning birth control over to the medical profession and for creating a "tradition of elite professionalism."

1239.5 Leathard, Audrey. The Fight for Family Planning; The Development of Family Planning Services in Britain 1921-74. New York: Holmes & Meier Publishers, 1980. 293 p. Index. Bibliography. (OCLC: 7283096)

A study of the history of birth control clinics in Great Britain and of the part played by the Family Planning Association. Includes a few interesting notes on M.S.

1240. Ledbetter, Rosanna. A History of the Malthusian League, 1877-1927. Columbus: Ohio State University Press, 1976. 261 p. Index. Bibliography. Footnotes. (OCLC: 2137182)

Ledbetter's scholarly work traces the history of the Malthusian League. Because of the belief of the laboring classes that poverty was caused by unequal distribution of wealth and not by overpopulation, the league failed to win the acceptance of the poor. Although M.S. acknowledged the help she had received from the league, she emphasized practical instruction in birth control and played down "economic doctrines." (See item 1241 for dissertation.)

1241. Ledbetter, Rosanna. "The Organization That Delayed Birth Control: A History of the Malthusian League, 1877-1927." Dekalb, Illinois: Northern Illinois University, 1972. 346 p. Order #AAD72-22792 Bibliography. (OCLC: 5280884) (Ph.D. Dissertation)

Although her main thesis is that the Malthusian League delayed birth control, the author nevertheless gives extensive evidence that the efforts of Charles Robert Drysdale, and Charles Vickery Drysdale, his son, were important in the shaping of the family limitation movement. Their secularism, social Darwinian theories, and conservative economic concepts were set and did not change with the times that brought about a widening breach between their group and the working classes. The league, which Charles Bradlaugh was primarily responsible for founding, organized Malthusian leagues throughout Europe. The leagues realized some success--especially in Holland--in furthering the spread of family limitation. Others, however, have stressed that family limitation was needed most for the "working poor"--those that the league viewed as "unfit." Margaret Sanger (p. 273) stated that "it was the name 'Malthus,' I concluded which kept the idea from spreading to the workers." Marie Stopes, who "ignored economic theories," emphasized the individual benefits to be derived from birth control and went on to lead the movement in England. (See also item 1240.)

1242. Lerner, Gerda. The Female Experience: An American Documentary. Indianapolis: Bobbs-Merrill Educational Pub-

lishing, 1977. 509 p. Index. Select Bibliography.
(OCLC: 2745868)

This interesting collection of documents is centered on the study of women's history. It contains the section of M.S.'s Autobiography that relates the story of Sadie Sachs.

Sanger, Margaret. "The Story of Sadie Sachs." in: The Female Experience: An American Documentary. by Gerda Lerner. Indianapolis: Bobbs-Merrill Educational Publishing, 1977. pp. 98-104. (OCLC: 2745868)

An excerpt from M.S.'s An Autobiography. (See item 952.) The excerpt relates that Sadie Sachs died from a self-induced abortion--the incident which sparked M.S.'s involvement with birth control.

1243. Lerner, Max. "Max Lerner." in: Population Control: For & Against, introduction by Harold H. Hart. New York: Hart Publishing Co., Inc., 1973. Index. (OCLC: 693319)

In this interesting pro-birth control essay (pp. 8-33), Lerner notes that M.S.'s coined term "birth control" may have alienated potential followers and that the term "family planning" has been more effective.

1243.5 Lieberman, Janet J. "Short History of Contraception." American Biology Teacher, 35 Sept. 1973: pp. 315-18+. Ill.

Gives a concise world view of subject. Includes brief history of M.S.'s efforts (under "Pioneers of Birth Control") and a picture of her in front of the Brooklyn Court of Special Sessions (January 1917).

1244. Lindemann, Constance. "Margaret Sanger and the Birth Control Movement." Women and Health, 3.2 March-April 1978: pp. 12-13, 16-21.

A critical review of David M. Kennedy's Birth Control in America. (See item 1165.) Lindemann uses "data," "book interpretation," and "critique and alternative interpretation data" to show that Kennedy's interpretation "appears to be based on sexist ideology."

1245. Littlewood, Thomas B. The Politics of Population Control. Notre Dame, Ind.: University of Notre Dame Press, 1977. 232 p. Index. Bibliography. Notes. (OCLC: 2983718)

This book discusses political motivations for birth control in the United States, motivations that began in the 1960's. The book asks if birth control has been used as a method of black genocide. M.S.'s motivation is seen as eugenic.

1246. Llewellyn-Jones, Derek, M.D. Human Reproduction and Society. New York: Pitman Publishing Corp., 1974. 547 p. Bibliography. Index. (OCLC: 1186479)

The author, a member of a World Health Organization team, has written a book dealing with "demographic and social problems of human reproduction" and the "challenge posed by exponential population growth." Included is a chapter on the history of contraception.

1247. Lynn, Mary C., ed. <u>Women's Liberation in the Twentieth Century</u>. New York: John Wiley & Sons, 1975. 139 p. No Index. No Bibliography. (OCLC: 1288346)

This interesting collection of readings on American feminism includes a selection from M.S.'s <u>Woman and the New Race</u>.

1248. McGovern, James R. "Anna Howard Shaw: New Approaches to Feminism." <u>Journal of Social History</u>, 3.2 Winter 1969/70: pp. 135-54.

The commitment of Anna Howard Shaw to feminism is seen as springing from her childhood, which centered on a strong domineering father. M.S. is also cited. She is viewed as a feminist leader whose background was similar to Shaw's and as a woman who took on strong male "characteristics."

1248.5 "Margaret Sanger: Registers of Papers in the Manuscript Division of the Library of Congress." (Manuscript Division, Research Department) Washington: Library of Congress, 1977. 62 p. (OCLC: 2263355)

Contains a biographical note and is a basic searching tool for using the M.S. manuscript collection given by M.S. and others to the Library of Congress, 1942-66: (Approx. 130,000 items.)

"A microfilm edition of these papers on 145 reels is available on interlibrary loan through the Library's Loan Division." United States Library of Congress. Manuscript Division.

1248.6 Masel-Walters, Lynne. "Birth Control as Obscenity: Margaret Sanger and 'The Woman Rebel'." 24 p.

Paper presented at the 61st annual meeting of the Association for Education in Journalism (Seattle, Washington, August 13-16, 1978) Aug. 1978. Not Seen.

1249. Meltzer, Milton. "Hughes, Twain, Child, and Sanger: Four Who Locked Horns with the Censors." <u>Wilson Library Bulletin</u>, 44.3 Nov. 1969: pp. 278-86.

M.S. is included as one of those who fought censorship.

1250. Millstein, Beth. "Dauntless Family Planner." <u>New Directions for Women</u>, 7 Autumn 1978: p. 19.

A brief biography of M.S., with portrait.

1251. Morehouse, William M. "The Speaking of Margaret Sanger in the Birth Control Movement from 1916 to 1937." Purdue University, Ph.D. Dissertation, 1968. 218 p. Order #AAD68-12590, DAI Vol. 29/03-A p. 989. No Index. Bibliography. (OCLC: 1023317)

This valuable work closely examines the public speaking of M.S. and "considers her writings and her organizational activities" in order to view the "speeches in their proper social setting." Includes excerpts form many of M.S.'s more important speeches.

1251.5 Norback, Judith, ed. <u>Sourcebook of Sex Therapy, Counseling and Family Planning</u>. New York: Van Nostrand, Reinhold, 1983. 331 p. Index. (OCLC: 2909457)

Volume contains a directory of U.S. population research and family-planning training centers.

1252. O'Connor, John J. "TV: 'Portrait of a Rebel.' Life of
      Margaret Sanger." New York Times, 22 April 1980:
      Sect. C p. 22 col. 3-4.
      Review of television movie "Portrait of a Rebel."
1253. O'Connor, John J. "TV: 'Woman Rebel,' A Portrait of Mar-
      garet Sanger: Story of Birth-Control Leader on PBS;
      Piper Laurie Stands Out in Title Role." New York Times,
      25 May 1976: p. 71 col. 1.
      Produced, directed, and written by Francis Gladstone.
1254. Payne, Robert. The Life and Death of Mahatma Gandhi.
      New York: E. P. Dutton & Co., Inc., 1969. 703 p.
      Index. Bibliography. (OCLC: 24181)
      This biography of the Indian spiritual leader, Mahatma
      Gandhi, includes an account of his meeting with M.S. in
      1936. Gandhi could not accept birth control but insisted upon
      chastity. He was so exhausted by the conversation that he
      was taken to the hospital in "a state of collapse."
1254.5 Petchesky, Rosalind Pollack. Abortion and Woman's Choice:
      The State, Sexuality, and Reproductive Freedom. New
      York: Longman, 1984. 404 p. Index. Notes. (OCLC:
      9620135)
      This is a well-documented, feminist view of the historical,
      legal, economic, and cultural aspects of abortion. M.S. is
      criticized for her support of "doctor's only" legislation for
      her eugenic ideas, and for her anti-abortion feelings.
1255. Petersen, William. Population. New York: Macmillan Co.,
      1969. 735 p. 2nd ed. Index. Bibliography (OCLC:
      3830)
      In Chapter 14, "The Trend of Fertility in Industrial Coun-
      tries," author relates M.S.'s efforts and those of others in
      the history of birth control. Page 489 has picture of M.S.
      taken upon release from jail.
1256. Pickens, Donald K. Eugenics and the Progressives. Nash-
      ville, Tennessee: Vanderbilt University Press, 1968. 260
      p. Index. Bibliographical Essay. (OCLC: 260510)
      "M.S.: The Radical and the Restoration of Nature"
      (Chapter 5).
      This book presents a concise treatment of American
      eugenists (1859-1930) and it discusses their interrelationship
      with intellectual history. Chapter 5, with emphasis on Mar-
      garet Sanger and her writings, links the birth control move-
      ment to that history.
1256.5 Polenberg, Richard. "The Second Victory of Anthony Com-
      stock?" Society, 19.4 May/June 1982: pp. 32-38.
      Polenberg discusses the "Comstockian denial" that there is
      any difference between the ending of a pregnancy and the
      prevention of one. The author presents M.S.'s stand on abor-
      tion.
1257. Polgar, Steven. "Introductory Statement: The Objectives
      and History of Birth Planning." International Journal of
      Health Services, 3.4 Fall 1973: pp. 557-60.

This review of the history of birth control attempts to introduce the "goals and ideologies" that have been part of the movement. M.S. is seen as having linked birth control with "the emancipation of women."

1258. Potts, Malcolm; Diggory, Peter; Peel, John. Abortion. Cambridge: Cambridge University Press, 1977. 575 p. Index. References. (OCLC: 2645117)

Traces the history of abortion and discusses the techniques associated with it. M.S.'s account of the death of Sadie Sachs is among those accounts used as pleas for safe abortion.

1259. Rama Rau, Dhanvanthi. An Inheritance; The Memoirs of Dhanvanthi Rama Rau. New York: Harper & Row, 1977. 305 p. No Index. No Bibliography. (OCLC: 3003848)

These fascinating memoirs of the Indian feminist include her work with the All-India Family Planning Association and the International Planned Parenthood Federation. The memoirs also include the author's contacts with M.S. (M.S. pp. 243, 251, 255, 257, 261, 263, 264, 274, 286, 294, 295, 296).

1260. Raven, Susan and Weir, Alison. Women of Achievement: Thirty-Five Centuries of History. New York: Harmony Books, 1981. 288 p. Index. (OCLC: 6790418)

Contains a brief biographical sketch of M.S.

1260.5 Reagan, Patricia A. "In Search of Health History, Margaret Higgins Sanger: Health Educator." Health Education, 13 July/Aug. 1982: pp. 5-7.

Both a brief biography and an assessment of M.S.

1261. Reed, James. "Birth Control and the Americans, 1830-1970." Ph.D. Dissertation, Harvard, 1974. Not seen. (See item 1167 for book.)

1262. Reed, James. "Doctors, Birth Control, and Social Values: 1830-1970." in: Vogel, Morris J. and Rosenberg, Charles E., eds. The Therapeutic Revolution: Essays in the Social History of American Medicine. Philadelphia: University of Pennsylvania Press, 1979. pp. 109-33. Notes. (OCLC: 5286547)

As the title suggests, Reed details to some extent the positions of doctors confronted with the necessity "[of defending] the highest moral standards of the community." Reed also tells us why M.S.'s fight for birth control was a necessity.

Most doctors acted as social arbitrators. They viewed birth control as a threat both to society and to the medical profession. Lay women such as M.S. were the major instruments of change. They were aided, however, by doctors. Robert Latou Dickinson was one who helped. In 1937 he managed to obtain "an affirmative resolution" on birth control from the AMA. And physician John Rock helped in the development of the pill; as a Catholic, he saw it as a "natural" method of contraception.

1263. Reifert, Gail and Dermody, Eugene M. Women Who Fought: An American History. 1978. 233 p. Bibliography.

(OCLC: 4490328) For information contact Eugene Dermody, Cerritos College, 11110 Alondra Blvd.; Norwalk, California. This work is meant to supplement male-oriented American history texts. It describes the accomplishments of the "other half." Pages 187-190 contain a biographical sketch of M.S.

1264. Renshaw, Patrick. The Wobblies: The Story of Syndicalism in America. Garden City, New York: Doubleday & Company. 1967. 312 p. Index. Footnotes. (OCLC: 233456)

Contains a brief account of M.S.'s role in the evacuation of strikers' children from Lawrence, Mass.

1265. Ris, Hania W. "The Essential Emancipation: The Control of Reproduction." in: Beyond Intellectual Sexism; A New Woman, a New Reality. Joan I. Roberts, ed. New York: David McKay Co., Inc., 1976. (OCLC: 2072874)

In a scholarly essay, which includes "The Role of Margaret Sanger" (pp. 85-110), Hania Ris, M.D. carries the struggle for reproductive control from the past to the issues of today, including abortion.

1266. Robertson, William H., M.D. "Contraception: Past, Present and Future." Alabama Journal of Medical Science, 12.4 Oct. 1975: pp. 316-21.

Relates some of the history of contraception, describes the present state of contraception, and views the possible future of contraceptive methods.

1267. Robinson, Donald. The Miracle Finders: The Stories Behind the Most Important Breakthroughs of Modern Medicine. New York: David McKay Co., Inc., 1976. 332 p. Index. Bibliography. (OCLC: 2388165)

In this popular history of medical researchers, Robinson acknowledges M.S.'s role in Gregory Goodwin Pincus' and Min Chuch Chang's development of the pill.

1268. Ross, Pat, Comp. Young and Female; Turning Points in the Lives of Eight American Women: Personal Accounts Compiled with Introductory Notes by Pat Ross. New York: Random House, 1972. 104 p. No Index. Table of Contents. (OCLC: 548058)

In this book aimed at young readers, Ross includes an excerpt from M.S.'s An Autobiography.

1269. Rossi, Alice S., ed. The Feminist Papers: From Adams to de Beauvoir. New York: Columbia University Press, 1973. 716 p. Table of Contents. References. No Index. (OCLC: 640900)

An anthology of abridged feminist writings. Each writing is introduced by a biographical, sociological essay. Contains an excellent introductory essay on M.S. plus excerpts from My Fight for Birth Control and Woman and the New Race.

1270. Rothman, Sheila M. Woman's Proper Place; A History of Changing Ideals and Practices, 1870 to the Present. New York: Basic Books, Inc., 1978. 322 p. Index. Notes. (OCLC: 4055952)

The author sees M.S.'s career as part of the development
of the 1920's "wife-companion" concept. Rothman discusses
M.S.'s problems with the progressives and sees Sanger's reliance on physicians and her support of "doctor's only" bills
as leading to the failure of the clinic movement.

1271. Rowbotham, Sheila. A New World for Women: Stella Browne;
      Socialist Feminist. London: Pluto Press, 1977. 128 p.
      Index. (OCLC: 3399855)
      This work provides many important insights into the radical
      movements in the U.S. and England. It investigates the in-
      teractions occurring between M.S. and others as birth control
      advocates, and it looks at their feminist aspirations. M.S.
      published Stella Browne in the New Generation, June, 1925,
      p. 62.

1272. St. John-Stevas, Norman. The Agonizing Choice: Birth
      Control, Religion and the Law. Bloomington: Indiana
      University Press, 1971. 340 p. Index. (OCLC: 200190)
      Written by a devout Catholic, this text presents what the
      author calls an "objective account" of birth control. Of great
      value is the extensive treatment given the Christian and Roman
      Catholic views of, and responses to, birth control. Author
      views the practice of birth control as raising a moral dilem-
      ma--"the limits which morality should seek to impose on an
      ever-advancing technology, which offers both a promise and
      a threat to the humanity of man."

1273. St. Johns, Adela Rogers. Some Are Born Great. Garden
      City, New York: Doubleday & Co., 1974. 297 p. No
      Index. (OCLC: 1009315)
      These personal reminiscences of St. Johns include one of
      M.S. as one of the "great" women St. Johns has known. St.
      Johns stresses the importance of M.S.'s physical beauty and
      confesses she disliked M.S. because of Sanger's lack of a
      sense of humor (M.S., pp. 189-206).

1274. Schneir, Miriam, ed. Feminism: The Essential Historical
      Writings. New York: Random House, 1972. 360 p.
      No Index. No Bibliography. (OCLC: 239916)
      This collection of readings on feminism includes a selection
      from M.S.'s Woman and the New Race.

1275. Scott, Anne Firor, ed. The American Woman: Who Was She?
      Englewood Cliffs, New Jersey: Prentice-Hall, Inc., 1971.
      182 p. No Index. No Bibliography. (OCLC: 116512)
      Pages 155-58 contain a passage form M.S.'s Woman and the
      New Race (New York: Truth Publishing Co., 1920), pp. 51-
      56, copyright 1920 by Brentano's, copyright renewed 1948 by
      Margaret Sanger.

1276. Seaman, Barbara. The Doctors' Case Against the Pill. New
      York: Peter H. Wyden, Inc., 1969. 279 p. Index.
      (OCLC: 30564)
      A post-M.S. look at what's happening in the birth control
      field. Dr. Alan F. Guttmacher, president of Planned Parent-
      hood-World Population, is one of many influential doctors
      quoted by the author.

1277. Seaman, Barbara and Seaman, Gideon, M.D. Women and the
Crisis in Sex Hormones. New York: Rawson Associates
Publishers, Inc., 1977. 502 p. Index. Notes. (OCLC:
2968656)
The authors outline the dangers of "hormone therapy,"
suggest nutritional alternatives during menopause, and recommend that the birth control pill be replaced by other methods.
M.S. is credited with having raised money for Gregory
Pincus' research on the "pill." She is also credited for her
role in the birth control movement. But she is blamed for
giving control of contraceptive information to physicians.

1278. Silverstein, Elliot. "From Comstockery Through Population
Control: The Inevitability of Balancing." North Carolina
Central Law Journal, 6 Fall 1974: pp. 8-47.
Silverstein discusses court cases important to the birth
control movement.

1279. Simons, Herbert W. "Requirements, Problems and Strategies;
a Theory of Persuasion for Social Movements." Quarterly
Journal of Speech, 56.1 Feb. 1970: pp. 1-11.
Simons has undertaken the task of analyzing the role of
persuasion in social movements.

1280. Smith, Anita. "Ancient and Modern: A Brief History of
Contraception." Nursing Mirror, 142.8 26 Feb. 1976: pp.
55-56.
A review of the history of contraceptives.

1281. Smith, Mary. "Birth Control and the Negro Woman." Ebony,
23.5 1968: pp. 29-37.
An interesting account of the black American's view of
birth control. "Black genocide" is discussed. Mention is
made of Martin Luther King Jr.'s acceptance of the Margaret
Sanger Award in Human Rights. His speech is quoted. In
it he compares the civil rights movement to "Margaret Sanger's
early efforts."

1282. Smith, Page. Daughters of the Promised Land; Women in
American History. Boston: Little, Brown and Company,
1970. 392 p. Index. Notes. (OCLC: 98374)
This work includes a sketchy and questionable account of
M.S. (Some odd information--e.g., M.S. four months pregnant when married to William Sanger? Contradicts the dates--
cites Lader and Meltzer as documentation--but not in these.)

1283. Sochen, June. Movers and Shakers: American Women Think-
ers and Activists 1900-1970. New York: Quadrangle/The
New York Times Book Co., 1973. 320 p. Index. Bibliographic Notes. (OCLC: 748623)
Study of selected women intellectuals whose actions during
this century were significant and noteworthy.

1284. Sochen, June, ed. The New Feminism in Twentieth-Century
America. Lexington, Mass.: D.C. Heath & Co., 1971.
208 p. (OCLC: 240212)
In a volume dedicated to reporting the role of women in
American history, pages 42-45 contain M.S.'s "The Case for

Birth Control." (See item 573, reprinted from the Woman Citizen, Feb. 23, 1924.)

1284.5 Soloway, Richard Allen. Birth Control and the Population Question in England, 1877-1930. Chapel Hill: University of North Carolina Press, 1982. 418 p. Index. Bibliography. (OCLC: 7773575)

Includes many references to M.S.'s involvement with England's birth control movement.

1285. Spitzer, Walter O. and Saylor, Carlyle L., eds. Birth Control and the Christian: A Protestant Symposium on the Control of Human Reproduction. Wheaton, Illinois: Tyndale House Publishers, 1969. 590 p. Index. Bibliography. (OCLC: 16711)

In his foreword, Carl F. Henry, editor-at-large of Christianity Today, states: "The papers presented to the symposium on the Control of Human Reproduction ... represent an effort by evangelical leaders to stay abreast of current developments and to appraise them from an authentically biblical point of view." M.S.'s role in the rise of birth control organizations is noted (p. 451 in the "Historical Review" section).

1286. Stoddard, Hope. Famous American Women. New York: Thomas Y. Crowell Company, 1970. 461 p. Index. (OCLC: 77281)

Contains a well-written short biography of M.S. aimed at young people.

1286.5 Stwertka, Eve and Stwertka, Albert. Population: Growth, Change and Impact. New York: Franklin Watts, 1981. 87 p. Index. Bibliography. (OCLC: 7572484)

General work for young people covering the population problem. References to the courageous work of M.S.

1287. Suitters, Beryl. Be Brave and Angry: Chronicles of the International Planned Parenthood Federation. London: International Planned Parenthood Federation, 1973. 424 p. Index. (OCLC: 1213322)

Suitters was librarian for the IPPF in London from 1964 to 1970; her "chronicles" are drawn from the records of the federation. This is a valuable look at the workings of the IPPF and of M.S.'s part in founding it and influencing it.

1288. Symonds, Richard and Carder, Michael. The United Nations and the Population Question 1945-1970. New York: McGraw-Hill Book Co., 1973. 236 p. Index. Footnotes. (OCLC: 297782)

This book considers the role of the League of Nations--and the agencies of the United Nations--regarding the population question. Included is an interesting discussion of M.S.'s part in the World Population Conference (Geneva 1927). The discussion reveals the difficulties she encountered.

1289. Taylor, Howard C., Jr., M.D. "Responsibility of the Obstetrician-gynecologist for Lay Education." American Journal of Obstetrics and Gynecology, 104.3 1 June 1969: pp. 301-09.

In tracing the development of physician concern for lay education, Dr. Taylor includes three areas: "maternity education," "education in cancer prevention," and "education in family planning." Except for Dr. Robert L. Dickinson, physicians left birth control in the hands of M.S. and her followers.

1290. Vaughan, Paul. The Pill on Trial. New York: Coward-McCann, Inc., 1970. 244 p. Index. (OCLC: 97780)
This examination of the history and safety of the birth control pill discusses M.S.'s connections with Dr. Gregory Pincus and Katharine McCormick; the two developed the pill.

1291. Veerhusen, Pamela G. "The Role of the Condom in Planned Parenthood Programs." in: The Condom: Increasing Utilization in the United States. Myron H. Redford, et al., eds. San Francisco: San Francisco Press, Inc., 1974. (OCLC: 1415033)
The birth control movement was dominated by women. M.S.'s fight (pp. 186-93) was aimed at giving women control of their own bodies and their own fertility. The diaphragm was "The Method"--the condom merely a prophylactic and not to be trusted for controlling births.

1291.5 "Voices in the Population Debate." Scholastic Update (Teacher's Edition), 116.14 2 Mar. 1984.
Portraits and biographical sketches of persons concerned with birth control (including M.S.).

1292. Wallace, Irving; Wallace, Amy; Wallechinsky, David; Wallace, Sylvia. The Intimate Sex Lives of Famous People. New York: Delacorte Press, 1981. 618 p. Index. (OCLC: 7168736)
This book popularizes the lives of well-known people by attempting to reveal their sex lives. A sketch of M.S. is included. Sanger is also named in sketches of Havelock Ellis and H. G. Wells.

1293. Wardell, Dorothy. "Margaret Sanger: Birth Control's Successful Revolutionary." American Journal of Public Health, 70.7 July 1980: pp. 736-42. (Discussion, Vol. 71, Jan. 1981: p. 91)
This well-done biographical sketch of M.S. also includes some brief assessments of M.S.'s major biographers. (See also items 1171 & 1294.)

1294. Wardell, Dorothy. "Wardell's Response." American Journal of Public Health, 71.1 Jan. 1981: p. 91.
In response to a letter to the editor, Wardell defends M.S. against the charges of racism and anti-Semitism. (See items 1293 & 1171.) Sanger's "eugenic rhetoric" was an effort to gain support for the birth control movement.

1294.7 Weinhouse, Beth. "The Life They Saved Was Yours." Ladies' Home Journal, Jan. 1984: pp. 30, 32.
Brief sketch of "women" in 1883. M.S.'s actions to save women from "sexual servitude."

1295. Weisbord, Robert G. "Birth Control and the Black American:

a Matter of Genocide?" Demography, 10.4 Nov. 1973: pp. 571-90.
Weisbord presents "an analysis of black leadership opinion on birth control"; he denies the genocide theory.

1296. Weisbord, Robert G. Genocide?: Birth Control and the Black American. Westport, Conn.: Greenwood Press, 1975. 219 p. Index. Bibliography. Notes. (OCLC: 136987)
Weisbord examines the question of genocide as it relates to birth control. He finds the charge of genocide against black Americans unfounded, but he decries the racism that is apparent in matters concerning sterilization. Weisbord admires M.S. but sees "her flirtation with eugenics and nativism" as "a blot on her movement's otherwise excellent record."

1297. Werner, Vivian. Margaret Sanger: Woman Rebel. New York: Hawthorn Books, Inc., 1970. 128 p. Index. Illus. (OCLC: 73117)
Biography for young adults. Many of the excellent photographs contained in the volume are from the Sophia Smith Collection (Smith College).

1298. White, Abraham. "Gregory Goodwin Pincus (1903-1967)." Endocrinology, 82.4 April 1968: pp. 651-54.
A short biography of Gregory Pincus.

1299. Williams, Doone and Williams, Greer. Every Child a Wanted Child: Clarence James Gamble, M.D. and His Work in the Birth Control Movement. Boston: Francis A. Countway Library of Medicine, 1978. 445 p. Index. No Bibliography. (OCLC: 3943398) (Edited by Emily Flint)
This biography of Clarence James Gamble tells the story of the physician's sincere belief in Christian giving. He gave money--and himself--to the cause of birth control. Page 243 tells us of "...his conviction that the best way to promote birth control of any kind was to send out field workers to find the interested people, lay and medical, and bring them together in community organizations and clinics." This work presents most of Gamble's adult life and continues through the activities of the Pathfinder Fund which he founded. Throughout the volume, Dr. Gamble's interaction with, and cooperative support of, Margaret Sanger are noted. Readers are referred to the index for a listing of the birth control/planned parenthood organizations with which Dr. Gamble was associated throughout the world.

1300. Wood, Clive and Suitters, Beryl. The Fight for Acceptance: A History of Contraception. Aylesbury, England: Medical and Technical Publishing Co. Ltd., 1970. 238 p. Index. Bibliography. (OCLC: 196156)
Traces the history of contraception from the earliest times and compares the work of M.S. with that of Marie Stopes.

Titles of Materials Written by Margaret Sanger

Note: References are to item numbers, not page numbers.

"Abortion in the United States"   66
"Address by Mrs. Margaret Sanger"   1037
"Address of Welcome to the Sixth International Neo-Malthusian and
   Birth Control Conference"   597
"Address to the Japanese People"   1081
"The Aim"   54
"All Together--Now!"   369
American Conference on Birth Control and National Recovery.   Bio-
   logical and Medical Aspects of Contraception   841
"Another Woman"   96
"An Answer to Mr. Roosevelt"   263
Appeals from American Mothers   420
"Are Birth Control Methods Injurious?"   384
"Are Preventive Means Injurious?"   88
"Asia Discovers Birth Control"   1098

"The Ban"   67
"Birth Control"   845
"Birth Control and Racial Betterment"   385
"Birth Control and the Working Woman"   194
"Birth Control and Woman's Health"   264
"Birth Control in Soviet Russia"   874
"The Birth Control League"   89, 97
"Birth Control or Abortion?"   373
"Birth Control--Past, Present and Future"   427, 428, 429
"The Birth-Control Raid"   678
"Birth Control Steps Out: A Note on the Senate Hearing"   744
"Birth Control Through the Ages"   989
"A Birth Strike to Avert World Famine"   403
"Birthday of the Review and of Havelock Ellis"   532
"Blood and Oil"   68
Book Reviews   535, 574, 594, 649, 746
"Breaking into the South--A Contrast"   395

"The Call to Women"   405
"Cannibals"   69

"Message to the President of the United States" 599
"The Militants in England" 83, 92
"Morality and Birth Control" 364
"The Morality of Birth Control" 479
"More Justice!" 101
Motherhood in Bondage 648
"Motherhood--or Destruction" 74
"Mrs. Sanger in Rebuttal" 748
"Mrs. Sanger's Magazine" 195
"Mrs. Sanger's Opinion; To the Editor of the New York Times" 433
"My Fight for America's First Birth-Control Clinic" 1124
My Fight for Birth Control 740

"National Security and Birth Control" 873
"The Need for Birth Control" 650
"The Need of Birth Control in America" 592
"The New Feminists" 55
The New Motherhood 474
"A News Letter From Margaret Sanger" 782
"The Next Step" 679
"No Defense Fund" 114
"No Gods" 93
"No Healthy Race Without Birth Control" 425
"No Masters" 102
"Not Suppressed" 84

"The Old and the New" 103
"On Picket Duty" 56, 63, 75
"One Week's Activity in England" 601
"One Woman's Fight" 104
"An Open Letter to Alfred E. Smith" 371
"An Open Letter to Judge J. J. McInerney" 258
"An Open Letter to Social Workers" 824
"Opinions" 115

"A Parent's Problem or Woman's?" 387
"The Passing of a Hero" 577
The People of the State of New York, Respondent, Against Margaret
    H. Sanger... 257
"A Personal Glimpse of Havelock Ellis" 572
The Pivot of Civilization 475
"A Plan for Peace" 783
"Politicians vs. Birth Control" 426
"Pope's Position on Birth Control" 781
The Practice of Contraception 741

Appendix I.

Major bills (with sponsors) Favoring Birth Control

5/26/30	S.4582	Gillett	71st Cong.
4/04/32	H.R.11082	Hancock	72nd Cong.
4/21/32	S.4436	Hatfield	72nd Cong.
6/06/33	S.1842	Hastings	73rd Cong.
6/08/33	H.R.5978	Pierce	73rd Cong.
1/03/35	H.R.2000	Pierce	74th Cong.
1/10/35	S.600	Hastings	74th Cong.
2/12/35	H.R.5600	Pierce	74th Cong.
2/12/36	S.4000	Copeland	74th Cong.
2/20/36	H.R.11330	Gassaway	74th Cong.

Appendix II.

Pro-Birth Control Hearings Held in the United States Congress

S.4582	Feb. 13-14, 1931	9 speakers
H.R.11082	May 19-20, 1932	15 speakers
S.4436	May 12-20, 1932	10 speakers
S.4436	June 24-30, 1932 (confidential)	4 speakers
H.R.5978	Jan. 18-19, 1934	18 speakers
S.1842	Mar. 1-20-27, 1934	13 speakers

(Also: Economic Security Bill, 5/22/35--4 pro-birth control speakers--Senate Finance Committee)

Author Index

Subject Index

Abbott, Leonard 163, 220
Abortion
  America, in 1225
  Case study 867
  History of 1236, 1254.5, 1258
  Japan, in 1121
  Lader, Lawrence, on 1155
  Legalized, call for 132
  Reproductive control, as method of 1265
  Sanger, Margaret, on 66, 84, 373, 388, 429, 842, 981, 983,
    1063, 1064, 1098, 1254.5, 1256.5
  Self-induced, death from 1242
  Struggles with the issue of 1197.5, 1239
  Sulloway, on 1128
  Techniques discussed 1258
Abstinence (sexual) see Continence (sexual)
"Address to the Japanese People" 1084
Advertisements 1
Albany, N.Y. 356, 545, 554, 622
  Hearings 561, 562, 629, 687
Albert and Mary Lasker Foundation Awards 1030, 1053, 1054, 1055,
    1057
Alcohol, Effects of 98
Aldrich, Winthrop W. 981
All-India Family Planning Association 1259
American Birth Control Conference, First see First American Birth
    Control Conference
American Birth Control League
  Aims 441, 461, 475, 585
  Birth Control Clinical Research Bureau,
    merge with 974, 978
    protests raid on 702
  Commissioner of Health, refuses to address 724
  "Doctor's Only Bill" 582
  Eugenics, and 831
  Incorporated 521, 522
  Jones, Eleanor D., chosen president 669, 672
  Judge withholds approval of incorporation 505
  Marion, Kitty, honored 731
  Meetings 608, 632, 641, 653, 724, 727, 729, 967, 977
  National Broadcasting Company, and 724, 729
  National Committee on Federal Legislation for Birth Control, on
    739, 756

Birth Control Movement
  Abortion, accused of condemning 1225
  Attacks on 751, 1006
  Change from feminist oriented to male controlled 1215, 1216
  Court cases discussed 1278
  England, in 1223, 1284.5
  Eugenic movement, as 1218.3; linked with 1256
  Examination and analysis of 1173
  "Goals and ideologies" 1257
  History of 989, 1145, 1187, 1219
    See also Birth Control, history of
  Legal and social gains 1024
  Legal decisions, in 1128
  Major dates listed 1186
  Moore, Hugh, impact on 1237
  Sanger, Margaret, career of 1189; early efforts in 1205; en-
    trance into 972; role in history of 1208
  Victory of 942.5
  World War I, growth during 419
  See also Birth Control
"Birth Control" (Moving Picture) 346, 348, 357, 358, 359, 360, 361
Birth Control Pill see Contraceptives, Oral
Birth Control Review
  Anniversary 532
  Arrests for selling 370, 382, 383, 394, 398
  Blossom, Frederick, resignation of 367
  Ceases publication 835, 836, 994
  Introduced 195, 260
  Marion, Kitty, honored 730, 731, 732
  Possible merger 662, 665, 666, 671, 673, 674
  Sanger, Margaret, resigns as editor 684
"Birth Controller"
  Dickinson, Robert L., as 1167
  Gamble, Clarence J., as 1167
  Pincus, Gregory, as 1167
  Sanger, Margaret, as 1167, 1271
Birth Rate
  Decline of 958, 961, 965; fear of 753, 797, 823, 830, 840; Japan,
    in 1113; reversal of 891
Birth Rate Commission, Federal see Federal Birth Rate Commission
Birth Strikes
  Margaret Sanger calls for 403, 405, 406, 408
Black American
  Birth control, view of 1281, 1295, 1296
Black Genocide
  Birth control, used as a method of 1245; charge unfounded 1296
  Discussed 1281
  Theory denied 1295
Blacklist 661
Blackwell's Island (Jail, N.Y.) 104, 154, 312, 314, 315, 316, 317,
    318

Hearings 580, 755, 759, 787, 788, 789, 790, 801, 804, 807, 808, 809, 810, 812, 813, 852, 853, 861, 863, 865
  Opposition of 714
  Sanger, Margaret and Mary Ware Dennett, encounters with, discussion of 1181
Condom 1185
  Prophylactic, merely a 1291
Conference of the International Planned Parenthood Federation, Seventh see Seventh Conference of the International Planned Parenthood Federation
Conference on Contraceptive Research and Clinical Practice, 1936 926, 942.5
Congregational Church, Trinity see Trinity Congregational Church
Congress, U.S. see U.S. Congress
Connecticut (Hartford)
  Hearings 551, 552, 556
Connecticut (New Haven) 589, 798, 799, 800
Conservatism
  Birth control movement, and 1165
Consultation
  Premarital 1119
Continence (sexual)
  Ineffective 586, 592, 606
  Physicians should stress 323
Contraception
  History of 1176, 1243.5, 1246, 1266, 1300
  Male 1197; research on new methods of 1179
  See also Birth Control
Contraception Law
  New York State, attempts to appeal or change 1185
Contraceptive Methods 741, 785, 847, 849, 885, 956, 1025, 1052, 1058, 1070, 1154
  History of 1219, 1266
  Male, research on new 1179
  Research discussed 942.5
  See also Birth Control, Harmless Methods
Contraceptive Practices 844
Contraceptive Research, Conference see Conference on Contraceptive Research and Clinical Practice, 1936
Contraceptives
  Campaign for 1175.5
  Clinical Research Bureau, and 651
  Commercial interests 858, 861, 864, 866
  Effectiveness of 587, 604, 786, 873, 960
  History of 1127, 1218.3, 1280; popularized 1218
  Illustrated compilation 785
  Law, and the 979
  Legality of 935
  Non-prescription 1185
  Oral see Contraceptives, Oral
  Pessary called dangerous 584

North Carolina (Elizabeth City)   395, 401

Ogburn, William F.   616
Ohio (Cleveland)   228, 417
One Little Boy   574
Oregon (Portland), Margaret Sanger arrest in   226, 228
Ottesen-Jensen, Elise   1122, 1143
Overpopulation   630
   Eugenics, and   818
   Problem of   1138, 1139, 1219; in India   1143; in Japan   1143
   War, and   614, 656, 842

Pankhurst, Emmeline   151
Parenthood League, Voluntary   see   Voluntary Parenthood League
Parents' Exposition (Grand Central Palace, N.Y.C.)   658, 659, 660
Park Theatre (N.Y.C.)   357, 452, 454, 479
Paterson, N.J.   273, 275, 276
Paterson Philosophical Society (Paterson, N.J.)   273, 275, 276
Pathfinder Fund
   Gamble, Clarence J., founded by   1299
   McKinnon, Edna Rankin, work with   1202
Patterson, Robert P.   518
Paul, Saint   138
Pearl, Raymond   616, 630, 823
Pennsylvania (Hazelton), Margaret Sanger arrest in   30
Pennsylvania (Philadelphia)   274
Pennsylvania (Pittsburgh), Birth Control League   352
Pennsylvania Conference of Birth Control   500
Pensions
   Poor mothers, for   127
   Unfit, for   643
People v. Byrne   820
People v. Sanger   820
Pessaries Case, Japanese   see   U.S. v. One Package Decision
Pessary   584
   See also   Diaphragm
Peterson, Houston   649
Philadelphia, PA   274
Philosophical Society, Paterson   see   Paterson Philosophical Society
Physicians
   Birth Control, change of attitude toward   811; control of   573,
      582; views of   1262
   Catholic   762
   Clinical Research Bureau, response to raid on   691, 695, 697,
      700, 715, 718
   Continence, should stress   323
   Contraceptive information, control of   1277

Contraceptives, oral, speak about 1276; right to prescribe 410.
1005; due to efforts of Margaret Sanger 1111
Education, cancer prevention, concern for 1289; family planning,
concern for 1289; lay, concern for 1289; maternity, concern
for 1289
Inactivity of 871
Male controlled planned parenthood campaign, as leaders of 1215
New York State of Appeals decision, and 379
Sanger, Margaret, reliance on 1270
Women, hostile reactions 395
"Physician's Only Bill" see "Doctor's Only Bill"
Physicians' Opinion 766
Pierce, Walter 852, 857, 860, 863, 865
Pierce Bill 852, 857, 860, 863, 865
Pierson, Richard N., M.D. 974
"The Pill" see Contraceptives, Oral
Pinchot, Gertrude M. 324, 598, 609, 623
Pincus, Gregory, M.D.
    Biography 1298
    "Birth Controller," as 1167
    Contraceptives, Oral, and 1158, 1182, 1183, 1191, 1226, 1230,
        1277, 1290
    Tribute to 1226
    Writings, chronological bibliography of 1226
Pissont, Elizabeth, arrest 690, 698
Pittman, Mrs. Ernest 554
Pittsburgh, PA. 352
Pius XI (Pope), Encyclical 743, 758, 781
Planned Parenthood
    Clinics, effectiveness of in underdeveloped areas 1142
    Programs, role of condom in 1291
    Term, as a 1037, 1056
Planned Parenthood, Citizen's Committee for see Citizen's Committee
    for Planned Parenthood
Planned Parenthood, International Federation of see International
    Federation of Planned Parenthood
Planned Parenthood, National Committee for see National Committee
    for Planned Parenthood
Planned Parenthood, New York State Federation for see New York
    State Federation for Planned Parenthood
Planned Parenthood Conferences see
    Fifth International Conference on Planned Parenthood
    Seventh International Conference on Planned Parenthood
    Sixth International Conference on Planned Parenthood
    Third International Conference on Planned Parenthood
Planned Parenthood Federation, International see International
    Planned Parenthood Federation (Association)
Planned Parenthood Federation, Seventh Conference of the Inter-
    national see Seventh Conference of the International Planned
    Parenthood Federation
Planned Parenthood Federation of America 1048, 1056, 1072, 1088,
    1129, 1166

Federal Council of Churches of Christ, Report 760, 761, 762, 764, 768, 770
Protestant Symposium on the Control of Human Reproduction, papers 1285
Protestants, community interaction, and 1104
Publishing Company, New York Women's see New York Women's Publishing Company
Puerto Rico 821, 822
Purity Congress, International see International Purity Congress
Pusey, William Allen 586

Queens County Jail (Long Island City, N.Y.) 317, 318, 321, 322, 336, 337, 338, 339, 340, 341, 368

Race Suicide 263, 266, 439, 602, 814, 815, 987, 1028
    Fear of 1217
Racial Improvement see Eugenics
Racism
    Birth control linked with 1216
    Sterilization, apparent in 1296
Racist, Margaret Sanger defended against label as 1294; labeled as 1171
Radical, Margaret Sanger as 1221; as feminist 1172
Radical Movements, insights into 1271
Radicalism 161, 376, 784, 899, 1083
    Birth control movement, and 1165
    Margaret Sanger and 1120
Radicals, birth control movement, influence on 1163
Radio Broadcasting 575, 724, 729, 735, 1087
Railroad Strikes see Strikes, Railroad
Rave, Carl, arrest 711
The Rebel Woman 1006
Reitman, Ben 224
Remer Birth Control Bill (N.Y.) 687, 707
Reproduction, Human see Human Reproduction
Reproductive Control, history of struggle for 1265
Revolution 95
    Violence, and 153
Rhythm 832, 844
Rhythm Method 832, 844, 901, 1023, 1052, 1090, 1147
"Right to Choose Campaign," Margaret Sanger related to 1189
Robinson, William J. 182, 224, 776
Rock, John, M.D.
    Birth control movement, as aide to 1262
    Contraceptives, oral, and 1158, 1198
Rockefeller, John D., Jr. 69, 75
Rodman, Henrietta 182

Sanger, Margaret
    Bibliography 1248.5
    Biographers, assessment of 1293
    Biographical chronology of life 1217.8
    Biographical note 1248.5; brief 1044
    Biographical novel 1209
    Biographical sketches 721, 736, 828, 837, 851, 910, 970, 992,
        1059, 1133, 1154, 1170, 1180, 1234, 1260, 1260.5, 1263, 1269,
        1282, 1291.5, 1293
        Popularized 1292
        See also Sanger, Margaret, Obituaries
    Biographies 955, 1169, 1174, 1186, 1190, 1207, 1211, 1233, 1238,
        1250, 1286, 1297
        Major 1162, 1163, 1164, 1165, 1166, 1167
    Birth of celebrated 1217.8; 100th anniversary of 1188
    Birth control, history of, efforts in 1255
    Birth Control League of New York, break with 367, 380, 381
    "Birth Controller," as 1167, 1271
    Blacklisted 661
    Blossom, Frederick, dispute with 367, 380, 381
    Canada, influence of in 1175.55, 1197.3
    Catalogs 1248.5
    Catholic Church, on 73, 472, 478, 660, 664, 743, 758, 762, 781,
        782, 822, 843, 844
    Censorship, as one who fought 1249
    Colloquy on 1188
    Contraceptives, oral, acknowledgment of 1267; role played in de-
        velopment of 1212, 1230
    Court cases recounted 1233
    Eugenic, motivation seen as 1245
    Eugenics, on 385, 402, 431, 475, 500, 573, 592, 600, 602, 635,
        643, 645, 1063
    Eugenics movement, connection with 1187
    Eugenics attack 815, 817
    Feminism, and 1120, 1172
    Feminists, cited as leader of 1248; on 55, 56, 63, 83
    Free love, on 62
    Funds for defense of 330
    Hunger strike, vows 289; will not undergo 313
    "Impetus behind the pill," as 1158
    Jail experiences
        Blackwell's Island (N.Y.) 314, 317, 318, 1124.5; anniversary
            of 1014, 1015
        Hazelton, PA 30
        Queens County Jail (Long Island City, N.Y.) 317, 318, 321,
            322, 336, 337, 338, 339, 340, 341
    Keller, Helen, on 1206
    Lader, Lawrence, interviews with 1236
    Lawbreaking, on 259
    Lawrence, Mass. strike 2, 3, 12, 13, 14, 15, 16, 17, 18, 21;
        children, role in evacuation of 1264
    Manuscripts 1248.5

Sanger, Margaret
  Marriage, on 62, 636
  Marries J. Noah Slee 581
  Materialism, on 79, 80
  Military, on 77, 262
  Morality, on 364
  Morality, sexual, and 1003
  Motherhood, on 74
  Moving Picture "Birth Control" barred 357, 358, 359, 360, 361;
      stars in 346, 348
  Neo-Malthusianism, on 475, 1204.5
  "New Morality," and 1120
  Obituaries 1161
  "Personal Philosophy" 1087
  Politicians, on 426, 536
  Profit motivation, accused of 240, 861, 866
  Prostitution, on 77
  "Racist," defended against label as 1294; labeled as 1171
  Radical, as 1221
  Radical beliefs 161, 784, 1120
  Radical feminist, as 1172
  Rama Rau's contacts with 1259
  Research Bureau, New York see Margaret Sanger Research Bu-
      reau, New York
  Response when named 1957 Humanist of the Year 1102
  Revolution, on 95
  Schools, on 85
  Sense of humor, lack of 1273
  Socialism 4
  Speaking, barred from 274, 356, 554, 564, 565, 566, 567, 622,
      798, 800, 1017, 1050, 1051, 1104; public, closely examined
      1251
  Speeches, close examination of 1251; excerpts from 1251; see
      Title Index for individual speeches
  Sterilization, on 637, 1054, 1057, 1063
  Suffrage movement, on 63, 92
  Trials
    Brownsville (N.Y.) 242-53, 255, 257, 258, 267, 268, 270,
        283, 284, 290, 292, 293, 295, 300, 301, 302, 307, 308, 309,
        311, 313; account of 1124.5; discussion of 1181
    Woman Rebel 196, 198-221
  Tributes to 342, 343, 351, 733, 772, 1045, 1046, 1133, 1134,
      1136, 1138, 1184; at her death 1161
  "Uplifter" of the poor, as 1203
  War, on 107, 108, 111, 262, 481, 596, 656, 842
  Women's organizer, as 1
  Works, pirated 261
Sanger, William
  Arrest 162, 163, 164, 165, 166, 167, 169, 173, 177, 188, 646
  Eugenics, on 350
  Lawrence, Mass. strike 19, 20
  Sanger, Margaret, relationship with 1190